STANDARDS: A CHRONICLE OF BOOKS FOR OUR TIME

STANLEY EDGAR HYMAN

STANDARDS:

A Chronicle of Books for Our Time

stand'ard (stăn'dĕrd), *adj.* **1.** Being, affording, or according with, a standard for comparison and judgment. . . . **2.** Hence: Having a recognized and permanent value; as, *standard* works in history; *standard* authors.
stand'ard (-dĕrd), *n.* **1.** Something elevated as a signal or beacon. *Obs.*

—*Webster's Second International Dictionary*

HORIZON PRESS   NEW YORK
A NEW LEADER BOOK

ACKNOWLEDGMENTS

So many people helped at one stage or another of the task that the result is a work of collaboration. *The New Leader*, personified in Myron Kolatch and a sequence of editors, gave me absolute freedom, and many courtesies and kindnesses in addition. Ben Raeburn of Horizon Press made the book possible by his enthusiasm, and assisted in the selection for it. Many friends and colleagues at Bennington College and *The New Yorker*, too many to list individually, followed the column regularly and helped with encouragement and advice. A number of colleagues, Bernard Malamud and Barbara Herrnstein Smith in particular, advised on books to review. Brendan Gill and Howard Nemerov advised on selection for this volume. Barbara Karmiller read books in advance for me, copyread each review, and advised on selection for this volume. My daughter, Sarah Hyman, ruthlessly copyread the manuscript. My late beloved wife, Shirley Jackson, winnowed out books for me, discussed each book with me before I reviewed it, corrected each review as I wrote it, and proofread each galley. She is largely responsible for any virtue or felicity these essays may have, and they are necessarily and lovingly dedicated to her memory.

To the memory of Shirley Jackson 1919-1965

CONTENTS

"UNDERSTANDED OF THE PEOPLE"

Much of the criticism of the New English Bible, it seems to me, has been wide of the mark. The voices of English teachers are loud in the land, proclaiming that the new translation lacks the power and beauty of the Authorized Version (AV), the King James translation of 1611. As an English teacher, I can join the chorus: It certainly does.

What it has instead is, first, far greater accuracy, in accord with the translators' aim to produce "a rendering which should harvest the gains of recent biblical scholarship." Second, it has much more clarity. Where Jesus on the cross was mysteriously offered a sponge soaked in vinegar put on hyssop, these translators find the vinegar to be sour wine, the hyssop to be marjoram, and one text that fixes the sponge on the end of a javelin instead of on any herb at all. Third, it comes in familiar language. When the Ephesian craftsmen who make shrines for Diana protest that Paul's Christian proselytizing menaces their trade, in AV they say: "Sirs, ye know that by this craft we have our wealth"; in the New English Bible (NEB) they say: "Men, you know that our high standard of living depends on this industry."

For the most part, the businesslike flatness of the NEB reflects the unliterary Greek of the New Testament, the *koine* or *lingua franca* of the Roman empire, better than the high poetry of the AV. It is quite effective for most of Acts, the scramblings of the apostles, or for the close-knit logical Greek of what the NEB calls (rejecting Pauline authorship) "A Letter to Hebrews." It is woefully inadequate for the ecstatic language of the mysteries in John's Gospel (instead of the marvelous "In the beginning was the Word, and the Word was with God, and the Word was God," we get jello: "When all things began, the Word already was. The Word dwelt with God, and what God was, the Word was"). It is even more inadequate to the illiterate ghetto Greek and surrealist apocalyptic vision of Revelation.

The NEB's tone is often quite ludicrous. Jesus chides Martha for "fretting and fussing" and tells the Pharisees what to do "when you give a lunch or dinner party" in Luke; he institutes the Eucharist in John with "Does this shock you?" Paul is charged with being "a perfect pest" in Acts; he asks the Corinthians to "at least be grown-up in your thinking," hopes to stay awhile and avoid "a flying visit" with them, and promises "I am not going to sponge upon you"; he tells the Ephesians not to copy "good-for-nothing notions"; he writes to Timothy that deacons should avoid "double talk" and that a rival teacher is a "pompous ignoramus." John the Baptist warns the soldiers in Luke: "No bullying, no blackmail"; the brother of the prodigal son tells their father that the prodigal has returned "after running through your money with his women"; the soldiers at the crucifixion in John says of Jesus' garment: "Let us toss for it."

One of the demands of the Reformation was the liturgical use of a Bible in the vernacular, and it is enshrined in Article 24 of the Thirty-Nine Articles of the Church of England, which says that the use of "a tongue not understanded of the people" is "a thing plainly repugnant to the Word of God." The translators of the NEB are thus consistent with the Protestant tradition when they conclude their introduction with the trust that "under the providence of Almighty God this translation may open the truth of the scriptures to many who have been hindered in their approach to it by barriers of language."

There are, however, many things that modern readers expect of a Bible besides clarity. One is majesty. When the centurion says to Jesus, "Speak the word only" in AV, it has a grandeur that "You need only say the word" lacks. "Of course religion does yield high dividends" reads like a vulgar parody of AV's "godliness" and "great gain." Jesus' "Woman, what have I to do with thee?" to his mother in John is majestic and awful, a reminder that primitive Christianity denounced kin ties to exalt cult ties, like the Bacchic *thiasoi* (covens); the NEB's "Your concern, mother, is not mine" is merely an Eton boy being snippy.

Another quality that can fairly be demanded of a Bible is mystery, much of which evaporates in the prosiness of the NEB. More than that, readers of good will can ask that a translation throw a veil of decent obscurity over the absurd, the barbaric, and the unworthy; that, in fact, at key points it not be in a language too clearly understanded of the people. The absurdities of the Gospel story of the trial and crucifixion of Jesus as history are all too clearly visible in the NEB: Judas' ridiculous public identification of Jesus, who was well known to his enemies; the impossible night meeting of the Sanhedrin; Pilate inscribing "Jesus of Nazareth King of the Jews" in three languages as a caption over the cross; and so forth. The New Testament's demonology is equally disenchanting in a clear light, whether it is the perfunctory temptation of Jesus by Satan or the unedifying miracle of the Gadarene swine.

More important, perhaps, is the book's anti-Semitism, which comes through much more clearly in the new translation, and makes it seem more likely, as the Dutch radical critics claim, that all the books of the New Testament are pseudepigraphic and second-century, written when the Christians had given up hope of winning the remaining Jews and were out to capture the gentile world. What the NEB calls "the secret of Christ" is that their covenant and Scripture are to be taken away from the Jews, for denying the Messiah, and awarded to the gentiles. The AV's "sign of circumcision" is undercut by the NEB as "the symbolic rite of circumcision." The AV's mysterious "beware of the concision" in Philippians, rendered by the Revised Standard Version of 1952 (RSV) as "look out for those who mutilate the flesh," in the NEB becomes, nastily, "Beware of those who insist on mutilation—'circumcision' I will not call it." We would not have understood Paul's comment on the circumcisionists in Galatians in the AV, "I would they were even cut off which trouble you," but the NEB makes it clear: "As for those agitators, they had better go the whole way and make eunuchs of themselves!" Jesus' withering of the fig tree because of its failure to bear fruit when he wanted it, so out of character in Matthew and Mark, is recognizably a curse on the Jews from Luke 3:9, where the "children of Abraham" are threatened: "Every tree that fails to produce good fruit is cut down and thrown on the fire."

Nor is anti-Semitism the only barbarism that the language might better veil. Whoever "sneers" at his brother "will have to answer for it in the fires of hell" (much stronger than the AV's "be in danger of hell fire"). "Slaughter them in my presence" as the end to the parable of the talents is even bloodthirstier than the AV's "slay them before me." Healing a leper in Mark, Jesus is no longer "moved with compassion" (AV) or "moved with pity" (RSV) but acts "in warm indignation." It is the same indignant Jesus, presumably, who says fiercely in Luke: "I have come to set fire to the earth, and how I wish it were already kindled!" Many will be shocked to find Paul writing again and again: "Slaves, obey your earthly masters with fear and trembling, singlemindedly, as serving Christ." The AV, translating "servants," conceals this unholy alliance of Christ with Caesar.

It was probably a mistake to translate *agape* as "love" throughout. The translators of the Old Testament into Greek in the third century B.C. (the Septuagint or LXX) adapted the word to mean "brotherly love," to avoid the unholy connotations of the Greek *eros*, and the writers of the New Testament used it throughout. St. Jerome translated it *caritas* in the Vulgate in the fifth century A.D., and the early English translators took their choice: Wycliffe preferred "charity"; Tyndale preferred "love"; the AV uses both. Neither is possible today: "charity" because it has all the connotations of giving outgrown snowsuits to the maid's children; "love" because it has all the connotations of *eros* that worried the LXX translators. We might do worse than adopt *agape* as an English word. Other decisions are less important but seem equally whimsical. The "magi" or "wise men" are now "astrologers," the devil "Mammon" is "Money," "Christ" is often "Messiah" and "Hades" often "Hades" rather than "Hell," "letter" is "written code," "anointed" is "initiated."

All this quest for clarity might well have gone further. A few harmless antiquated forms remain, perhaps for nostalgic reasons: "fatted calf," "woe betide," "fornication," "no mean city," and others. Along with them, at least three unnecessary obscurities have been allowed to remain. The "dogs" whose malpractices are warned against in Philippians and punished in Revelation are never explained; they are homosexual male prostitutes, as we know from Deuteronomy 23:17-18, where RSV calmly footnotes: "sodomite." Paul's "archons of this aeon," the Gnostic devils who

are the true crucifiers of Jesus in 1 Corinthians 2:8, are still concealed in the NEB as "the powers that rule the world." The "imprisoned spirits" Jesus proclaimed the tidings to while his body lay
dead in 1 Peter 3:19 are the souls in hell, whom in folklore he
rescues, although one would never know it from the NEB's translation.

In short, we have not yet attained to perfection. The New
English Bible sold its three million copies in the year of publication, as the Revised Version did in 1885 and the Revised Standard
Version in 1952, but if you look on the pulpits now, what do you
think you will find? That same old 1611 book.

THE INNOCENCE OF HENRY MILLER

After twenty-seven years, Henry Miller's first and most famous book, *Tropic of Cancer*, finally achieved its publication in Miller's country. Its appearance deserves an uncritical welcome, and our thanks for the courage (and commercial shrewdness) of Grove Press, which contested the book's banning from the mails. In her 1934 preface, Anaïs Nin warns against turning the "critical eye" on "a naked book such as this," and defines its function as liberation. If *Tropic of Cancer* had been published here in the 30s, amid the dreary wastes of proletarian literature, it might have had a liberating effect. By the time I read it, in the 40s, it had become an anachronism. Now, in the 60s, who can say what effect, if any, it will have?

After writing *Tropic of Cancer*, Miller went on to a series of Paris-published books, increasingly dishonest fantasies of Olympian virility and sexual athleticism; and another series of books of rather mixed value, published here, criticizing the culture. In recent years he has settled at Big Sur in California, become a proud father, and turned as soft and sentimental as the rest of us, struggling to keep the children from learning dirty words.

When he wrote *Tropic of Cancer*, Miller may have been just as soft inside, but he had a carapace. The book tells of his life as an impoverished writer and sponge in Paris. As autobiography, it is often relentlessly honest, describing the shifts by which he lived, from theft to posing for pornographic photographs, and neglecting few details ("My stool is always full of blood"). Miller luxuriates in sordidity with a kind of *gourmandise:* "I pause a few minutes to drink in the full squalor of the scene"; "I had been coming back to this quarter, attracted by certain leprous streets which only revealed their sinister splendor when the light of day had oozed away."

Mixed with the autobiography are long passages of violent rhetoric: fantasies about American women, diatribes against

Paris, rantings about the state of the world. The third major element consists of stories of his friends and acquaintances: the eccentricities of an Indian who supported Miller but treated him like a servant; the busy sex lives of half-a-dozen American expatriates; the ludicrous teachers at a school in Dijon where Miller briefly taught.

The voice is insistently prophetic, but the message seems remarkably shallow. In his worshipful introduction to the Grove edition, Karl Shapiro says that he had planned to compile a "bible" (to replace Holy Writ) from Miller's writings, only to discover that the project was already under way, and that one such scripture had already been published. As a guide to life, Miller offers us a number of formulas. He writes: "I made up my mind that I would hold on to nothing, that I would expect nothing, that henceforth I would live as an animal, a beast of prey, a rover, a plunderer." At the same time, we are not to forget "above all, *the ecstasy!*" At the end of the book, when Miller has stolen about a hundred dollars from his friend Carl, a "wonderful peace" descends on him, a true ecstasy of animality.

As a political prophet, Miller seems equally inadequate. He warns that American materialism "will drag the whole world down to the bottomless pit": "The ubiquitous bathtub, the five-and-ten-cent store bric-a-brac, the bustle, the efficiency, the machinery, the high wages, the free libraries, etc., etc." Miller argues a kind of class war in which blood must flow, but it might better be catsup.

At a concert, he thinks: "The woman with the red hat who is dozing over the rail—marvelous if she were to have a hemorrhage! If suddenly she spilled a bucketful on those stiff shirts below. Imagine these bloody no-accounts going home from the concert with blood on their dickies!"

It is as a prophet of sexual liberation that Miller has been chiefly celebrated, but here too there are problems. It is a liberation of monotonous promiscuity, an orgasm tabulation as mechanical as Kinsey's. Whatever its dubious delights, this revolution is only for the male, since the role of women is to be inferior, passive conquests. The only triumph for the woman is the affirmation of her own genitals, as when a whore named Germaine who became a life-giving symbol for Miller by a fetishistic worship of her own sex organ: "stroking it with her two hands, caressing it, patting it, patting it." Not very deeply repressed in Miller is a curious fastidiousness and prudery: he muses about "swell dames," in whose lives a good deal is "sordid as any garbage can, only they are lucky enough to be able to put covers over the can"; he reports with pleasure, of a friend who kicked his amorous wife in the belly, that it "took the wind out of her—and a bit of her sexy nonsense too."

Miller often seems more like a small boy telling whoppers than a sexual liberator. He constantly boasts of his emotional health in the book. "I am the happiest man alive," he announces on the first page. "I keep thinking of my really superb health," he remarks later. "It was healthy," Lawrence Durrell has said of *Tropic of Cancer*, "where Céline and Lawrence were sick"—but who on earth would consult Lawrence Durrell on emotional health? "There must be something about a healthy Gentile that excites the Jewish mind," Miller boasts, but this Jewish mind reserves judgment.

Most of Miller's sexual adventures in *Tropic of Cancer* are honest accounts of impotence or unconcern. A passionate encounter with an American girl in a public lavatory includes a failure to penetrate her, and ends as they waltz out into the vestibule: "I come all over her beautiful gown and she's sore as hell about it." At another time, Miller and his friend Van Norden share a fifteen-franc whore, but neither can achieve an erection, despite their determination to get their money's worth. Later in the book Miller goes home with a Negro girl from the telephone company, who falls sound asleep "as I was climbing over her," and eventually Miller gives up and goes to sleep himself. When Miller returns to Paris after the Dijon teaching, he is offered a girl but isn't interested: "I was too excited."

This low potency combines incongruously with the wildest sexual boasting ("I shoot hot bolts into you, Tania, I make your ovaries incandescent"). The one convincing sexual adventure described is an encounter with a prostitute, in which Miller is preoccupied with resisting her impatience ("I wanted to stretch it out. I wanted full value for my hundred francs") while at the same time keeping a wary eye on the money in his pants pocket.

The deepest sexual experiences in *Tropic of Cancer* are actually voyeuristic. Van Norden tells Miller that a few nights before he had trained a flashlight on a girl's shaven genitals and stared at them for ten minutes, and that fascinated study is the book's key scene. When Miller and Van Norden tackle the fifteen-franc whore, Miller gives up first, then: "I get down on my knees behind Van Norden and I examine the machine more attentively." Toward the end of the book Miller and another friend go home with two whores who strip and do somersaults on the floor (some of the incidents in *Tropic of Cancer* do not lend themselves well to synopsis). Miller finds himself staring at the genitals (unshaven) of one of the girls, which sends him into a trance and several pages of philosophic speculations about life, death, and eternity, but provokes no other action. With women, Miller's role is consistently passive: "the dame next to me has two fingers in my fly"; "she's clutching it like a lifesaver"; "Marcelle was tickling me in the crotch all the while."

Deeper than the impotence, the voyeurism, and the passivity is a strong latent (or not so latent) homosexuality. When Miller and some friends find a woman waiting in the bed of one of them, they throw her out and the four men go to bed together. "I find myself wondering what it feels like, during intercourse, to be a woman," Miller writes. His characteristic reaction to being propositioned by a girl (in this case Marcelle the tickler) is to spend the night drinking with the boys. Miller's typical situation is living with a man and his girl; then, when she moves out, the two men settle down happily to drink hot toddies around the fireside and talk about Whitman. Toward the end of the book, Van Norden gives up chasing women and preaches masturbation in a cored apple instead. "I was amazed," Miller comments.

Under the hardboiled surface, Miller's vision of the whores and pimps in the world he describes is incurably romantic. The whores crave men and want to "writhe in ecstasy," or their eyes "seemed to be swimming in sperm"; the pimps suffer spiritually over the sullying of their beloveds ("to taste another man's breath"; "to taste those bruised lips"). Realistically Miller knows that the whores are frigid and that their passion is feigned, that the pimps have a good businessman's concern for the merchandise, but the inner small boy denies the knowledge.

For a book so sex-obsessed, its author seems oddly innocent

and pure. The only real lust he shows in *Tropic of Cancer* is for food, and Miller's true erotic fantasies are of sweetbreads and fried liverwurst, sirloin steaks and "wonderful hams cushioned in white fat." "You only think about food," a friend charges. "I not only think about food all day," Miller admits to the reader, "but I dream about it all night." No woman's hams, cushioned in white fat, need apply.

If Miller is not much of a prophet or liberator, he is not much of a writer either, although he has his moments. His characteristic style is a mosaic of cliché: "And since we didn't have to put on a false front we could laugh about the incident to our heart's content." The rhetorical passages are mostly empty wind; the anecdotes about friends and acquaintances eventually become monotonous and boring.

There are exceptions. Sometimes Miller writes a sentence of bitter truth like a blues lyric ("To get a hat that fits now you have to walk to the electric chair"), or achieves an elegant phrase ("the Mongols of the North, glazed like eggplants"), or produces a passage of genuinely apocalyptic eloquence and fury (there is one about worms and bugs taking over the Folies-Bergère). At least one narrative in the book is a comic masterpiece: the story of a Russian princess pursued by Miller's friend Fillmore. She insisted that she first had to be adequately stimulated, proposing a visit to a brothel enactment of the rape of Leda by the swan, since "the flapping of the wings excited her terribly."

The plain truth is that, unbanned, *Tropic of Cancer* is not very interesting. In Paris, Miller made what he calls "the heroic descent to the very bowels of the earth, the dark and fearsome sojourn in the belly of the whale." He came up, however, not reborn like Jonah or Jesus, but the same old Brooklyn adolescent. "Art consists in going the full length," Miller writes. He could not be more wrong. Art may deal with the whole range of experience, but it consists in ordering that experience by means of form. It is thus a moral act, the replacing of disorder with order. It is in *that* sense, a want of craft, that *Tropic of Cancer* is an immoral book, not in the scenes on which it casts the beam of its dim little flashlight.

HOMER'S SHINING RAIMENT

What do we want of a translation of *The Odyssey* in our time? If the answer is an English poem of vigor and beauty, aptly conveying the vigor and beauty of the original, then Robert Fitzgerald's version is all that we could ask. He has found a surprisingly good equivalent for the Greek hexameters in a very loose blank verse, with lines as long as eight feet.

At its best, Fitzgerald's *Odyssey* is as free and as splendid as George Chapman's in 1615. There are innumerable felicities. How exciting it is to read "Now who in thunder?" for "Ah me, who?" or "Athena came as a god comes, numinous, to the rites," for "Athena came to accept the sacrifice." How brilliant, and how nervy, to call shooting an arrow through the axes "the needle shot," or to translate the curious pun predicting that Irus, the beggar who challenges the disguised Odysseus, will be no-Irus, as "By god, old Iros now retiros."

Like Chapman, Fitzgerald is particularly effective on low life and verbal abuse, yet equally effective at moments of high emotion. Penelope cries "until she had tasted her salt grief again." Telemachus pictures his father dead:

> *a man whose bones are rotting somewhere now,*
> *white in the rain on dark earth where they lie,*
> *or tumbling in the groundswell of the sea.*

Fitzgerald's translation appears with no introduction, so that his theory has to be induced from his practice. One of the characteristics of *The Odyssey* that he did not wish to convey is its patterned geometric style, the constant repetition of fixed phraseology. Witness his treatment of the conventional epithets. Homer (if we may so designate the authors of *The Odyssey*) never tires of calling Athena *glaukopis* (originally "owl-eyed" or "owl-faced," but generally translated "grey-eyed" or "flashing-eyed"). Fitzgerald quickly tires, and plays such variations on it as "her eyes shone like the sea" or "cast a grey glance." Instead of saying endlessly that Odysseus is *polytlas,* "much-enduring," Fitzgerald specifies: "who had borne the barren sea" or "who had borne the long war." The constant *pepnymenos,* "wise," for Telemachus displeases Fitzgerald, and he either omits it entirely or renders it "clear-headed," "prudently," "perceptive," or "with his clear candor."

With one of the most common epithets for Odysseus, *polymetis,* "of many wiles" or "of many schemes," Fitzgerald is remarkably acrobatic. He translates it "the strategist," "the great tactician," "the man of all occasions," "that resourceful man," "the master of improvisation," "that sly and guileful man," "brought his ranging mind to bear," "who had it all timed in his head," "the master of many crafts," "the great master of invention," "the master improviser," "the master of subtle ways and straight," "the man skilled in all ways of contending," and "the wiliest fighter of the islands."

Fitzgerald keeps the two phrases that were once brilliant imaginative strokes and are now the clichés of Homeric translation: Philip Worsley's "winedark" sea for *oinopa,* "wine-faced"; and Andrew Lang's "honey-hearted" wine for *meliphrona,* "sweet to the heart." For the epithets that make no sense in the poem, Fitzgerald has a variety of solutions. The absurd description of the treacherous murderer Aegisthus as *amymonos,* "faultless," he simply omits. The embarrassing term for the mother of the cowardly beggar Irus, *potnia,* "Lady," he softens to "gentle." When Menelaus is called *boen agathos,* "good at the war-cry," when getting out of Helen's bed, Fitzgerald gives up and translates it "clarion in battle."

Fitzgerald is equally resourceful with other Homeric conventions. He sometimes makes the long formal similes more naturalistic by breaking them into short ejaculations, such as (for the suitors):

> *Fawns in a lion's lair! As if a doe*
> *put down her litter of sucklings there, while she*
> *quested a glen or cropped some grassy hollow.*
> *Ha! Then the lord returns to his own bed*
> *and deals out wretched doom on both alike.*

At other times he makes a simile seem playful and improvised by beginning it "Think of," or boldly turns it into a metaphor.

One of the most formal geometric patternings in *The Odyssey* is a device that the scholars call "ring-composition," the framing of a scene in the same words. Thus the episode of the hiding of the arms begins and ends (in A. T. Murray's close translation): "So goodly Odysseus was left behind in the hall, planning with Athene's aid the slaying of the wooers." Impatient of any exact repetition, Fitzgerald weakens this effect, beginning with Odysseus "studying the ground for slaughter," and ending "Odysseus waited with his mind on slaughter."

An ancient Greek form of address, *Daimoni*, originally meant "Daemon-possessed," but by Plato's time it had become a purely conventional "Good sir." In *The Odyssey* it still has enough of the old magic to be used only when the person addressed is doing something peculiar. Fitzgerald does everything with it from "Are you mad?" through "Little devil," to "Captain, shake off this trance."

Inevitably, in Fitzgerald's thousands of lines, there are inconsistencies of tone. His translation has an archaic effect on the page because he keeps the Greek spelling instead of the more familiar Latin spelling, even with well-known names ("Phoinikians" for Phoenicians), and renders the Greek *chi* by means of "kh" ("Akhilleus"). Some of his words are comparably archaic: "nape cord," "corse," "benison," "steading" (that classic of Lang-Butchery), even "doorhook" for key.

Others are British-slangy: the Cyclops registers "fuddle" and calls Odysseus "twiggy"; Antinous hits the disguised Odysseus with a stool and the other suitors say "A poor show, that"; Odysseus tells Penelope, after their reunion, "I am off up country." Still others are peculiarly American: Sisyphus is "roustabout" to a boulder, Argos pastureland is "bluegrass," a Phoenician adventurer is "a plausible rat," Eumaeus greets Telemachus with "You made it back!" and the suitors tell Telemachus that his guests are "what the cat dragged in." (It seems surprising that Fitzgerald does not go all the way with M. I. Finley and render "cattle-raiding" as "rustling.")

Where Homer has a slave say that the suitors have "loosened my knees" with toil, Fitzgerald says, in our idiom, "They've made me work my heart out"; but he does not change "it lies upon the gods' great knees" to the equally idiomatic "it lies in the lap of the gods." When Odysseus explains that the wine Maron gave him was so excellent that it could be diluted with twenty parts of water, Fitzgerald, who cannot bear the thought, changes it to "brandy." (The ancient Greeks habitually drank their wine in highballs, two parts of water to one of wine, and it must have been rather like Manischewitz.) When Odysseus checks his bow to see if worms have weakened it during the years of disuse, Fitzgerald ingeniously makes them "termites."

Sometimes the language has a fine sprightliness. Odysseus tells Irus: "Old as I am, I might just crack a rib or split a lip for you." Melantho tells Odysseus: "You must be crazy, punch drunk, you old goat." At other times the language is entirely inadequate, as when Penelope says of the likelihood of her marrying the supposed beggar, "How very, very improbable it seems," or the bed is described as "Their secret!"

Fitzgerald's blank verse is extremely good. When he goes into random couplets in the Lay of Demodocus he is less successful, and the short-line quatrains that Hermes and the Sirens sing lean toward musical comedy. Occasionally the blank verse misses fire, and we get clumsy and inadequate lines like Odysseus' revelation to Telemachus:

> *I am that father whom your boyhood lacked*
> *and suffered pain for lack of. I am he.*

At some point we must face the question of fidelity to the text. As Chapman did, Fitzgerald adds many lines largely improvised or entirely his own. He adds words to suggest extraneous meanings, or to interpret where Homer does not (remarks are introduced with "jesting" or "gruffly"). Some passages are not so much translated as paraphrased.

Fitzgerald's language is sometimes weaker than seems necessary, and sometimes stronger. When Helen says that the Trojan War was caused by "dog-faced me" (*kynopidos*), it should be rendered "bitch that I was" (the Greeks shared the canine insult with us). Fitzgerald translates weakly "wanton that I was," although he is free enough with "bastard," "whore," "harlot," and "trull," where they are not in the text, and he sprinkles speeches liberally with "damned" and "damn it."

Fitzgerald chooses to translate the puns in certain proper names: the Phaeacians are Tipmast, Sparwood, Seareach, etc.; a spring is at Clearwater; the Dawn's horses are Firebright and Daybright; disguised Odysseus tells his father that he is Quarrelman son of King Allwoe. He chooses just as firmly not to translate others: Antinous is never unmasked as Foe of Reason, Arete as Virtue, Polyphemus as Loud Roarer, Melantheus as Black God, or Oenops as Wine Face.

Finally, Fitzgerald omits a few things we can hardly do without. The beautiful image of Odysseus, cast ashore on Phaeacia, as a "seed" of fire (developing out of earlier similes of thistledown and chaff) is lost when Fitzgerald freely translates "spark." When Nausicaa loads her dirty laundry onto the cart, Fitzgerald calls it "soiled apparel," because it is; but Homer called it "bright" or "shining," because in fairyland even the dirty laundry glistens. When Odysseus and his men come to the land of the Lestrygonians, he sends scouts to learn (in Murray's translation) "who the men were, who here ate bread upon the earth." This standard Homeric periphrasis for the human condition here has a terrible irony, since the Lestrygonians are cannibals. Fitzgerald's "to learn what race of men this land sustained" loses it all.

In other words, Fitzgerald's *Odyssey* buys its poetic effectiveness at a certain cost. His theory of Homeric translation is, apparently, that it is more important to transmit the poem's power and eloquence than its stylization, that something comparable to the resonance of the Greek is of more value than pedantic fidelity to each word. He may very well be right. No one will ever say of his translation what Richard Bentley said of Pope's: "It is a pretty poem, Mr. Pope, but you must not call it Homer." This is unquestionably Homer, if not all of Homer. Fitzgerald's version is a superb poem to read, but it runs where we must sometimes trot.

BLACKS, WHITES, AND GRAYS

The striking photograph that serves as the jacket design for *Nobody Knows My Name* reveals James Baldwin through a broken window, standing in what is apparently the foundation of a demolished house. He wears a T-shirt, and his face displays a look of infinite sadness, as though he bore all the suffering in the world on his slumped shoulders.

It strikes the perfect note for this collection of magazine articles written over the past seven years, and it raises all the issues: a composition in blacks, whites, and grays; the writer in the foreground of his scene, ambiguously observer and observed; the return of the native son to Harlem. The essays divide into a first group, concerned with the Negro question, and a second group largely literary. The literary ones tend to be better, although the racial essays are often shrewd, tough-minded, and eloquent. Here is a paragraph that upset a considerable number of readers in its magazine publication:

> Harlem got its first private project, Riverton—which is now, naturally, a slum—about twelve years ago because at that time Negroes were not allowed to live in Stuyvesant Town. Harlem watched Riverton go up, therefore, in the most violent bitterness of spirit, and hated it long before the builders arrived. They began hating it at about the time people began moving out of their condemned houses to make room for this additional proof of how thoroughly the white world despised them. And they had scarcely moved in, naturally, before they began smashing windows, defacing walls, urinating in the elevators, and fornicating in the playgrounds. Liberals, both white and black, were appalled at the spectacle. I was appalled at the liberal innocence—or cynicism, which comes out in practice as much the same thing. Other people were delighted to be able to point to proof positive that nothing could be done to better the lot of the colored people. They were, and are, right in one respect: that noth-

ing can be done as long as they are treated like colored people. The people in Harlem know that they are living there because white people do not think they are good enough to live anywhere else. No amount of "improvement" can sweeten this fact. Whatever money is now being earmarked to improve this, or any other ghetto, might as well be burnt. A ghetto can be improved in one way only: out of existence.

Baldwin's title, *Nobody Knows My Name,* is nowhere identified in the book. It comes from the defiant last stanzas of the greatest of all blues songs, Bessie Smith's "Young Woman's Blues." She sings:

> *I'm a young woman, and ain't done runnin' round,*
> *I'm a young woman, and ain't done runnin' round.*
> *Some people call me a hobo, some call me a bum,*
> *Nobody knows my name, nobody knows what I've done.*
>
> *I'm as good as any woman in your town,*
> *I ain't no high yaller, I'm a deep yaller brown.*
> *I ain't gonna marry, ain't gonna settle down,*
> *I'm gonna drink good moonshine, and run these browns down.*
>
> *See that long lonesome road, don't you know it's gotta end?*
> *And I'm a good woman, and I can get plenty men.*

The blues pervade the book. Baldwin explains that when he suffered a kind of breakdown in Europe, two Bessie Smith records helped him to recover. He writes: "I had never listened to Bessie Smith in America (in the same way that, for years, I would not touch watermelon), but in Europe she helped to reconcile me to being a 'nigger.'" Her recording of "Backwater Blues" is used as a literary touchstone: a story by Richard Wright is "as spare and moving" as the song; a passage by Jack Kerouac is in comparison "thin, like soup too long diluted." Baldwin also quotes blues lyrics by "Ma" Rainey and others.

As the blues singers do, Baldwin talks a great deal about himself in the book, but the self is usually the artificial *persona* or mask of the blues. In this sense the new collection is less frank and personal than its predecessor, *Notes of a Native Son,* and only in the sections on Wright and Norman Mailer, ironically, does some-

thing of Baldwin himself appear. He writes of his first meeting
with Mailer in 1956: "I was then (and I have not changed much)
a very tight, tense, lean, abnormally ambitious, abnormally intelligent, and hungry black cat." (We have seen that lean and hungry
black cat in Baldwin's landscape before, notably in the Harlem
gutters in *Go Tell It on the Mountain,* but never realized that it
was the author himself.)

Baldwin continually projects himself onto the scene he is describing. In "A Fly in Buttermilk," an account of the only Negro
boy at an "integrated" Southern high school, Baldwin displays the
parents' motivation as ambition for the boy to get an adequate
education rather than any kind of racial crusading. In the title
essay, Baldwin generalizes about "just what made Negro parents
send their children out to face mobs":

> Those Negro parents who spend their days trembling for their
> children and the rest of their time praying that their children
> have not been too badly damaged inside, are not doing this out
> of "ideals" or "convictions" or because they are in the grip of a
> perverse desire to send their children "where they are not
> wanted." They are doing it because they want the child to
> receive the education which will allow him to defeat, possibly
> escape, and not impossibly help one day abolish the stifling
> environment in which they see, daily, so many children perish.

This is true, and it clears the air of a certain amount of do-
goodism, but it is only a part of the truth; many Negroes who
buck the mobs are motivated partially, or even wholly, by "ideals"
and "convictions." Baldwin can see only part of the truth because
an "abnormally ambitious" young Negro, himself, keeps getting
into the forefront of his scene.

The subjects of Baldwin's novels have been notably masked
and elusive. The first, *Go Tell It on the Mountain,* disguised its
story of a boy's conversion to homosexuality as a religious conversion; the second, *Giovanni's Room,* symbolically accepted Negro
identity in the guise of a white man accepting his repressed homosexuality. Problems of identity are just as tricky in the essays.
There is nothing in *Nobody Knows My Name* as bold as the essay
in *Notes of a Native Son* that is written with an ironic white "we,"
but observe the dance of pronouns in a lecture to a white audi-

ence about the Negro: "This is because he has had to watch you, outwit you, and bear you, and sometimes even bleed and die with you, ever since we got here, that is, since both of us, black and white, got here."

Baldwin writes of a crisis of identity earlier in his life: "I could not be certain whether I was really rich or really poor, really black or really white, really male or really female, really talented or a fraud, really strong or merely stubborn." As does the protagonist of *Go Tell It on the Mountain*, whose identifications ranged from St. John the Divine to Mildred in *Of Human Bondage*, Baldwin has a complex ambivalence that will not let his personality come to rest anywhere.

Baldwin's vision of race relations in the United States also has its St. John elements and its Mildred elements. "The Southerner remembers," he writes, "historically and in his own psyche, a kind of Eden in which he loved black people and they loved him" (that is: historically before the Civil War; psychologically before puberty). The expression of this thwarted love, in Baldwin's obsessive imagery in the book, is lynching and castration: "hanging from a tree, while white men watched him and cut his sex from him with a knife"; "that black man, sexless, hanging from a tree"; "the sex torn from its socket and severed with a knife." What Baldwin's Negro asks of white America, quite simply, is that it stop making him either a mammy or a eunuch, and recognize him as a man. "*Negroes want to be treated like men*," Baldwin writes in desperate italics.

If the book's racial message is ultimately simple, its literary message is more complicated. Primarily it involves a coming to terms with Richard Wright, the author Baldwin identifies as his spiritual father. Three of the book's fifteen essays are memoirs of Wright, the last of them the only thing in the book previously unpublished. "His work was a road-block in my road," Baldwin writes, as Henry James called Maupassant a lion in his path. Baldwin mocks Wright in the memoirs, exposes his absurdity as a social thinker, cruelly notes the replacement of his friends by "dreary sycophants" in his last years, even identifies Wright's "real" impulse toward American Negroes: "to despise them." Yet there is no reason to doubt that, with characteristic ambivalence,

Baldwin feels and always felt the love and respect for Wright that he claims, and his judgment of Wright's work is very perceptive: the work is flawed by "gratuitous and compulsive" violence, but "Wright's unrelentingly bleak landscape was not merely that of the Deep South, or of Chicago, but that of the world, of the human heart."

Baldwin dismisses Wright's novelette "The Man Who Lived Underground," and says that the work that proved "an immense liberation and revelation" for him was *Black Boy*, "one of the major American autobiographies." *Black Boy* is a very impressive book, but it was "The Man Who Lived Underground," appearing in *Cross-Section* in 1944, along with the fiction of Ralph Ellison about the same time, that freed American Negro writing from the fetters of naturalism, and thus made Baldwin possible. The new tradition was symbolist fantasy, and it came in from modern European literature, but a native symbolist poetry in the Negro folk tradition stood waiting to receive it—the blues. "I have always wondered," Baldwin told an interviewer in 1953, "why there has never, or almost never, appeared in fiction any of the joy of Louis Armstrong or the really bottomless, ironic and mocking sadness of Billie Holiday." The combination had always been in the blues; with Ellison and Baldwin it became the major strain in American Negro writing.

As this confusion about his own literary tradition suggests, Baldwin is not educated enough (by education I do not mean schooling) for his intelligence, ambition, and talent. He shows little acquaintance with the great literature of the past, apart from the Bible, and he will quote Emerson or T. S. Eliot with an innocent "Someone said." His remarks about American immigration and racial stereotypes show a considerable ignorance of history and anthropology. Baldwin's prose falls frequently into cliché ("a match in the powder keg") or jargon ("the aforementioned coterie"). Sentences ramble or have no subject, and one whole essay, "Notes for a Hypothetical Novel: An Address," wanders ruinously from its topic. It is discouraging to note that the shapeliest and most eloquent essay in the book is the earliest, a fine review of André Gide's *Madeleine* that appeared in 1954.

No one can doubt Baldwin's enormous talent. *Go Tell It on*

the Mountain showed us the sharpness and range of his perceptions, and *Giovanni's Room* their depth and emotional truth. Any number of sentences and passages in this book carry absolute conviction. But few whole essays do. Baldwin needs to read more literature and to work harder at its discipline, form. More than that, he must decide more firmly who he is and what he is, and stand in that identity. If the blues he uses for his title says "Nobody knows my name," there is also a blues beginning "My first name is James."

THE BEST OF HEMINGWAY

When a writer who has been important to you dies, if you want to get the taste of the tributes in the mass-circulation magazines out of your mouth ("He was a cherished colleague of ours," said *Life*), the thing to do is to go back and read his best work.

I first read Ernest Hemingway in high school, in the early 1930s, and I can still recall the excitement of the experience, although I had no idea why the books gave me such pleasure. In college, along with every other ambitious English major in the nation, I studied Hemingway's prose, with its short sentences, its sparse modifiers, and its rhythmic repetitions; I tried, with very little success, to copy it. The first Christmas present I gave my wife was Hemingway's collected stories, just out. Since then I have read each book as it appeared, not often with joy, and have followed the celebrated public career, sometimes with disgust, but each time I encounter a Hemingway story in an anthology I remember the greatness of his talent and achievement. I never met Hemingway. By the time it might have been possible, he was "Papa" Hemingway the international playboy, and I did not particularly want to.

After the shock of reading of his death (and *Time* did not spare the bloody details) I sat down and read the work I have always thought Hemingway's best, his first novel, *The Sun Also Rises*, and the short stories. *The Sun Also Rises* seems to me Hemingway's only completely honest novel. If, as they say, there is a thin shy ectomorph buried inside every stout hearty endomorph, *The Sun Also Rises* uncovers him. More than that, in boldly choosing for his subject matter the love between an impotent man and a frigid promiscuous woman, Hemingway found a truly representative and deeply disturbing metaphor for the human condition.

The prose is no less than masterly. Its syntax is parenthetical and conversational rather than "literary." Hemingway writes:

"The lady who had him, her name was Frances, found toward the end of the second year that her looks were going." The style is stripped and economical, using the simplest of means and vocabulary, presenting observed behavior and conversation with a minimum of comment or analysis. Every detail functions. We are told of Robert Cohn: "He stood up from the table his face white, and stood there white and angry behind the little plates of hors d'oeuvres." The technique is like that of a mosaic. When a meal is eaten, Hemingway identifies every dish; when his characters walk through Paris, he names every street and what they see on it. Hemingway demonstrates Mies van der Rohe's "Less is more" in his marvelous use of understatement in the book. The moving last scene of Book I, when Brett Ashley and the narrator, Jake Barnes, confess their love for each other and part miserably, concludes: "The door opened and I went up-stairs and went to bed."

The ironic themes of *The Sun Also Rises* are introduced by means of a few repeated key words: fun ("We *will* have fun," Brett says); luck ("It's rotten luck" is Jake's strongest commiseration); value ("You must get to know the values," the Count says). "Life is ritual," Lionel Johnson used to tell Yeats, and in *The Sun Also Rises* it truly is. In addition to the organized rituals of the bullfight and the fiesta, drinking, eating, fishing, even playing bridge, are made ceremonial and numinous.

The book's important subplot involves Robert Cohn, the outsider and Jew on the fringe of the group. "He's quite one of us," Brett says of the Count to Jake, and it is something no one would say of Cohn. Cohn provokes everyone's nastiness in the book; as Jake says, "Cohn had a wonderful quality of bringing out the worst in anybody." "I hate his damned suffering," Brett explains.

In one sense, as the book makes clear, Cohn is an innocent steer, gored by the bulls because they cannot get at their real tormenters. In another sense, he is the uninitiate, and any contact with him is a pollution. After her affair with Cohn, Brett seems always compulsively bathing; talking to him, Jake thinks only "I wanted a hot bath in deep water"; when Cohn beats up the bull-fighter, Pedro Romero, the latter can wash away the beating only in the bull-ring; after her affair with Romero, Brett says, "He's wiped out that damned Cohn." Robert Cohn is based on a known prototype, but Hemingway has written a good deal of himself into the character. He is that aspect of the artist that is perpetually wounded and alienated, the outsider, what John Berryman called "the imaginary Jew."

In the main plot, the relationship of Brett and Jake, there is a terrible pain and poignancy. Castrated in the war, Jake is the true bullfight steer. He says of his wound: "I try and play it along and just not make trouble for people." When he thinks about Brett, Jake cries himself to sleep like a child. The key action of the book is Brett's renunciation of Romero for the boy's own good, the first truly unselfish act of her life. "I do feel such a bitch," Brett says when she goes off with Romero; "I feel rather good, you know," she says when she gives him up. In renouncing Romero, Brett voluntarily assumes a frustration like Jake's involuntary one, and at the end of the book we see the two of them in heartbreaking fraternal embrace in a cab. "We could have had such a damned good time together," Brett cries, and Jake answers, as the motion of the cab presses Brett against him, "Isn't it pretty to think so?"

Like *The Sun Also Rises*, the best stories are chronicles of defeat and loss, their endings deeply moving because every word in the story has built to the final effect. "My Old Man," a boy's account of his love for his father, a crooked jockey, is written in a marvelous first-person narrative style derived from *Huckleberry Finn*. Its authenticity and truth to a boy's emotions are overwhelming. When the jockey is killed in a steeplechase race, the narrator says:

> My old man was dead when they brought him in and while a doctor was listening to his heart with a thing plugged in his ears, I heard a shot up the track that meant they'd killed Gilford. I lay down beside my old man, when they carried the stretcher into the hospital room, and hung onto the stretcher and cried and cried, and he looked so white and gone and so awfully dead, and I couldn't help feeling that if my old man was dead maybe they didn't need to have shot Gilford. His hoof might have got well. I don't know. I loved my old man so much.

Waiting for the ambulance, the boy hears two horseplayers agree that "He had it coming to him on the stuff he's pulled," and the boy comments bitterly in the story's last line: "Seems like when they get started they don't leave a guy nothing."

"The Undefeated," the story of an old bullfighter's failure at a comeback, carries the same absolute conviction. I have no idea what thoughts go on in a bullfighter's mind in the ring, but they must certainly be the ones the story gives (as I find the emotions of the wounded lion in "The Short Happy Life of Francis Macomber" entirely convincing). Lying with his horn-wound at the end, refusing to let them cut off his bullfighter's pigtail, Manuel says: "I was going good. I was going great." This is not Spanish idiom, but it is something truer, the equivalent in our culture for what a bullfighter would say, and it has an absolute rightness.

Another superb story, "In Another Country," is about an Italian fencing champion, getting machine therapy for his mutilated hand during the First World War. In the course of the treatment his wife dies, and the story ends with a beautiful dying fall, with the fencer sitting at the therapy machine, surrounded by cheery photographs of hands like his completely restored, and the narrator's comment: "The photographs did not make much difference to the major because he only looked out of the window."

A wildly imaginative story, "The Light of the World," is about an encounter of two boys with some whores in a railroad station. Two of the whores compete in lying about their intimacy with the boxer Stanley Ketchel, whom they call "Steve." Their absurd boasts (in the language of *True Romances*), their copious tears, and their nasty abuse of each other are grotesquely funny, yet as an expression of what Freud called "the omnipotent wish," they are oddly touching. When one of the whores concludes with dignity: "Leave me with my memories. With my true, wonderful memories," a miracle has occurred through Hemingway's art, and lies have become truth.

The last of the stories I think first-rate, "The Short Happy Life of Francis Macomber," is about an American hunting in Africa who funks, then achieves courage for the first time in his life, and is immediately shot by his wife. Macomber is another look at Cohn, the American who never grew up, the artist as outsider. The prose is less firm than it is in Hemingway's earlier stories; his wife's awful remarks to Macomber are less harrowing than the awful remarks everyone makes to Cohn because less obviously the product of inner hurt; and the ending is weak and inadequate. Nevertheless, the story is so beautifully structured, its vision of delayed and short-lived initiation into manhood so powerful, that it triumphs anyway.

Along with these five thoroughly successful stories, parts of others are memorable: the beautiful camping and fishing detail of the "Big Two-Hearted River" stories, and the fine boxing detail of "Fifty Grand"; the marvelous dialogue with the landlady in "The Killers"; the endings of "After the Storm" and "A Clean, Well-Lighted Place"; the sensitivity to a child's mind in "A Day's Wait"; and some of the lovely fragments into which "The Gambler, the Nun, and the Radio" shatters.

There are fine scenes and parts, too, in the later novels, but after *The Sun Also Rises*, I think, none is a complete success. From *A Farewell to Arms* to *The Old Man and the Sea*, they show a progressive emotional softening, an increasing self-indulgent slackness of the prose, less and less control of the id's fantasy gratifications and the ego's defense mechanisms. "Famous at twenty-five; at thirty a master," Archibald MacLeish has written of Hemingway, but he omits the melancholy conclusion: over the hill at thirty-five.

Hemingway is not the first American writer stifled by fame and wealth. In the self-disgust of the autobiographical protagonist in "The Snows of Kilimanjaro," he suggests that some inner failure demands the outer stifling. The question of whether the individual or the culture is primarily responsible when a writer like Hemingway does not mature beyond his early work, or improve on its excellence, is ultimately unanswerable and pointless. If despite his great gifts Hemingway never became Melville or Tolstoy, Joyce or Proust, he nevertheless left us, in *The Sun Also Rises* and a handful of short stories, authentic masterpieces, small-scale but immortal. I urge you to read them.

A NEW LIFE FOR A GOOD MAN

Bernard Malamud's *A New Life* is the first new novel of consistent excellence that I have found since I began regular reviewing,
a lovely oasis after an interminable crawl through the hot sands. It
is the story of S. Levin, a thirty-year-old failure, who leaves New
York to be an English instructor at Cascadia College on the West
Coast. The novel covers one year of rich experience, and at its end
we see Levin, fired and disgraced, setting off for San Francisco
with his booty: a second-hand Hudson, the wife of the chairman
of his department, her two adopted children, and Levin's own
child inside her.

   A New Life, as a fable of redemption or rebirth, is accurately
titled. "One always hopes that a new place will inspire change—in
one's life," Levin says tentatively when he arrives in Cascadia.
Later, "he felt like a man entering a new life and entered." At the
height of his affair with Pauline Gilley, she says, "Oh, my darling,
we must do something with our lives." When he despairs of her,
he thinks of her as "the small town lady who talked of a new life
but had been consistently afraid of it." When she determines to
leave her husband, she says to Levin: "I want a better life. I want
it with you."

   The action of the novel is Levin's development into a kind of
saint. To the outward eye, he is a typical *schlemiel:* he steps into
cow pies, teaches with his fly open, makes the ruinous remark
every time. But in truth he is a holy *schlemiel,* God's innocent, a
Fool in Christ. Levin attains to sanctity (and I think that this
represents a considerable advance for Malamud) not through denying and mortifying the flesh, as does the anchorite Frank Alpine
in *The Assistant,* but through indulging the flesh, and his adultery
is a holy adultery.

   It begins in lust, and after his first adventure with Pauline in
the forest, Levin thinks vulgarly: "his first married woman, sex

uncomplicated in a bed of leaves, short hours, good pay." The affair progresses, and Levin suddenly realizes: "The truth is I love Pauline Gilley." It then goes beyond love, or beyond what Levin understands as love, to the sacrificial acceptance of responsibility: feeling his love gone, he nevertheless accepts the burden of Pauline and her children. "Why take that load on yourself?" Pauline's husband Gerald challenges, itemizing the disadvantages, and Levin answers, in the true voice of a Malamud saint: "Because I can, you son of a bitch." It is a classic progress from *eros*, fleshly love, to *agape*, the spiritual love of one of God's creatures for another.

Malamud's vision of life in the novel redeems its ugliness and nastiness with humor, and redeems the humor with charity. Cascadia College is a dreadful place, narrow and mean, but it is also a terribly funny place where "there are no geniuses around to make you uncomfortable," fly-casting is taught for credit, and a textbook containing Hemingway's story "Ten Indians" is banned on the pretext that it might offend, "as degrading the American Indians." Gerald Gilley is a repulsive careerist, a golf-mad professor who is compiling a picture-book of American literature, but he is a comic masterpiece of a careerist, and Levin's ultimate understanding is that Gilley too is a suffering fellow human, and his final feeling for him is compassion.

Where the sex scenes in Malamud's earlier books were always interrupted at their climax, constituting a prolonged tease of the reader, or else were consummated under the aegis of death, producing an unlovely *liebestod* effect, here (although traces of the old bad habits remain) sex is funny, earthy, and sometimes beautiful. Before becoming involved with Pauline, Levin has had: an encounter with a waitress in a barn, ruined at the dramatic moment when a disappointed rival steals their clothes; a wrestle with an unmarried colleague on the floor of his office, broken off by Levin out of an obscure compassion; and a gay weekend with a student named Nadalee, resulting in her efforts to get her class grade raised from a C to a B. His involvement with Pauline is hardly more glamorous: he is disturbed by her flat chest; at one point in the affair he has excruciating muscle spasms in bed with her; at another point she is temporarily frigid, and he thinks bitterly, "Now we have truly come to adultery." At the novel's end, in one of the most wonderfully embarrassing scenes in modern fiction, Gerald warns Levin of Pauline's constipation and menstrual irregularities. Funny, awful, it nevertheless is love, and beauty, and value.

Levin's past, when it is finally confessed to Pauline, seems unnecessarily melodramatic: his father a thief, Harry the Goniff; his mother insane and a suicide; himself a gutter alcoholic. Levin's future, as we can picture it at the end of the novel, is less extreme: Pauline will develop breasts in pregnancy; Levin, with a new identity, will again have a first name; their life together will be responsible, hard-working, and devoted. If this is not joy, the topgallant delight that Father Mapple's sermon promises the righteous in *Moby-Dick*, it is a happy ending nevertheless, and perhaps as much as our shabby modern world can promise anyone.

Malamud's technical mastery is impressive. His apparently episodic novel is tightly woven, mostly by means of foreshadowing. When the chairman of the department warns Levin against dating students or prowling among faculty wives, the weekend with Nadalee and the affair with Pauline are implicit in his warning, as though created by it ("Nay, I had not known sin, but by the law," says St. Paul, "for I had not known lust, except the law had said, Thou shalt not covet"). When Levin arrives in Cascadia, the Gilleys take him to their house for dinner, and Pauline spills the tunafish casserole in his lap; when he has changed into a fresh pair of pants, the little boy wets on them. It is an uproarious scene, and announces Levin as the book's *schlemiel*, but it is also the annunciation of his future role as husband and father, victim and protector, of the woman and child who pour their love in his lap.

Some of *A New Life* is scandalously funny. C. D. Fabrikant, the department's scholar, is rarely seen except on horseback, and gallops off by way of punctuating his remarks. Levin first meets the dean carrying a bag of grapefruit, and as in an old silent movie, while they talk they scramble for the grapefruit after the dean has walked into a telephone pole, then scramble again when Levin walks into a tree. Like that of Malamud's best stories in *The Magic Barrel*, the humor is wild and surrealistic. The cold bare trip back to town with the waitress cursing Levin is nightmarish comedy, as is his later fruitless effort to expose a plagiarist, with the suspected plagiarist following him around and jeering.

At the height of his emotional disturbance, Levin walks into a bar, orders "Love," and when the bartender goes in search of the bottle, madly flees. When Levin goes to confront the wronged husband in his hotel room, Gerald greets him earnestly with: "Pardon the small room." In the terrible period when Levin has bravely given up Pauline, and is tormented by erotic dreams, Malamud writes:

> Amid such pleasures Mrs. Beaty's white cat fell in love with him, laying a broken-feathered bird at his door, fat headless robin. He asked the landlady to keep the cat out of the house but pussy in love was faithful, finding more ways in than he could block off, depositing another bloody-breasted bird. "Eat my heart," he cried and kicked the beast down the stairs. Ascending on three legs she delivered a mangled rat, then went into heat, her raucous cries sounding through the house.

Malamud's expressionist device, which he shares with several of the best writers of our time, is writing dreams, fantasies, and even similes as though they were literal realities. When he reads a theme of Nadalee's about swimming naked, "Though Levin's legs cramped after a too hasty immersion in cold water, he jumped in after her and spent most of the night swimming with Nadalee." When Gerald describes trout-fishing to Levin, his office becomes a mountain stream.

Malamud's work has some of the bitter comedy of Yiddish literature, some of the preoccupation with sin and redemption of Russian literature. It particularly resembles the work of that remarkable Soviet-Jewish writer, Isaac Babel, who combines both traditions, and combines them *within* the current of modern European literature. *A New Life*, in its progress from affair to bondage, may remind readers of *A Farewell to Arms*, but Malamud faces up to problems that Hemingway kills Catherine to evade. It has some of the grubby comedy of the British Angries, the compassion of Salinger, the moral earnestness of George P. Elliott. Yet this novel, like Malamud's work generally, remains unique, in its totality sharply unlike the work of anyone else.

Certainly there are flaws. *A New Life* is too slow getting started, and the book is half over before its action really begins. There are infelicities of style and syntax, although fewer than in the earlier books, and occasional weaknesses of diction, as when Malamud gets fancy and writes "dew" for "tears." Some of the plot, in which Levin becomes a candidate for chairman of the department and meets espionage with counter-espionage, is absurd, although Malamud saves himself at the worst point by writing a human and moving confrontation scene between Levin and the woman colleague who has just gone through his files.

In progressing from *The Natural* to *The Assistant* to *A New Life*, Malamud has achieved a new mature acceptance. Pauline is the Iris of *The Natural*, no longer scorned; Levin rakes leaves with the frenzy of Frank Alpine, but he has an insight into his nature and destiny that Frank never achieves. In a sense, Malamud has moved from the story of Samson, punished for the misuse of his powers, to Job, suffering because chosen to suffer, to Jesus, suffering voluntarily to redeem. If Malamud continues to find modern plots to embody his powerful redemptive themes, I know no limit to what he can accomplish.

MARIANNE MOORE AT SEVENTY-FOUR

She is the Great Lady of modern poetry, an institution as timeless and lovely as the Brooklyn Bridge near which she lives. *A Marianne Moore Reader* is a sampler that puts all her skills on display, and afterwards sends us scurrying back to her other books. "From forty-five to seventy / is the best age," she tells us in "Marriage," quoting Trollope, but surely seventy-four is the best age for a retrospective show—and what a show it is.

The first third of the *Reader* consists of selections from the *Collected Poems*, two complete later volumes of verse—*Like a Bulwark* and *O To Be a Dragon*—and five recent poems. Here is "Silence," that beautiful tribute to her father's tact, which must be quoted entire:

> *My father used to say,*
> *"Superior people never make long visits,"*
> *have to be shown Longfellow's grave*
> *or the glass flowers at Harvard.*
> *Self-reliant like the cat—*
> *that takes its prey to privacy,*
> *the mouse's limp tail hanging like a shoelace from its mouth—*
> *they sometimes enjoy solitude,*
> *and can be robbed of speech*
> *by speech which has delighted them.*
> *The deepest feeling always shows itself in silence;*
> *not in silence, but restraint.*
> *Nor was he insincere in saying, "Make my house your inn."*
> *Inns are not residences.*

A gem of autobiography, one says? Yet the notes show that Miss Moore created it, miraculously, out of a reminiscence by Miss A. M. Homans of *her* father, and the inn quotation from Edmund Burke.

Here too are "Ireland," with its "linnet spinet-sweet," and

that powerful and delicate tribute to fortitude, "Nevertheless,"
with its famous ending (which I will always hear in Miss Moore's
brave small reading-voice):

> *What sap*
> *went through that little thread*
> *to make the cherry red!*

Among so many triumphs, perhaps the finest of all is "In Distrust
of Merits," the most eloquent and permanent poem to come out of
the Second World War. It is interesting to learn from the interview with Donald Hall, reprinted in the *Reader,* that Miss Moore
now finds "In Distrust of Merits" too formless to call a poem, referring to it as "testimony," and explaining, "Emotion overpow-
ered me." The poem is too long to quote here, but if its chiseled
and radiant ten-line stanzas are formless, a barrel of Moore Form-
lessness ought to be dispatched to all the poets.

The apparent subjects of Miss Moore's poems are most often
exotic animals: the pangolin, the plumet basilisk, the ostrich, the
Indian buffalo, the frigate pelican, and innumerable others. They
are all exactly detailed, since, as she tells us in "Four Quartz Crys-
tal Clocks," "The lemur-student can see / that an aye-aye is not /
an angwan-tíbo, potto, or loris." There is a lesser, but substantial,
richness of botanical life in such poems as "Virginia Britannia,"
and a preoccupation with the art of music in such poems as "Pro-
priety." Magnificently alive as her animals, plants, or musical
compositions are, they are not really her subjects, but occasions
for reflections on the human world, or parables, what she calls in a
poem about Italy, *"mythologica esopica."* Thus "The Paper Nauti-
lus" begins:

> *For authorities whose hopes*
> *are shaped by mercenaries?*
> *Writers entrapped by*
> *teatime fame and by*
> *commuter's comforts? Not for these*
> *the paper nautilus*
> *constructs her thin glass shell.*

Miss Moore's subtlety of form is unrivaled in our time. She
says in the preface to the *Reader* that she prefers end-stopped

lines, but the stanza above shows how jauntily her lines can run on. As T. S. Eliot wrote in his introduction to her *Selected Poems* of 1935, she is "the greatest living master" of the light or inconspicuous rhyme, rhyming on an unaccented syllable or even on an article. Some of her poems are syllabic rather than accentual, like French poetry, with stanzas in which each line has a fixed number of syllables (perfectly so in the eight stanzas of "The Fish" and the twenty-seven stanzas of "The Jerboa," less regularly so in such poems as "Nine Nectarines and Other Porcelain"). Her art inheres where William Blake said it must, in "minute particulars," and her moral is Blake's moral, "Everything that lives is holy."

Many excellent poems are omitted from the *Reader*, among them "No Swan So Fine," "The Past is the Present," "Novices," "Elephants," and most of the syllabic ones, including "The Jerboa." Almost all of the wonderful poems on aesthetics are omitted, even her most famous poem, "Poetry," with its bold beginning, "I, too, dislike it: there are things that are important beyond all this fiddle," and its classic formulation, "imaginary gardens with real toads in them." Miss Moore may have grown tired of "Poetry," but surely *we* have not. She has revised one poem for the occasion, "The Steeple-Jack," with an additional stanza and a few word changes, and she has, I think, revised it for the better.

The later poems included are on the whole less impressive than the poems of the *Collected* volume. Sometimes they go flat and prosy, as in parts of "The Staff of Aesculapius"; or fall into doggerel, as in parts of "Hometown Piece for Messrs. Alston and Reese"; or become Ogden-Nashery, as in the end of "The Arctic Ox (or Goat)." Instead of those "rigorists," the Lapp reindeer, the hero is now apt to be President Eisenhower, "our / hardest-working citizen." Yet "Rosemary" is a lovely poem, "No Better Than a 'Withered Daffodil' " has much of the old economical perfection, and "Sun" (almost the latest written) is magnificent. Miss Moore effortlessly defies retirement.

The critical prose in the *Reader* includes four essays from *Predilections*, along with some later articles and reviews. It shows the same fine eye for detail that the poetry does. Miss Moore is a real critic, with a rich insight into poetry, not only the Moorish, such as Cowper's "The Snail," but work that is worlds apart from

hers, such as Eliot's "Ash Wednesday." It is a shame that more of
the essays from *Predilections* could not have been included, particularly those on Wallace Stevens and W. H. Auden, and the delightful reminiscence of the *Dial*. Perhaps the Pound essay, which
dates, could have been omitted to make space for one of two of
them.

The later prose is sometimes, as in the 1956 "Idiosyncrasy and
Technique," almost a mosaic of quotations, a commonplace book.
At least one of the late pieces, Miss Moore's excessively kind review of George Plimpton's contrived and worthless *Out of My
League,* should not have invited preservation. But all of the critical prose has Miss Moore's enchanting pawky quality (as in the
gnomic comment on obscurity, "One should be as clear as one's
natural reticence allows one to be"), and she is sometimes gently
stern, as when she whispers that Beat poetry might be better still
were it not so formless and exhibitionistic.

The *Reader* includes three other things worth having. One is
a liberal selection of about two dozen fables from Miss Moore's
translation of *The Fables of La Fontaine*. La Fontaine would
have seemed the perfect subject for her, since they are both besti-
ary fabulists, but actually he is her inferior, and his prosy didacti-
cism fetters her imagination. These translations are best where she
is very free, as in "The Fox and the Crow," or where La Fontaine
is very Moorish, as in the moral to "The Serpent and the File," or
where she is preoccupied with her own music, as in the harmonies
beginning "Bitch and Friends":

> *A bitch who approached each hutch with a frown.*
> *Since a-shiver to shelter an imminent litter,*
> *Crouched perplexed till she'd coaxed from a vexed benefactor*
> *A lean-to as a loan and in it lay down.*

A real treasure in the book is her exchange of correspondence, first printed in *The New Yorker,* with the Ford Motor Company regarding a name for its new car. She proposes "Hurrican
Hirundo," "The Intelligent Whale," "Mongoose Civique," "Utopian Turtletop," and a hundred others—for the car eventually
named "Edsel." We see her receiving the confidential sketches,
done in what she calls "toucan tones," studying them upside

down, and discovering in them "a sense of fish buoyancy." It is a priceless encounter between the frail lady poet and the mammoth corporation, and in the war of wits the Ford Company had about as much chance as Goliath had.

The final item is the interview by Hall that appeared in *The Paris Review* early in 1961. In it Miss Moore is modest, referring to her "so-called poems" or "observations"; she is sparse and eloquent, explaining, "We did foregather a little," or remarking of Hart Crane's *The Bridge*, "he could have firmed it up"; she is even still loyal to the Edsel, explaining, "It came out the wrong year." (Perhaps it would have done better named "Utopian Turtletop.")

More than anything, she is Marianne Moore. In common with her, I lived for many years in Brooklyn (although my Brooklyn was not as bounded by Presbyterian churches as hers seems to be), and I am a fan of the former Brooklyn Dodgers. I claim these ties with pride, because she confers distinction on everything she touches. She is inimitable, and a very great lady. Give *A Marianne Moore Reader* for Christmas to all the people you respect, or love.

IN THE JUNGLES OF BROOKLYN

Daniel Fuchs' three novels of American Jewish life—*Summer in Williamsburg, Homage to Blenholt,* and *Low Company*—appeared in the 1930s, along with Henry Roth's *Call It Sleep.* As it did, they got lost in the swamp of proletarian literature. They sold 400, 400, and 1,200 copies respectively, but a few people knew and valued them, and a small Fuchs cult has developed over the years. Roth's book was successfully reissued in 1960, and now Basic Books has brought out a one-volume edition of all of Fuchs' (*Three Novels by Daniel Fuchs*). Although these novels are better written than *Call It Sleep,* they are less ambitious and "serious," although very well worth reading or rereading.

Summer in Williamsburg, published in 1934, is the inevitable autobiographical first novel. The young hero, Philip Hayman, puzzled by the suicide of a neighbor, is assigned the task of understanding by an unlikely local sage, Old Miller. Miller says:

> If you would really discover the reason, you must pick Williamsburg to pieces until you have them all spread out on your table before you, a dictionary of Williamsburg. And then select. Pick and discard. Take, with intelligence you have not and with a patience that would consume a number of lifetimes, the different aspects that are pertinent. Collect and then analyze to understand the quality of each detail. Perhaps then you might know why Sussman died, but granting everything I do not guarantee the process.

This assignment becomes the novel. The pertinent aspects of Williamsburg are: Philip's uncle Papravel, a gangster engaged in wrecking one bus service to the Catskills on behalf of another; Sam Linck, the janitress' son, a married truck driver engaged in a very messy affair with a Polish waitress; Philip's friend Cohen, "the poor simp," who characteristically jumps off the Williamsburg Bridge, unsuccessfully, because he has spilled herring on a rented tuxedo; Philip himself, involved with high-class-uptown-Yankee-Doodle Ruth and unhappily-married Tessie; Philip's family; and many others.

All this is given a mild social significance: Cohen falls into Communist party circles as briefly and senselessly as he falls into the East River, and Papravel defends himself and his mobsters as just another small business trying to make a living. Cohen's misadventures and Papravel's bland piety are quite funny, the Linck households are convincingly sordid, Philip's fumblings at life are often moving, but somehow the material never comes together in the synthesis and enlightenment Fuchs means to produce. The book ends on Papravel's joy at his business success, but nothing else is resolved, certainly not Sussman's suicide. The image of Williamsburg life that the reader takes away from the novel is a vision of the guinea pigs that roam the floor of the filthy Linck apartment, nibbling at dropped food and scurrying with fright at every shouted curse.

Homage to Blenholt, published in 1936, is neater in that all of its strands are tied together at the end. Max Balkan, who aspires to Renaissance grandeur and hopes to achieve it by selling revolutionary ideas to industry, and his sister Rita's fiancé, Mendel Munves, an amateur etymologist who aspires to a life of dedicated scholarship, are reconciled at the book's end to the realities of life in Williamsburg, marriage, and a partnership in a delicatessen. Fuchs attempts to symbolize both the aspirations and their absurdity in the figure of Blenholt, a crooked politician who has just died. Max sees him as "a great man," "Tamburlaine in New York," a symbol of "high-handed adventure," and attends his funeral as an act of homage. In a savage comic scene, the funeral turns into a riot, in which Max gets trampled and his glasses are broken.

Blenholt is too cruel a parody to symbolize Max and Mendel's aspirations for a life richer than the one they see around them. A more effective symbol appears in Heshey, a boy in the apartment house, who revenges himself on the bully, Chink, by trapping him in a dumbwaiter and bombarding him with garbage. It is a scene that is every weakling's wishful fantasy, and Max properly identifies himself with Heshey, as does the reader.

The book's final reconciliation with the world's demands is foreshadowed in its early pages, when Max sees a fantastic figure walking down the street, and it turns out to be two pregnant women walking arm in arm, a vision of his and Mendel's future. At the end, Max's noble old father silently protests his son's surrender, thinking "that this death of youth was among the greatest tragedies in experience and that all the tears in America were not enough to bewail it." The author answers him in the book's final line, "But all the same the evening sun that day went down on time," and we realize that we are being asked to accept the triumph of the world, the death of the dream, as natural and perhaps even as welcome. We are left with a warm domestic comedy, an earlier and more engaging *Marjorie Morningstar*.

Low Company, published in 1937, moves from Williamsburg to Coney Island, and, as an uglier gangster novel than the first, thoroughly justifies its title. Its gangsters remain unconvincing figures who say, "If you give us ten thousand dollars we will do to the other fellow as we were supposed to do to you," but now they are ominous. More sharply than Papravel and his mob, they are designed to symbolize capitalism. Herbert Lurie, who owns a dress store and is the only understanding intelligence the book has, tells Shubunka, a brothel-keeper being run out of business by the syndicate: "Business is business. It's the same goddammed thing in my line, only a little less lousy." The book deals with the interwoven fates of half a dozen characters who meet in Ann's soda parlor: Lurie; Shubunka; Louis Spitzbergen, who owns the houses Shubunka uses; Moe Karty, a compulsive horse-player; Shorty, an unsuccessful lecher; and others.

In the course of the novel's action the gangsters almost kill Shubunka and drive him out of town; Lurie breaks with his fiancée after seeing her heartlessness in refusing to give Shubunka refuge; Shorty is beaten up by a stout Russian corsetière he has tried to rape; Karty is beaten almost to death by his brothers-in-law for embezzling their money and losing it on the horses; and Spitzbergen is grotesquely murdered by Karty in a pathetic and ineffectual attempt at a hold-up. For all the violence and horror, the only gain is Lurie's perception:

> Lurie knew now that it had been insensible and inhuman for him, too, simply to hate Neptune and seek escape from it. This also was hard and ignorant, lacking human compassion. He had known the people at Ann's in their lowness and had been re-

pelled by them, but now it seemed to him that he understood how their evil appeared in their impoverished dingy lives and, further, how miserable their own evil rendered them. It was not enough to call them low and pass on.

What remains in the reader's mind from *Low Company* are two authentically chilling scenes, the brilliantly-lit deserted boardwalk where Shubunka flees the killers, and the nightmarish, slobbering death-struggle of Karty and Spitzbergen in a BMT washroom.

In the Brooklyn jungles of Daniel Fuchs, every hoodlum and pimp, every horse-player and brothel-landlord, sees himself as an honest businessman, righteously proclaiming "There is still a God over America," as he drives a competitor out of business or beats a relative unconscious. It is a world drenched in sex, but it has surprisingly little joy. In the nearest thing to a "love story" in the novels, the courtship of Max and Ruth in *Homage to Blenholt,* Ruth's pretty memory is of Max fondling her breast, "playing with it like a potato pancake." The normal means of communication in this brutal world is cursing and screaming, in a vocabulary consisting mainly of "mean," "rotten," and "snotnose." The ultimate mood is sad reconciliation: Sam Linck's wife and mistress somehow adjust to each other; even Heshey and Chink make up; Lurie accepts human nature.

Sometimes Fuchs captures a life I can remember with the relentless and embarrassing accuracy of Nichols and May, as when Philip explains to Tessie, "I feel that a funny I lives in my body." At other times we get something close to the travesty of "The Goldbergs," with Mrs. Balkan shouting "Mother, schmother," or instructing her daughter Rita to call a suitor who owns a meat market "darling." But Fuchs is not really in the naturalistic tradition of Michael Gold's *Jews Without Money,* nor do his novels "do for Jewish life in Brooklyn in the 1930s," as the jacket foolishly suggests, "what James T. Farrell did for the Irish of Chicago in his Studs Lonigan trilogy."

Fuchs' true tradition is that of Nathanael West and Henry Roth in the 30s, the symbolists and fantasists, a tradition he shares with many of the finest young writers of our time. He is best when he is most bold and imaginative, most garish and grotesque: the guinea pigs, Blenholt's funeral, Chink in the dumbwaiter, the death of Spitzbergen. Fuchs was never quite bold *enough*, never really understood his literary heritage, never achieved a firm center for his sprawling natural history. His talent is considerable, and his later works might have been the triumphs that bits of these books promise. But Fuchs never wrote any more novels. Instead, as he tells us proudly in the preface to *Three Novels,* he gave up, and quit his fourth in the middle. He decided "to become rich" instead, and took to writing for the slick magazines, and then for Hollywood. Fuchs now lives in Beverly Hills, and he won an Academy Award in 1955 for the script of *Love Me or Leave Me*. The question of whether he ever really had the talent to be a major novelist remains unanswered.

Meanwhile the tone of machine politics in New York has changed a lot since Blenholt wore a white linen suit with yellow tie and blue shirt. These days Carmine De Sapio writes to the *Times:* "The employment of semantics in order to create a gratuitous dichotomy ill becomes the *New York Times*." Now Williamsburg and Coney Island are full of Puerto Ricans, and if they call each other "snotnose" it is in an alien tongue. It is a remote and archaic past that comes to life again in these pages.

THE SADNESS OF CESARE PAVESE

"The fame Vittorini has won in America, has it made you jealous? No. I am in no hurry. I shall beat him in the long run." So Cesare Pavese wrote in his diary late in 1949, at a time when not one of his books was available in English. A few months later, at the age of forty-two, he killed himself and achieved in death the American public that he had not been able to achieve in life. Three of the four novels of his last period, which he called "symbolic realism," were published in the United States in 1953 and 1954. The fourth, *The House on the Hill*, translated by W. J. Strachan, and the diaries, *The Burning Brand: Diaries 1935-1950*, translated by A. E. Murch, appeared in the United States in 1961.

In the style of the best Italian films, Pavese works by understatement and implication. Nothing seems to happen in the foreground of *The House on the Hill*. The narrator, a forty-year-old schoolteacher taking refuge in the countryside from the bombing of Turin, encounters some anti-Fascists staying at an old inn, among them his former mistress and her illegitimate son, who may be his son too. When the adults are arrested by the Germans and the boy runs off, the narrator goes dispiritedly back to his native village. Nothing dramatic has happened, we never learn the fates of the boy and his mother, yet the suggestions and resonances of the story are profoundly moving.

The narrator, Corrado, is utterly inadequate in his relationship with the woman, Cate. During their affair Cate's "sole appeal was sex, sex somewhat tediously and embarrassingly manifest," and he had failed her as a lover. Now he fails her as a friend and potential husband, deeply attracted but fearful of something "elemental and savage, a woman in her prime." His contemptible reaction to her arrest is to think "I could still save myself" and to flee to safety. He eventually concludes: "I do not know whether Cate, Fonso, Dino and all the others will ever return. Sometimes I hope they will and then I get in a panic."

The boy, Corradino, is surely Corrado's son, and Corrado's failure to be a father to him is perhaps even greater than his failure with Cate. Knowing better, he accepts Cate's transparent assurance that he is not Dino's father, and he cultivates the boy in a chummy relationship involving no responsibilities. When Dino runs off, Corrado thinks only: "If I had Dino here with me, I could still give him his orders." The problem is Corrado's own immaturity. He wants not a son, but a companion for roaming the woods, where "all notion of woman and the burning mystery of sex was out of place." Cate tells him, "You are just like a boy," and later clarifies it: "You are not capable of love."

As Corrado is less than a husband and less than a father, so is he less than a man in the existentialist situation of the Resistance, which demands action against the enemy. "We should rise in revolt and throw bombs," he tells Cate, but when she acts on his words, he says, "You've become a real bolshie." At the novel's end he recognizes himself as a failure who "ran away from the Germans and from sorrow and remorse." "No one has any rights over us," Corrado had said, denying all human ties; "We are in the world by chance." During a bombing he thinks: "I would like to have been a root, a worm, and gone underground." His reward at the end is bitter self-contempt, the recognition that he was saved only because he was "the most useless of them."

In Pavese's world of myth and irony, *The House on the Hill* is a powerful anti-Odyssey, in which a weakling Odysseus is returned to his long-lost wife and son, only to lose them again through impotence and ineffectuality. Corrado's disengagement from the world, Pavese makes clear, is the disengagement of catatonia, not of philosophic freedom. The diaries show that to some degree the figure is autobiographical. As Corrado did, Pavese spent 1943 and 1944 in the Piedmont countryside; two of his close friends were active in the Resistance and were killed by the Germans; he records his feelings of "bewilderment and nothingness" during those years. "A man, a woman, a boy," the diaries note at one point, and at another: "A house on the crest of the hill, dark against the crimson sky—the place that evokes your passion."

Much of the book's power inheres in those two symbols, which in different terms are the Holy Family and Calvary. Other symbols in the book seem more contrived. A bomb is a "maddened fire-bird"; the Germans are "bony, green like lizards"; a fearless rat on a rubbish heap in Turin embodies all the horror of war. Phalliform scarlet flowers explicitly represent sexuality—as winter comes they die, and new flowers of hope will appear in the spring. "Under the rotting leaves on the hillside, the first flowers would soon be coming through."

No symbol in *The House on the Hill* is as powerful as the two terrible human bonfires in *The Moon and the Bonfires*, Pavese's last novel and perhaps his best. But nothing in *The Moon and the Bonfires* is quite so poignant as the scene here when Dino nestles up against Corrado in the dark, and Corrado feels that "I had lost myself for a moment among the stars and in the night space."

The diaries reveal that for a while at least Pavese was a member of the Italian Communist Party, but surely he was the least political of Communist novelists. "My stories are always about love or loneliness," he wrote in 1938. Even later, when he wrote novels of the War and the Resistance, they became inner events: the war an externalization of the torn self, the Resistance an initiation into manhood and a test of the initiate's capacity to love and to act. Ultimately *The House on the Hill* is an existentialist allegory of the human condition, the loneliness and terror man feels as a dying animal, the humiliation and disgust he feels as a nasty one.

The Burning Brand: Diaries 1935-1950 makes very melancholy reading. A good deal of it is devoted to general problems of writing and literature. The most common image for writing is pain and torment: "poetry is an ever-open wound." About other writers Pavese is sometimes very perceptive, as when he remarks of Balzac, "He is never comic or tragic, he is curious," or discovers that Faulkner's metaphors are Elizabethan. Pavese's long discussions of myth and ritual, of Frazer and Jane Harrison, make clear how conscious his symbolic effects are, as do such definitions of his intention as "Narrating realities as though they were incredible."

Many of the entries are bitter wisdom about life. "Living is like working out a long-addition sum," Pavese writes, "and if you make a mistake in the first two totals you will never find the right answer." A later entry adds gloomily, "Mistakes are always initial." "Youth ends," Pavese writes bleakly at twenty-nine, "when we perceive that no one wants our gay abandon." Sometimes the tone is ruefully comic, as when he observes: "When a man is suffering people treat him like a drunkard: 'Get up, now; come on; that's enough; be on your way; not like that; that's it. . . .' "

There is little political discussion in *The Burning Brand* until 1946, when Communism appears as a subject. "A meeting of the Party has all the characteristics of a religious rite," Pavese notes in 1947. "We listen to be assured of what we already think, to be exalted by our common faith and confession." In 1948 there are traces of Marxist thinking, of a rather existentialist sort, such as: "To *know* the world one must *construct* it." In 1949 Pavese is questioning the limits of "dialectical materialism," and by the next year he quotes the opinion of unidentified persons that "Pavese is not a good communist." There is a wry aptness to a wild slip in an editorial footnote, which describes Pavese's 1935 imprisonment for anti-Fascism as "sentenced to prison for anti-communist activities."

At times the diaries talk about nothing but sex, and one sad affair succeeds another. Pavese is quite frank about his sexual difficulty, a history of premature ejaculation that made him unable to satisfy women and determined him never to marry. There is a terrible anguish in his recognition that "no woman ever finds pleasure with me, or ever would," combined with his conviction that sex "is the central activity of life, beyond question." At one point Pavese is convinced that he is cured; at another he resolves: "One can do without it." Most touching, perhaps, is the absurdity of what he calls "an old dream": "To live in the country with a beautiful woman—Greer Garson or Lana Turner—and lead a simple, perverse life."

Page after page cries out in pain: "But it is agony," "Loneliness is pain," "I am filled with distaste for what I have done," "I have a live coal in my breast," "The greatest misfortune is loneliness." There are few years without thoughts of suicide. "My basic principle is suicide," Pavese writes in 1936. "The worst thing a suicidal type of man can do," he remarks the next year, "is not killing himself, but thinking of it and not doing it." In 1938 he notes bitterly, at the end of a long recital of failure: "You will never have the courage to kill yourself. Look how many times you have thought of it." And so the diaries go, endlessly toying with the subject, until 1950, when we find a sudden note of decisiveness: "There is only one answer: suicide." The last entry in the book, just before his death, notes: "All it takes is a little courage."

Why did Pavese kill himself? There are so many answers—sex, politics, loneliness, self-disgust, depression—that the question might better be: How did Pavese manage to live so long? One image that Pavese presents for himself and his writing is almost unbearably painful. He imagines:

> A man alone in a hut, eating the grease and gravy from a cooking pot. Some days he scrapes it with an old knife, on other days with his nails; there was a time when the pot was full, the food good; now it is stale, and to get the taste of it the man gnaws his broken nails. He will do the same tomorrow and the next day.

Pavese was a greatly talented writer, and one fervently wishes him the American success he longed for. But how disturbing these books are to read, and how terribly sad.

O'FAOLAIN'S WONDERFUL FISH

Sean O'Faolain (formerly Seán O'Faoláin; still earlier, John Whelan), is not nearly so well known in this country as Frank O'Connor and other Irish fiction writers markedly his inferior. It seems unlikely that the publication of his latest fine volume of short stories, *I Remember! I Remember!*, will do much to correct this. At sixty-two, O'Faolain is perhaps the foremost living Irish writer. Posterity at least will know it.

Unlike Goldsmith and Sheridan, Moore and Wilde, Joyce and Yeats, Shaw and O'Casey, O'Flaherty and Miss Bowen, as well as innumerable others, O'Faolain has remained living and working in Ireland. For a time in the 1930s he lived in London, but he soon returned. O'Faolain spends a lot of time in Italy and he has been teaching and lecturing in the United States in recent years, but he has never been a member of the Irish literary emigration. His roots remain in Ireland, where, incidentally, two of his books are banned.

O'Faolain has a small but genuine talent, and his polished, subtle, and effective short stories include some of the finest of our time. He is a minor writer, as George Herbert, say, is a minor writer. He is not Yeats or Joyce, and like every contemporary Irish writer he has had to spend a good deal of effort getting them off his back. What distinguished Yeats and Joyce from all their contemporaries was not their imaginative power, but the possession of a first-rate mind that turned that imagination in the right direction: Yeats toward the spare, tuned-off-the-note verse of his mature years; Joyce toward the drastic confrontation of language that culminated in *Finnegans Wake*. O'Faolain has their brains without comparable imaginative resources. Other Irish writers, notably O'Casey and Seumas O'Kelly, had the imaginative power without the shaping intelligence.

Although he has remained in provincial, narrow, and puri-

tanic Eire, O'Faolain is the least provincial of Irish writers. He is
educated (a Harvard M.A.) and literate, his work is thoroughly
European, and his masters are not the peasant storytellers by the
turf fires, but Chekhov and Maupassant. His subject matter, however, is entirely Irish. It is in fact the Irish revolution, and to the
extent that that is now a diminished theme, the only theme with
which he can replace it is memory, nostalgia.

O'Faolain's first book, a brilliant collection of seven short
stories entitled *Midsummer Night Madness,* appeared in 1932.
The Troubles pervade all of them, but the stories are political
only to the extent that their subject matter is the tension between
the violent times and the constants of human passion. Three of the
stories—"Midsummer Night Madness," "The Small Lady," and
"The Bombshop"—are masterpieces, and what one remembers
from them is not the desperate and mindless killing by Tans and
Sinn Feiners, or Free Staters and Irregulars, but the richness of
life in pockets of the violence: Old Henn, the Anglo-Irish liber-
tine in his decrepit pride; the traitorous small lady naked and
passionate in the rain before the revolutionaries execute her; the
cozy fire the young lovers of "The Bombshop" light for the comfort of Mother Dale's staring corpse.

Each of the three novels O'Faolain wrote in the 1930s is impressive, but none is wholly successful. The first, *A Nest of Simple
Folk,* tried to chronicle three generations of change, 1854 to 1916,
through the life of Leo Foxe-Donnel. It suffers from over-
ambitiousness in trying to make Leo embody too much Irish history; at various times he is a peasant, an Ascendancy rake, a Fe-
nian revolutionary, a village laborer, a town shopkeeper, and so
forth. The strength of the book is its sense of nature as history and
destiny, what Leo's wife calls "the mad black blood that is in you."

O'Faolain's second novel, *Bird Alone,* is a gloomy love story
set in "those dead years," the years after Parnell's death. The narrator becomes a "bird alone, a heron without a mate," as much
from Parnell's death and the failure of political hope as from the
melodramatic death of his beloved carrying his unborn child—in
fact, it is the same story told on two symbolic levels.

The third and last novel, *Come Back to Erin,* is about a living
anachronism, Frankie Hannafey, a revolutionary gunman who has

been on the run in the hills, or in jail, from 1916 to 1936, first from the Tans, then from the Free Staters, finally from the Eire police. "I thought that was all over and done with years ago," says his American half-brother, not unreasonably. Eventually the author transports Frankie to New York, where he dabbles in high life and glamorous romance before returning to Ireland, his true love, and a job as, of all things, a Warble Fly Inspector.

Since 1940, O'Faolain has written no more novels, although he has published volumes of short stories, biography, travel, literary criticism, and cultural history. In the early 1940s he edited *The Bell*, a literary and political monthly. In 1948, after *The Bell* was stilled, he wrote a letter to the *New York Times Book Review*, announcing that "Irish literature is passing through years both hard and lean." That had been clear much earlier, when Frankie Hannafey appeared at the Starlight Roof of the Waldorf in a borrowed dinner jacket.

I Remember! I Remember!, as its title accurately shows, is suffused with the theme of memory. All but one of its eleven stories are about the ironies of remembrance. An ambitious and successful architect is upset in "A Shadow, Silent as a Cloud" when a waitress turns out to have shared his childhood at a country house, and all his youthful dreams of love return to challenge him. "A Touch of Autumn in the Air" is about an old man's vivid memories of an insignificant sensual experience in his childhood, suddenly recalled by a sweetshop odor, and the narrator comments: "It was plain, at last, that he was thinking of all those fragments of his boyhood as the fish scales of some wonderful fish, never-to-be-seen, sinuous and shining, that had escaped from his net into the ocean." In "The Younger Generation," the bishop's pastoral letter turns into a childish letter to his dead mother, and then he realizes that he writes "not to the living but to the dying and the dead." In "Two of a Kind" an Irish sailor and his legendary aunt in Brooklyn get together to lie and reminisce, and the lighthouse in Limerick that he describes to her is one that he has just seen in a toyshop on Eighth Avenue.

Three stories stand out from the rest. "Love's Young Dream" seems to me the best thing in the book, a superb story. The narrator recalls his adolescent involvement with two girls: his cousin

Philly, whose innocent and moving love for him he rejected callously, and Noreen, the wild daughter of his aunt's servant, who treated him as he treated Philly. Almost nothing happens—Philly fades out of the story, Noreen runs off to London with a man—but the tension mounts unbearably until the climax, when Noreen's mother, "her eyes out on pins," rips to shreds the blouse the narrator has brought for her daughter. The story concludes with the quiet statement that all this happened forty years before, that the narrator is now married with grown children, that the cottage has been torn down and replaced by a car park, but that somehow these memories are more real than the rest of his life.

The title story, "I Remember! I Remember!," is a delicate and beautiful tale of two Irish women: Mary, married to a wealthy American, and her crippled sister Sarah, who cannot stir out of her house but has total recall. Mary's marital unhappiness, subtly hinted, is sharpened by her memories of youthful joy. Her wounds are rubbed raw by Sarah's pitiless reminder of every event in Mary's past and present, "untrue in the way that a police report is untrue, because it leaves out everything except the facts." The story ends with Sarah's recognition that, for no reason that she can understand, her sister will never revisit her.

"No Country for Old Men" is O'Faolain's bold attempt to wrestle with his theme in comic terms. Two elderly businessmen who took part in the 1916 Rising forty years before, now manufacture Celtic Corsets, decorated with designs from the Lindisfarne Gospels. Through a series of accidents, they find themselves across the border in Northern Ireland, in the company van with a pink corset painted on each side, involved in an I.R.A. raid on a police barracks. They are captured and jailed, to their delight, and the story ends with one hero writing the other's biography. Ireland, in Yeats' words, is "no country for old men," whereas the young are "proud and ignorant and lovely," as the old once were. Revolutionary Ireland, O'Faolain says, is with O'Leary in the grave, and its fossils are inspecting cattle for warble flies or merchandising patriotic corsets.

O'Faolain's images are powerful and compelling. At Mary's final announcement, she hears from Sarah "a noise like a drip of rain, or melting snow, or oozing blood." The narrator of "Love's

Young Dream" realizes that everyone imprisoned in childhood "must, blind-eyed, gnaw his way out, secretly and unaided." When the images are used as symbols, they are equally effective. In "The Sugawn Chair," the old peasant chair, which the narrator's parents comically fail to reseat with straw ropes, beautifully represents the love and innocence of their youth. The thrush that the bishop repeatedly hears cracking a snail against a stone is a perfect symbol for the vulnerability of the universal dream.

There are less successful stories in the book, and sometimes a weak ending. But the general level is very high. The nostalgic voice of Sean O'Faolain is the true voice of Ireland in the 1960s, and as long as he continues to publish, the Irish Renaissance lives on.

THE WASH OF THE WORLD

When Djuna Barnes' *Nightwood* was first published in 1937, Clifton Fadiman reviewed it with wild enthusiasm in *The New Yorker*. On the strength of that review, this college freshman promptly read the book and agreed that it was one of the great novels of our time. In a retrospective column at the end of the year, as I recall, Fadiman retracted—he had thought less of *Nightwood* on second reading. I was left, so to speak, holding the bag of Fadiman's former opinion, and I think my sense that book reviewers speak with something less than divine omniscience dates from that event. In the quarter of a century since I have told anyone who would listen (including my students, who *have* to listen) that *Nightwood* is a marvelous book. I never quite dared reread it, though, lest I share Fadiman's fate. It has now been republished in *The Selected Works of Djuna Barnes;* I have reread it, and it is just as great as I remembered, or as Fadiman ever said.

The other things in *The Selected Works* are not of its caliber. Nine of the 16 stories that Miss Barnes has published in earlier volumes are included, as a collection entitled *Spillway*. The only omission I regret is "Nigger," that devastating squint at Southern race relations. Otherwise the stories are a good representation. The commonest tone is of scarcely controlled hysteria: "I tried to put my arms around her, but she struck them down crying 'Silence!'" The events are gothic and melodramatic: a woman with an idiot child takes to her bed and joins it in idiocy; a gentle tailor strangles a rabbit to please his fiancée.

Some of the images and metaphors are poetic in the best sense: "A great war painting hung over the bed; the painting and the bed ran together in encounter; the huge rumps of the stallions reined into the pillows"; "The waiting room was empty, dark and damp, like an acre risen from the sea"; a woman's bony knees under a skirt are "two sharp points, like the corners of a candy box." A few touches are beautifully effective. Moydia, in "The Grande Malade," wears a tight bodice on which, "just between the breasts, was embroidered, in very fine twist, a slain lamb." When her fiancé dies suddenly, Moydia becomes *tragique*," and her sister comments, as the point of the story, "She sugars her tea from far too great a height." When the little tailor has strangled his rabbit, he stands shaking, "his heart wringing wet."

Only one of the stories, however, seems to me successful as a whole. That is "A Night Among the Horses," which begins magnificently with a man in evening dress, carrying top hat and stick, creeping through the underbrush of a great estate. Horses thunder by him, "their legs rising and falling like savage needles taking purposeless stitches." He is the horses' groom, dressed as a gentleman to be the consort of his employer, a lady who laughs showing "nostrils scarlet to the pit," and twits him for being "girlish" when he asks what she wants of him. He suddenly perceives her as a praying mantis, flees into the shrubbery, and is trampled to death by his horses, who fail to recognize him in the strange costume. It is a superb story of "debased lady, debased ostler, on the wings of vertigo," a serious and tragic *Lady Chatterley*.

The third item in *The Selected Works* is a three-act verse drama, *The Antiphon*, first published in 1958, after 20 years of silence from the author. This remarkable work shows the family reunion of Augusta Burley Hobbs and her four grown children in the ruined Burley mansion in England at the start of World War II. It is patently intended as symbolic, introduced with a coy Cautionary Note advising the reader that "this play is more than merely literal." The ruined mansion, with its tumbled wall and paneless windows, is obviously the modern world, and Augusta's dead husband Titus, an open polygamist (as is Wendell Ryder in Miss Barnes' 1928 comic novel *Ryder*), seems to be the author having a go at God the Father. The nasty family relations, too, appear to be offered as representative, and the daughter, Miranda, generalizes to her mother: "Every mother, in extortion for her milk— / With the keyhole iris of the cat—draws blood."

It would be hard to find a more unattractive family. Titus was genuinely evil, killing a dog his wife was holding, raping Mi-

randa when she was 16. His sons Dudley and Elisha, if more cowardly, are equally evil. In a chilling scene they put on pig and ass
masks and cruelly maul and abuse their mother and sister. At the
end of the play they are revealed to have come back to Burley to
murder Augusta, and they flee. Augusta herself is insanely selfish,
snatching Miranda's clothing and finery, answering her recollec-
tions of the paternal rape with "I don't care what you've done, I
forgive me," and eventually killing Miranda and herself, to shouts
of "You are to blame, to blame, you are to blame." At the curtain,
the third son, Jeremy, who has brought Miranda back and provoked the violence, leaves the stage "with what appears to be indifference."

The language of *The Antiphon* is sometimes extraordinarily
obscure: "It's true the webbed commune / Trawls up a wrack one
term was absolute"; "His dear weight to bruit my case in alt";
"And I ripped public for the scapegoat run." At other times the
language is spare and eloquent, as in Augusta's apology for not
weeping:

> *It's not I wouldn't, it is that I cannot.*
> *My natural showers have wept unnatural moons:*
> *I'm grinned away, to catch my sons' attention.*

The blank verse lines are almost all end-stopped, and Miss Barnes
breaks the monotony with many shorter lines of one, two, or three
feet. Reminiscences of Shakespeare are everywhere, along with
Miltonic catalogues and even touches of Dylan Thomas. Eliot's
statement that Shakespeare and Milton make blank verse impossible for the playwright in our times has become a commonplace
of criticism. Apparently no one ever told Miss Barnes, and she
almost brings it off.

Nightwood is the interplay of a group of people, almost all of
them homosexual, in Paris in the 1920s. Four principal characters
cluster around the young girl Robin Vote: Nora Flood and Jenny
Petherbridge, who in their different fashions love her; Felix Volk-
bein, a Jew and spurious baron who was briefly married to her;
and "Dr." Matthew O'Connor, a Catholic homosexual and unli-
censed practitioner who brings them all together and shares their
confidences.

The doctor, who appeared earlier as a minor character in *Ryder,* dominates this book with the brilliance of his speech and the weight of his personality. The key chapter, "Watchman, What of the Night?," in which Nora appears in the doctor's sordid room at three in the morning to question him about the night world into which Robin has disappeared, is at once a classic of modern rhetoric and a scene of shattering poignancy. Nora sees the doctor lying in his dirty bed, wearing a woman's nightgown and a blonde curly wig, surrounded by rusty, broken instruments and empty perfume bottles. His dream is of babies and knitting in a pretty cottage, and as he tells Nora of his life of haunting urinals to pick up men, he draws out her own confession and is able somewhat to console her. With his mad vision of himself as Christ's younger brother, the doctor is a spurious priest who can hear confession but lacks the power to grant absolution.

The doctor's eloquence is more Elizabethan than anything in *The Antiphon.* "Our bones ache only while the flesh is on them," he tells Nora. Sometimes he speaks in the voice of Mad Tom in *Lear:* "Ho, nocturnal hag whimpering on the thorn, rot in the grist, mildew in the corn." His description of the lesbians kneeling in the toilets at night, alternately cursing their lovers and their own genitals in a terrible imprecation, is bloodcurdling. His comic monologue on the *gourmandise* of male homosexuality, produced in an effort to stop Nora's crying, is simultaneously funny and awful. His account of the Tuppenny Uprights, the numb old prostitutes under London Bridge, is nightmarish. "Go Down, Matthew" is a chapter title, and it is at once a homosexual joke, a call to prayer, and a command to descend into Inferno. The doctor is the mad tormented Dante of our sexual underworld, and his last words in the book are: "Now *nothing, but wrath and weeping!*"

The other characters, fine as they are, cannot rival his vitality. Jenny, the birdlike little woman who steals Robin from Nora, a looter of the emotional lives of others, is a masterful creation. Nora, "an early Christian" by temperament, is so "rotten to the bone for love of Robin" that she says that at the Resurrection she will recognize only her. Robin herself is innocent and promiscuous, playing at home with toys and marbles or drinking herself into a stupor in the streets, until at the end of the book she sud-

denly collapses into madness and becomes a dog frisking with
Nora's dog. Felix devotes all his life to the sickly and mentally
deficient child, "an addict to death," that Robin produced to mark
their brief marriage.

Felix and his son Guido extend the book beyond the torments
of homosexuals to make it a powerful lament for all the maimed,
the suffering, the insulted and injured. The key image is of the
agonized heart. "If one gave birth to a heart on a plate," the doctor says, "it would say 'Love' and twitch like the lopped leg of a
frog." Of himself: "You beat the liver out of a goose to get a *pâté;*
you pound the muscles of a man's *cardia* to get a philosopher."
When we cannot see the suffering human heart, it is hidden under
some protective covering. Laughter, Miss Barnes says, is "the second husk into which the shucked man crawls." "I was doing well
enough," the doctor tells Nora bitterly, "until you kicked my stone
over, and out I came, all moss and eyes." All of the book, in fact, is
what the doctor says he takes in, the "little light laundry known as
the Wash of the World."

Some of Miss Barnes' profundities are pseudo-profundities,
and her rhetoric occasionally falls into bathos. The end is not an
adequate catharsis for the pity and terror that the book evokes; no
more than Dr. O'Connor can Miss Barnes grant absolution. *Nightwood* is not such a fully achieved tragedy as Nathanael West's
Miss Lonelyhearts, but *Miss Lonelyhearts* is the only comparable
work of our time. In the years since the 30s we have had nothing
to equal those two great cries of pain, in their combination of
emotional power and formal artistry. The writers who have copied
Djuna Barnes—Truman Capote, William Goyen, and so many
others—have her surface without her depth. In *Nightwood,* at
least, she produced a masterpiece.

MOVIEGOING AND OTHER INTIMACIES

I missed *The Moviegoer* by Walker Percy when it came out in 1961. It was Percy's first published novel, although he was 45, and had written two earlier novels, unpublished and, he says, "very bad." I was not the only person who missed it, since Knopf did not push the book very hard, reportedly because the head of the firm was "baffled and somewhat irritated" by it. When *The Moviegoer* received the National Book Award as the "most distinguished" work of fiction published in 1961, there were howls of rage, as though the umpire had made a bum call against the home team.

I am not fully able to evaluate the choice, since I have not read all the eleven books nominated. Of the ones I know, some seem unsuitable because they are too successful to need the award, such as J. D. Salinger's *Franny and Zooey;* others are the work of promising young writers who have not yet demonstrated their staying power, such as Joan Williams' *The Morning and the Evening.* In my view, the award should recognize a distinguished book by the author of a body of work deserving recognition. On that basis, had I been a judge, I should have voted for William Maxwell's *The Chateau* or Isaac Bashevis Singer's *The Spinoza of Market Street.* But I have now read Percy's novel, and there is no question but that the judges—Lewis Gannett, Herbert Gold, and Jean Stafford—made a responsible and defensible choice. Probably the solution is, as Lewis Nichols suggested in the *New York Times,* to turn the award formally into a first-novel prize, or else to have two awards, as was done once in the past, one for the year's most distinguished work of fiction and one for the best first novel.

In any case, in calling *The Moviegoer* to the attention of a wider public, the National Book Award has performed a service. Like George P. Elliott's *David Knudsen,* Percy's book is a detailed pathology of modern neurosis, but unlike Elliott's it embodies its pathology in a realized fictional form. The book's narrator-pro-tagonist, Jack Bolling, is a young Louisiana stockbroker of good family, undergoing very considerable emotional difficulties. Al-though he has a wallet full of identity cards, he has no sense of identity, and much of the time he has no sense of inhabiting a real place at a real time. Only four activities give him any illusion of meaningfulness, and he has reduced his life to them: "I spend my entire time working, making money, going to movies and seeking the company of women." "What do you think is the purpose of life—to go to the movies and dally with every girl that comes along?" his aunt asks him. "No," Jack answers, but only because he doesn't think that there is any purpose of life.

Women stir him, particularly their beautiful bottoms or "splendid butts," and he spends quite a lot of time chasing them, but he does not appear anxious to catch any. When, after an elab-orate campaign, a girl fends him off, he seems more relieved than not. "The truth is that nowadays one is hardly up to it," he con-cludes unhappily at another point. In an experience that Percy has said is autobiographical, Jack spent his college years "propped on the front porch of the fraternity house, bemused and dreaming." He suffers from what he calls "invincible apathy," combined with periodic severe depression. He is obsessed with death, not the fear of death, but the sense "that everyone is dead," himself particu-larly. It is visibly the wish for death, and Jack thinks of "the grandest coup of all: to die."

On this neurotic disturbance Jack erects a sizable mystique. One of its three features is the concept of "the search," which transforms his aimless and apathetic rambling into a quest for identity and value. Another is a concept of "repetition," a deliber-ate "re-enactment of past experience toward the end of isolating the time segment which has lapsed." The third is a concept of "rotation," defined as "the experiencing of the new beyond the expectation of the experiencing of the new."

All of these heady ideas result in moviegoing. "The movies are onto the search," Jack says, "but they screw it up." Seeing a western film in the same seat in the same theater in which one saw a western film fourteen years before, in the same season, is "a successful repetition." Seeing a western film in the company of the invalid half-brother one loves *and* a girl one is pursuing, a "fine big sweet piece," is "a good rotation." Once Jack drove into a Louisiana village to see a movie in which the characters drive into a Louisiana village to see a movie, a triumphant "repetition within a rotation."

Jack sees all experience, even the death of his brother, in terms of remembered movies, and he acts in the stances of movie heroes. Movies "certify" the reality of places they show. Jack goes to see them alone, or if he goes with anyone, "it is understood that we do not speak during the movie." In his mind, Jack explains and justifies his behavior in dialogues with movie actors. He sometimes identifies a person he meets as "a moviegoer, though of course he does not go to the movies."

Pleased to learn "that a significantly large percentage of solitary moviegoers are Jews," Jack becomes a metaphoric Jew: "Anyhow it is true that I am Jewish by instinct. We share the same exile. The fact is, however, I am more Jewish than the Jews I know. They are more at home than I am. I accept my exile." Jack insists that his life is so unreal that he goes to the movies to find reality, but his descriptions of the experience make it clear what special reality he is searching for, what major situation requires repetition—it is the uterine state, and the book's title translates as *The Womb-Returner.*

The heroine of *The Moviegoer* is Jack's cousin Kate Cutrer, a thin girl with a "marvelously ample" behind. She is more desperately neurotic than he, although she repeatedly denies it, insisting "You're like me, but worse. Much worse," or "You're nuttier than I am." After an automobile accident in which she was unhurt and her fiancé was killed, Kate had a breakdown. Now she is a secret wino and an addict of barbiturates. Where Jack is sunk in apathy, Kate has periods of despair and terror; where he longs dreamily for death, she has true suicidal impulses, and she makes a try at suicide once in the book.

The Moviegoer is more than pathology because Jack and Kate are not only case histories but complex human beings. Percy's talent for the creation of character brings the minor characters just as vividly alive. They are: gentle Uncle Jules, "whose

victory in the world is total and unqualified"; bluestocking Aunt
Emily, who expects more of Jack because he and she used to read
the *Crito* together; Jack's formidable, beautiful secretary Sharon
Kinkaid, a comic masterpiece; half-brother Lonnie in his wheel-
chair, also "a moviegoer."

The book's language is sometimes quite fancy, as when Jack's
neck manifests "eschatological prickling," or a train corridor has a
"gelid hush" and "the peculiar gnosis of trains." Some sentences
are elaborately Jamesian. For the most part, however, the language is spare and effective, and Percy has a superb ear for
speech. He hears a Negro servant turn the word "is" into a diph-
thong "Harlem-style," or Alabama-raised Sharon protest "Ho no,
you son," report "I said nayo indeed," and euphemize "God damn"
as "Got dog."

Percy's use of symbolism shows a sure touch. The symbol that
dominates the book is New Orleans Carnival Week culminating in
the Mardi Gras parade, and its monstrous and mechanical gaiety
is the background against which the drama of neurotic quest is
performed. Some lesser symbols are subtler yet equally powerful:
the elderly married authors of a *Technique in Marriage* manual,
imagined "at their researches, solemn as a pair of brontosauruses,
their heavy old freckled limbs twined about one another"—a vision of the enlightened joylessness of our world; Aunt Emily lecturing Jack with a paperknife in her hand, its tip bent by him as a
child—an image of the inclined tree in the bent twig. A deserted
ocean wave in a playground, on which Jack often sits, is recognizably some life rhythm that has been stilled in him; Kate has a
nervous habit of tearing at the flesh around her thumbnail, which
might as readily be her heart.

More than in character, language, or symbol, the strength of
The Moviegoer lies in its clear firm line of action. Jack's Aunt
Emily, Kate's stepmother, puts him in the essentially false and
crippling role of Kate's keeper. He breaks out of it by taking Kate
to Chicago and going to bed with her on the train, the two of
them just barely managing it under "the cold and fishy eye of the
malaise," both terrified, both shaking like leaves. On their return,
Jack stands up to his aunt and answers her question, "Were you
intimate with Kate?" with the marvelous phrase, "Not very." He is

then free to create a valid relationship with her, a marriage in which they pool their neuroses democratically. At the end of the book, with Uncle Jules and Lonnie sacrificially dead, there is some hope that each, with the help of the other, will be better able to function in the world. At least they have no illusions about how hard the world really is.

There are flaws in *The Moviegoer*, certainly. One character, Sam Yerger, a figure of superhuman wisdom who imitates Amos 'n' Andy, is preposterous from start to finish, and a mistake. Sometimes Jack's philosophy, as when he meditates on "the genie-soul," is just blather. There are occasional pretentious attempts to make Jack's search seem not neurotic but deeply spiritual, along the lines of Percy's unfortunate statement, on receiving the National Book Award, that his novel shows Judaeo-Christian man as "a wayfarer and a pilgrim." These are minor failings in a work of considerable success. I think that *The Moviegoer* is a better novel than the work it most readily brings to mind, Albert Camus' *The Stranger*. It is patronizing and ridiculous to say of a 46-year-old man who has been late publishing his excellent first novel that he shows "promise." Walker Percy shows performance.

SOME QUESTIONS ABOUT HERMAN WOUK

"It is hardly an exaggeration to say that Jeanne had all but fallen in love with the author on reading the first seven pages of his manuscript." Who wrote that posy? Ouida? Frances Hodgson Burnett? Elinor Glyn? S. J. Perelman? No, it is the work of Herman Wouk, sometime Professor of English at Yeshiva University. It is from his enormous novel, *Youngblood Hawke*.

Is that the worst? Hardly. Here are a few other examples: "Being with this man, discussing his work, feeling that she was useful to him, was as close to heaven as she expected to come in this world"; "Frieda's tawdry self-defense about Paul disgusted him to his core"; "The first words she saw in Frieda's letter sent a red-hot stinging through her body"; "So Hawke ignored all the warning signs that Jeanne's mood was, to say the least, not attuned to a declaration from him"; "The cool feel of the tears on her cheeks aroused him in a bitter very strong way. She kissed him with shy tentative excitement, with cutting sweetness. Her body in his arms was angelic."

Is Wouk's prose always Victorian-girlish? No, sometimes it is Swiftian—Tom Swiftian. "A chorus of laughter showed the choice was popular," he writes. Speech mannerisms are the caricatures of boys' books: Hawke is from Kentucky, so that he speaks Amos 'n' Andy ("Mand ef Ah smoke uh see-gaw?"), although Wouk economically turns it off after a few lines and only recurs to it in moments of passion; Hawke's mother speaks quite another dialect, apparently Dogpatch ("get aholt of t'other end of that bed, I cain't get it downstairs myself"); a sophisticated European woman is identifiable by Consonant Mangle ("Vare is ze young genius?"); a crooked Southern businessman shows his hand by saying "binness" for "business" and "sumbitch" for some unidentifiable obscenity.

Isn't "sumbitch" pretty bold for Wouk? Yes. "I think you can report conversations realistically without going overboard on obscenity," Wouk told a hagiographer. "Frieda crackled out a filthy word" is the way he typically handles the problem in *Youngblood Hawke*. Hawke replies to a producer's obscenities "with some far rougher language from the Seabees or the Letchworth miners," at which "the producer was quite taken aback," although he later ripostes with "——!," glossed: "It was the dirtiest epithet that current English affords."

Didn't Aristotle say something about mastery of metaphor being a sign of genius? Yes, but he hadn't seen Wouk's similes, which manage the miracle of being bizarre and shopworn at the same time. Guests eat a buffet supper "like sharks at a dead whale," Hawke enters the suite of a Hollywood actress "like an ape let loose by a bored king in a French drawing room," unsuccessful playwrights are avoided during the first-night intermission "as though they were covered with the pustules of smallpox," Frieda cries with a look "like a little girl's when she has been struck by an indulgent father." Is that the worst Wouk can do? No, see what happens when some bored king lets him loose on the famous trope about burning one's candle at both ends: "The candle was invaluable, it was one's single sure possession. Properly trimmed and cared for it gave plenty of charming light from one end, for a long long time."

Hadn't you better synopsize the plot? Sure. A young genius of a novelist and playwright has an early meteoric success, gets overcommitted financially, drives himself to superhuman efforts, and dies. He has a long stormy affair with a married woman, but is kept from popping into bed with the sweet true girl he loves, as she loves him, by 783 pages of the most desperate contrivance. There is in addition a melodramatic subplot in which the hero's mother outwits the scoundrelly coal barons who have defrauded her and recovers a fortune. It is not really a novel but what Hawke calls one of his best-sellers, "a yarn," and an extraordinarily mawkish and boring yarn it is, written with the most dazzling ineptitude.

Some life in the characters, perhaps? None whatsoever. They are cereal-box cut-outs. Hawke himself is big, strong, handsome in a homely fashion, and well-nigh (it is hard to keep from falling into Wouk's language) irresistible to women. His brutal treatment of his mistress would be contemptible if he and she were not so visibly cardboard. The mistress, Frieda Winter, is a rich older woman of 39, beautiful, passionate, and hedonistic. When he breaks with her he feels "as though he had stumbled out of a cave into the sunlight," or "as though he had just tunnelled up out of a prison." The sunlight love, Jeanne Green (*Winter* and *Green*—get it?) is a brainy young girl, equally beautiful and passionate, but chaste. When she seems game for a roll in the hay with Youngblood, you can be sure that it is "the opiate in her cough medicine —she had taken a large dose upon coming home" that has temporarily weakened her moral fibre, and that she will be saved in the nick of time. The minor characters are equally conventional. Hawke's mother, Sarah, for example, is a stock Yiddisher Momma, bossy but wonderful, disguised as a mountain woman by the shrewd expedient of having her make a fabulous vegetable soup instead of chicken soup with noodles.

Is there really *nothing* good about the book? Nothing. It is the most fraudulent and worthless novel I have read in many years. *Peyton Place* is more honest. Wouk has announced that the figure of Youngblood Hawke was suggested by Balzac; he resembles Sinclair Lewis in a few details; there is a positive effort, in the first and last chapters of the book, to identify him with Thomas Wolfe. But these are transparent disguises—Hawke is unmistakably Herman Wouk. In common with Wouk he has written a bestseller about the navy, which won a Pulitzer Prize, and another about a girl who might be his sister, and has made an immensely successful play from the trial scene of one of his novels; he was a humorist in college and has a characteristic college-humor wit; he even buys his meat in Jewish delicatessens.

Why dissemble? Ah. *Youngblood Hawke* gives Wouk an opportunity to produce an Advertisement for Myself more grandiose than Norman Mailer's, to tell us for hundreds of pages that he is a literary genius who has "read almost all the important plays and novels in the world" and is a paragon of generosity and charity. It even allows him to write fan letters to himself (or to quote fan letters he has received) that class him with Dickens, Dostoevsky, Balzac and Twain. The solitary ring of honesty in the book is

Hawke's recurrent plea that the income of popular writers be more gently taxed as capital gains, and the long discussions of the vulnerability of tax dodges are more apt to bring tears to the reader's eyes than are the death scenes. The world of the rich successful writer eventually becomes the only world a rich successful writer knows, unfortunately. Having exhausted his Bronx background, his navy experience, and his family, in earlier novels, Wouk has no subject left but his inexhaustible narcissism.

Why then the enormous popularity of this book, which earned a million dollars before publication—serialized in McCall's, a Book-of-the-Month Club selection, sold to Readers' Digest Condensed Books and Warner Brothers, a first printing of 125,000? No one answer will do. Wouk is now a phenomenal merchandising success, sold as a detergent is sold. He can compete with the worst of television because he *is* the worst of television, without the commercials, a $7.95 Pay-TV. His readers really are the boobs Hawke describes, so "starved for an interesting story" that they will ignore the reviews to read him. They are yahoos who hate culture and the mind, who want to be told that Existentialism means that "you do what you goddam please," that current theatrical fashion is "pseudo-Freudian reconstruction," that young actresses offer themselves "with all the casualness of a housewife opening a can of soup."

Have we reached bottom yet? No. Nastiest of all, Wouk panders to the conviction of his moron-audience that the world of culture is homosexual, and that homosexuals are ludicrous and disgusting. Through his pages parade an endless stream: "Greenwich Village perverts," a "talented young sodomite" whose writing calls to mind "soiled nylon underwear," "a Hollywood pederast," "a notorious homosexual novelist about five feet tall," "sissies with bleached hair," "faggots in their skimpy Italian suits," simpering "pretty boys," tittering "homos," "fairies" uttering "little squeaks of carnal delight," a "fat old sodomite with red-dyed hair," "chirping and screeching faggots," and so on.

Couldn't these be Wouk's own feelings, not a pandering to his audience? Perhaps. But look what he does with the scene when Hawke is given a contract for his first book. The head of the publishing firm writes out a check at his desk for the advance, and the editor takes Hawke to a place like Twenty One for lunch and orders him a bottle of "vintage champagne." Wouk does not know much, but he has been around publishing long enough to know what would happen to a publisher's book-keeping if he wrote checks personally, and to know that vintage champagne is not the beverage at expensive lunches. But the panting reader expects a check on the spot and the flow of lovely bubbles, and Wouk pants along with him dutifully.

Doesn't Wouk stand for anything but venality? Yes. He stands for conventional American patriotism, and the proud conviction that "This country has no toiling masses." He stands for old-fashioned morality: female chastity is *right,* and Jeanne will be rewarded with the love of a good man for preserving her long-tried virginity; adultery is *wrong,* and Frieda will be punished for it by the death of her beloved son (he hangs himself in shame when he discovers it). Wouk's morality is less interested in honesty (those tax dodges) and charity (those chirping faggots) than it is in virtuous American womanhood. But doesn't Wouk offer himself to the world as a religious man? "A lot of empty mumbling is passed off as devotion," he wrote in *This Is My God.* Really?

A NOVELIST OF GREAT PROMISE

Television has destroyed boxing in our time, perhaps permanently, by killing the neighborhood clubs, at which young fighters learn their craft. As a result boys are brought up into the big time too soon, and acclaim and fortune are won by the semi-skilled, who then naturally continue to be semi-skilled. Consequently, we will probably never again see fighters with the effective artistry of Archie Moore or Ray Robinson.

In the literary arenas, the same thing is done by gushy reviewing. Philip Roth's first novel, *Letting Go*, is a case in point. In 1959, at the age of 26, he published his first book, *Goodbye, Columbus*, consisting of the title novella and five short stories. It was greeted with a cascade of adulation, of which some remarks quoted on the back of the paperback reprint are a fair sample. "One catches lampoonings of our swollen and unreal American prosperity that are as observant and charming as Fitzgerald's," Alfred Kazin wrote in *The Reporter*. "At twenty-six he is skillful, witty, and energetic and performs like a virtuoso," Saul Bellow wrote in *Commentary*. "What many writers spend a lifetime searching for—a unique voice, a secure rhythm, a distinctive subject—seem to have come to Philip Roth totally and immediately," Irving Howe wrote in *The New Republic*.

The next year, *Goodbye, Columbus* won the National Book Award as "the most distinguished work of fiction published in 1959." Roth was promptly awarded a Guggenheim fellowship, as well as a grant from the National Institute of Arts and Letters with a citation saying in part: "*Goodbye, Columbus* marks the coming of age of a brilliant, penetrating, and undiscourageable young man of letters." Undiscourageable? Who had tried?

The merits of *Goodbye, Columbus* and its author are immediately evident. The novella shows a sardonic wit, and the sharp eye of a born writer. The Patimkin way of life, with its white hair

"the color of Lincoln convertibles" and its 23 bottles of Jack Dan-
iels, each with a little booklet tied around its neck, decorating the
unused bar, has been rendered for all time. There are other sure
touches: the cherry pits under Neil's bare feet in the TV room;
the Ohio State sentimental record of the title. The long monologue by Patimkin's unsuccessful half-brother Leo at the wedding
is a masterpiece: funny, moving, perfect.

But the faults of *Goodbye, Columbus* are as readily seen.
The novella has no values to oppose to Patimkin values other than
a small Negro boy who admires Gaugin's Tahiti, which seems a
considerable overmatch. Some images are bad, such as Brenda's
treading water "so easily she seemed to have turned the chlorine
to marble beneath her"; the language is sometimes as inadequate
as: "I failed to deflate the pout from my mouth." Most important,
the novella shows Roth's architectonic weakness: many of the incidents do not advance the action; the end is not a resolution,
merely a running-down.

The stories show the same balance of strength and weakness.
"Defender of the Faith" is the only one of them that seems wholly
successful to me. "Eli, the Fanatic" reaches one high point of
power and beauty, when Tzuref replies to all the smooth talk
about the twentieth century with: "For me the Fifty-eighth," but
the rest of the story is rambling and diffuse. "The Conversion of
the Jews," with its pat moral, "You should never hit anybody
about God," is ultimately hokum, as "You Can't Tell a Man by the
Song He Sings" is immediately hokum. "Epstein" is slight farce,
an inflated joke.

The minor result of the shower of praise and coin that Roth
received was to make him arrogant. In a speech, "Writing American Fiction," at a 1960 symposium, he knocked off his elders and
betters: Malamud displays "a spurning of our world," Salinger
tells us "to be charming on the way to the loony bin," and so on.
The major, and really unfortunate, result has been to convince
Roth that he has nothing further to learn. Three years later, *Letting Go* appears with the same merits and the same faults as
Goodbye, Columbus.

Let us get the faults out of the way first. Since the novel is six
times as long as the novella, it shows Roth's architectural weak-

ness six times as strongly. It never in fact becomes a novel, with a unified dramatic action, but falls apart into two narratives which have only a pat complementarity: the failure of Gabe Wallach in the world of personal relations, specifically with the divorcée Martha Reganhart, despite every advantage; and the limited success of Paul and Libby Herz in the same world, despite every handicap. For the rest, it is a series of comic set pieces and vignettes: dirty diapers and high thought among the instructors at Midwest universities; Swedish modern and espresso in Jewish apartments in Brooklyn; the slides brought back from the European trips of Central Park West dentists.

The prose is still quite lame in spots. Characters experience "relief—though by no means total relief," and children eat, "manipulating their food like Muzak's violinists their instruments." There are letters that no one would ever have written, and long pedestrian explanations of past events by the author. In the style of college humor magazines, Roth will interrupt a scene to remark: "It's the little questions from women about tappets that finally push men over the edge." At the same time, there is a balancing pomposity; the book has no fewer than *three* epigraphs— by Simone Weil, Wallace Stevens, and Thomas Mann—any one of which would do for a dissertation on Covenant Theology.

A two-page history of the marital sex life of the Herzes has a clinical leadenness that would sink the most buoyant novel. Beyond that there is cocktail-party Freud. A pathetic event finally ends the liaison between Gabe and Martha. Martha's older child, Cynthia, pushes her younger brother, Mark, off the top of a double-decker bunk; the result is Mark's death. Roth spends laborious pages showing us why—it was penis-envy! Finally, Gabe's weakness is Hegelian essence: "He is better, he believes, than anything he has done in life has shown him to be." Not being the sum of his actions, Gabe is not really anything in the book.

The virtues of *Letting Go*—of Roth, really—are equally impressive. He has the finest eye for the details of American life since Sinclair Lewis. When Maggie Howells of Kenosha moves in with Gabe as an experiment in Bold Free Union, she comes with Breck shampoo, an Olivetti, an electric frying pan, a steam iron, and a copy of the *Oxford Book of Seventeenth-Century Verse*.

The Spiglianos (he is the chairman of Gabe's department) have eleven budgetary tins in their kitchen, one labelled: "John: Tobacco, scholarly journals, foot powder."

Roth's ear is just as remarkable as his eye. When Blair Stott, a Negro on pot, talks hip, it is the best hip, and a delight. When Gabe and Martha quarrel over money, every word rings true, and the reader can feel a sick headache coming on. No manner of speech seems to be beyond Roth's powers. An elderly Midwest woman says to Gabe: "You talk to the top professors and you see if they're not Masons." Paul recalls necking with a girl named Doris in high school, sitting in her darkened living room while her father called out from the bedroom: "Doris, is that you, dolly? Is somebody with you? Tell him thank you, dolly, and tell him it's the next day already, your father has to get up and go to work soon, tell him thank you and good night, dolly."

If Gabe is a thin Hegelian essence, Martha is a gorgeous rich *Existenz*. She *is* the total of what she does. "A woman at least realizes there are certain rotten things she's got to do in life and does them," Martha explains to Gabe. "Men want to be heroes." She is bawdy and vulgar, honest and decent, funny and heartbreaking. Gabe's effort, as he finally recognizes when he loses her, had been to turn her into a sniveling Libby. Martha's vitality dominates the book, and if Gabe's final "letting go" of the world is at all poignant, it is poignant chiefly in that he had a chance to keep Martha and failed it.

The best of *Letting Go* comes from the marvelous quality of Roth's imagination. A fellow-dentist with whom Gabe's father goes ice-skating is characterized in a phrase: he only makes "little figure eights, and all the time, smiling." The failure of Paul's father in the frozen foods business is one magnificent sentence: "One day, creditors calling at every door, he got into the cab of a truckful of his frozen rhubarb and took a ride out to Long Island to think; the refrigeration failed just beyond Mineola, and by the time he got home his life was a zero, a ruined man." At her low point, Libby, who has converted from Roman Catholicism to Judaism on marrying Paul, tries to commit suicide; when that fails she decides to make potato pancakes, "to bring a little religion into her house."

Two episodes of almost indescribable complexity, at once awful and uproarious, are the clearest sign of Roth's great promise. One is Libby's abortion, which becomes entangled with the effort of an elderly neighbor, Levy, to steal a job-lot of jockey briefs from another elderly neighbor, Korngold; it culminates in a horrifying and splendid scene when they both invade the Herz bedroom just after Libby comes home from the operation. The other is Gabe's mad effort to persuade a scoundrel named Harry Bigoness to sign a legal document that will enable the Herzes to keep their adopted baby. Eventually Gabe steals the baby in the night and drives it to Gary, Indiana, to confront Bigoness with it in the book's wild climactic scene.

Roth may be the Lewis of Suburbia, but he is potentially much more. His "Writing American Fiction" speech rejects all the easy affirmations of America, and concludes on Ralph Ellison's somber final image of the Invisible Man waiting underground. Roth really does know how hard life is. *Letting Go* concludes with Gabe, who has tried to do good without attachment, as Lord Krishna recommends in the *Gita*, left with little good achieved and no attachments either. I think that after he has seasoned longer, after another book or two, if he is prepared to learn from his mistakes, Philip Roth will be a first-rate novelist. Providing, that is, that all the matchmakers and promoters leave him alone.

NO COUNTRY FOR YOUNG MEN

"Powerful," says Mark Schorer on the bellyband of James Baldwin's novel, *Another Country*. Powerful it is indeed, in part, and to that extent Schorer, whose critical reputation may not survive his puff for Katherine Anne Porter's novel in the *New York Times Book Review*, here tells the truth. Other parts of *Another Country* are weaker and less convincing than anything Baldwin has yet published. As an enthusiastic admirer of his two earlier novels, I am sorry to find this, his most ambitious effort, a very mixed bundle.

The protagonist of *Another Country*, a young Negro jazz drummer named Rufus Scott, kills himself on page 88, and the rest of the book is taken up with the adventures and misadventures, mainly sexual, of the half dozen people who had been close to him. Of the important characters, only Rufus and his sister Ida are Negro, but almost everything in the book that is powerful and convincing deals with Negro consciousness.

That consciousness, as this novel shows it, seethes with bitterness and race hate. "Let the liberal white bastard squirm" is Rufus' most charitable feeling toward Vivaldo, his best friend; his less charitable feeling is a passionate desire for the extinction of the white race by nuclear bomb. Ida is even fiercer. She regularly affirms, in most coarse language, the total sexual inadequacy of whites, as well as their moral sickness and physical repulsiveness. In her view, the white male has an absolute dependence on Negroes of both sexes as sexual objects, and an inability to recognize them as anything but instruments for that function. To Cass Silenski, a sympathetic white woman, Ida describes Central Park at night as a great sexual jungle, but in truth that is her vision of New York, of the whole United States.

"Wouldn't you hate all white people if they kept you in prison here?" Ida asks Cass as they drive through Harlem. "Kept you here, and stunted you and starved you, and made you watch your mother and father and sister and lover and brother and son and daughter die or go mad or go under before your very eyes? And not in a hurry, like from one day to the next, but, every day, every day, for years, for generations?" Her conclusion follows logically: "I wish I could turn myself into one big fist and grind this miserable country to powder."

The other Negroes in the book share this bitterness and hatred without exception. A big Negro pimp who lives by beating up and robbing the white customers of his Negro whore clearly does so out of principle; before robbing Vivaldo, he stares at him "with a calm, steady hatred, as remote and unanswerable as madness." The Silenski boys are beaten up by Negro boys unknown to them out of simple racial hostility, and Richard, their father, automatically comments: "Little black bastards." Rufus' father, seeing his son's mangled corpse, remarks only: "They don't leave a man much, do they?" A musician who had been Rufus' friend, finding Ida out with a white man, calls her "black white man's whore" and threatens to mutilate her genitals twice, once for himself and once for Rufus.

The part of *Another Country* that carries absolute conviction is Rufus' neurotic destructiveness and self-destructiveness, and it is recognizably a warping of race hatred, a turning of it not against true enemies but against friends and against the self. The raw bitter scene published in *Partisan Review* in 1960 is the high point of the book. Displaying Rufus' paranoid suspiciousness and brutal treatment of Leona, the southern white girl who loves him, and his blind and vicious refusal to be helped by Vivaldo or anyone, it is utterly right and deeply moving, a tribute to the depth of Baldwin's understanding and to his great powers as a writer.

Many other parts of the book are weak and unconvincing, as though some lesser writer had done them. We have to take Rufus' talents as a jazz musician on faith, since Baldwin never shows him at work in any believable fashion. The lyrics of blues songs that fill the book, as characters play the phonograph, sing, or recall them, bear no organic relation to the action. They are merely decorative, and when a character follows a blues line with the comment, "Oh, sing it, Bessie," the reader feels that Baldwin is cheating him, and that he is being asked to believe that the inexpressible has just been expressed. *Another Country* is full of bits of stoic philosophy of the same spurious profundity: "Nobody's willing to pay their dues"; "Life is a *bitch,* baby"; "But it was only love which could accomplish the miracle of making a life bearable"; "Growing just means learning more and more about anguish"; "It can be borne, everything can be borne."

Some of the writing is bad by any standard, and exceptionally bad by Baldwin's own high standard. The flashback-within-flashback organization of the first part is confusing and slipshod. Many of the metaphors and similes have a compulsive sexual tone: a skyscraper is "blunt like the phallus," a boy's backside "seemed to snarl," a subway train goes through a tunnel "with a phallic abandon." They are no better when not sexual: a garbage truck is "like a gray brainless insect," 42nd street is a "great livid scar," after a marijuana party Vivaldo's mouth feels "like Mississippi in the days when cotton was king."

By far the worst writing in the book is in the big sex scenes. These are what Yeats called "disagreeable sentimental sensuality," or, if I may borrow a joke from Randall Jarrell, "*real* gardens with real toads in them." Since *Giovanni's Room* was distinguished by the delicacy and taste of its erotic scenes, I can only conclude that Baldwin has changed his ways in order to achieve a best-seller, as he surely will. I believe this to be a tragic error for this talented young writer, and I believe that anyone who encouraged or countenanced the decision is a scoundrel, and should be horsewhipped.

A few quotations are in order. The first big sex scene is the rape of Leona by Rufus, who has just picked her up, on a friend's terrace during a party. Here is a sentence that would not disgrace a Toffenetti menu: "He got hung up on her breasts, standing out like mounds of yellow cream, and the tough, brown, tasty nipples, playing and nuzzling and nibbling while she moaned and whimpered and her knees sagged."

In the next pairing, Ida goes home with Vivaldo, fries him a chicken, and pops into bed with him. The chicken is dismissed in a sentence, although it is the important symbolic act, but their relations in bed occupy seven lurid pages. Sometimes it is prettily "poetic": "She opened up before him, yet fell back before him, too, he felt that he was traveling up a savage, jungle river, looking for the source which remained hidden just beyond the black, dangerous, dripping foliage." Sometimes it is as glamorous as the *Daily Racing Form:* "He began to gallop her, whinnying a little with delight." At the end, it is pure *McCall's:* Ida looked "very much like a woman and very much like a shy, little girl."

Relations between Eric Jones, a homosexual actor, and Yves, a French youth with whom he cohabits, are *McCall's* all through. The scene of Eric shampooing Yves' hair is my favorite, but here is a typical paragraph from their big sex scene:

"And they moaned. *Soon,* Yves whispered, sounding insistent, like a child, and with a terrible regret. *Soon.* Eric's hands and mouth opened and closed on his lover's body, their bodies strained yet closer together, and Yves' body shook and he called Eric's name as no one had ever called this name before. *Eric. Eric. Eric.* The sound of his breath filled Eric, heavier than the far-off pounding of the sea."

When Eric returns to America, while waiting for Yves to follow, he takes up with Cass. Having titillated the reader with Negro man and white woman, white man and Negro woman, pederast and youth, Baldwin now gets to do bisexual and friend's wife: "He took her like a boy, with that singlemindedness, and with a boy's passion to please: and she had awakened something in him, an animal long caged, which came pounding out of its captivity now with a fury which astounded and transfigured them both."

Finally, in the most preposterous scene of all, Vivaldo "surrendered to the luxury, the flaming torpor of passivity, and whispered in Eric's ear a muffled, urgent plea." It is a shy little request to be anally violated, and Baldwin cheerfully does that scene too: "He moaned and his thighs, like the thighs of a woman, loosed, he thrust upward as Eric thrust down. How strange, how strange!" Afterwards, when they have a cigarette together, Vivaldo remarks: "You're trying to tell me something." I would say that he had got the message.

Eventually, *Another Country* turns out to be a parable of reconciliation, of sin and forgiveness. At the end, Ida and Vivaldo forgive each other's rambles and will live happily together; she will fry pork chops for him as well as chicken. We leave them tearfully clutched in each other's arms: "nothing erotic in it; they were like two weary children." In the book's final sentence, Yves strides happily toward Eric at the airport. Only Richard does not forgive Cass her fling, as we could have guessed from his remark about "black bastards." True, Rufus is dead, and Leona, back south, is probably in a madhouse, but they are the sacrifices who manure this crop of happiness.

One could not call *Another Country* a success (even Schorer did not) but it has considerable successes in it, along with the peep-shows. I hope that the hundreds of thousands who read it as pornography will profit from the Negro bitterness and fury to which they are incidentally exposed. Those of us who admire and respect James Baldwin hope that his clear eye will see through the role of cynical bedspring bard as it has seen through so many other imposed and degrading roles.

THE YIDDISH HAWTHORNE

If Sholom Aleichem is the Yiddish Mark Twain, Isaac Bashevis Singer is the Yiddish Hawthorne. I do not know how many reviewers have made that comparison before, since my sins are not great enough to require me to keep up with the reviewers, but the comparison is inevitable. Singer writes what Hawthorne called "romances" rather than novels, and moral fables and allegories rather than short stories. I cannot imagine anyone since Hawthorne writing such a tale as "The Gentleman from Cracow" in *Gimpel the Fool,* in which a generous stranger who corrupts and destroys the little town of Frampol is revealed to be Ketev Mriri, Chief of the Devils. Singer's third romance, *The Slave,* translated by the author and Cecil Hemley, is his most Hawthornian.

I do not read Yiddish; I am not familiar with much Yiddish literature, and I have not read Singer's first novel, *The Family Moskat.* The books that I know—*Satan in Goray, Gimpel the Fool and Other Stories, The Magician of Lublin, The Spinoza of Market Street,* and *The Slave*—seem to me incredible in mid-twentieth-century America. Singer has been in this country since 1935, on the staff of the *Jewish Daily Forward,* but America and the twentieth century do not exist in his work, except once as a fantastic vision in "The Little Shoemakers" in *Gimpel the Fool* when a half-crazed old Jew arrives in New York and takes it to be the pyramids of Egypt. Singer's subject is *shtetl* (Jewish village) life in Poland, sometimes in the seventeenth and sometimes in the late nineteenth century, and he brings it into being so powerfully that reading his books one soon comes to believe that our world *is* a fantastic vision.

Singer's style, in the tradition of Hawthorne and Melville, is often rhetorical and flamboyant, but there is not an ounce of fat on his prose. His characters sometimes bandy proverbs wittily, in the fashion of West Africans, and similarly he is sometimes folksy and proverbial. Singer's most characteristic style is one of sophisticated ironic juxtaposition, as in a sentence from *Satan in Goray:* "To divert the bride and raise her spirits, the women enthusiastically praised her beauty, stroked her hair, and quickened her with spoonfuls of moldy citrus preserve."

Singer seems almost the only writer in America who believes in the real existence of Satan. Or perhaps he doesn't. Three stories in *Gimpel the Fool* and two in *The Spinoza of Market Street* are narrated by demons, and the satanic forces are everywhere in the other stories and in the novels: inhabiting the characters as *dybbuks* (demonic possessions); tempting them as voices or appearing to dispute with saints; living underground in terror of men; even whirling a pious rabbi through the air and smashing his bones. In a few of the stories, particularly the finest of them all, "The Black Wedding" in *The Spinoza of Market Street,* the Evil One is obviously a metaphor for repressed sexuality, and Singer uses his mythology as a psychopathology with the insight of Euripides. At other times Satan and his forces seem as tangible as Moshe the Chimney Sweep.

The Slave is best seen against a background of the other two romances. *Satan in Goray* is an account of the Sabbatai Zevi messianic hallucination as it overwhelms the little *shtetl* of Goray in the seventeenth century. It is a work of power and brilliance, creating its almost-entirely-Jewish world with easy mastery, from the coarse jokes of the women's bathhouse to the mad messianic rhetoric of the missionary who comes to spread darkness in Goray.

Goray is a "town that lay in the midst of the hills at the end of the world," a town that "had always been isolated from the world." This is Singer's joke. Goray *is* the world, and his parable tells of its vulnerability to sin, the devil in the flesh. From the time of the Cossack pogroms in 1648 until 1666, Goray had been without a *shochet* (ritual slaughterer), and thus no Jew in it had tasted meat for eighteen years. When Reb Gedaliya settles down to be the new *shochet,* the Goray Jews feast on meat, and soon other pleasures of the flesh follow. Gedaliya preaches a religion of serving God through joy, and argues that since it is the end of days all the prohibitions of the Law have been repealed. The consequent excesses range from simple adultery to sodomy with

goats, and one diabolist even goes so far as to shave off his beard
and earlocks with a razor. Eventually Goray becomes "an ac-
cursed town," Gedaliya turns apostate in imitation of his master
Sabbatai Zevi, and the end of the novel is the pious moral of the
pamphlet on which it concludes: "Let none attempt to force the
Lord."

The Magician of Lublin, which I think to be Singer's finest
work, is not about the closed *shtetl* world, but about an infidel
Jew, Yasha Mazur, out among the nations in nineteenth-century
Poland. He is a performer: a magician, hypnotist, and acrobat.
Yasha lives his whole life "as if walking the tightrope": married to
a pious Jewish wife, Esther; having simultaneous affairs with Zeftel, the Jewish wife of a thief, and Magda, the Polish girl who
assists in his act, both of whom are in love with him; meanwhile
himself in love with Emilia, a highborn Polish lady. As Don Juan
did, "he lusted after women, yet hated them as a drunkard hates
alcohol."

In one terrible day, all of Yasha's life goes to pieces. He tries
an easy robbery and fails at it, damaging his foot so that he cannot perform; Emilia tells him "You stem from offal and you are
offal," and turns him away; Magda calls him a "dirty Jew" and
says she is leaving; he finds Zeftel in bed with a man; finally he
returns home to discover that Magda has strangled his trained
animals and hanged herself. Yasha has tasted the bitterness of the
world and "seen the hand of God."

As a result, he becomes Reb Jacob the Penitent, an anchorite
saint who bricks himself up in a cell, where he fasts, prays, and
gives audiences through the window. "You must have some sort of
covenant with God since he punished you directly on the spot,"
Emilia told Yasha when she heard the story of his unsuccessful
burglary. His inflamed and swollen foot, risen like dough, is the
punishment, and the yeast working in it is God's grace. Yasha,
who can "walk a tightrope, skate on a wire, climb walls, open any
lock," who can sign his name and shell peas with his toes, is a
Jewish Faust, and the book is a parable of the Enlightenment.
Yasha's covenant is the covenant of the Law, and when he is
knocked off his tightrope he flees to its security and reinforces it
with bricks.

The Slave is the most ambitious of Singer's romances so far. It is the story of Jacob, a pious scholar of Josefov in the seventeenth century, sold as a slave to a Polish peasant, and of his love for the peasant's daughter, Wanda, who passes as a mute to live with him as a Jewish wife, "Dumb Sarah." Its theme is universalism, the discovery by Jacob that even the most debased of the Polish peasants are fellow humans, created in God's image, and the humbling of his stiffnecked Jewish pride. Jacob first sees the peasants as subhuman, eaters of field mice, indulgers in abominations, shameless in debauchery, and soulless. A description of a cowherds' drunken party as Jacob sees it is truly Swiftian in its bestiality. Yet, through Wanda, he discovers universal humanity and feels compassion for the cowherds.

Beyond that, Jacob discovers his fellowship with "all living things: Jews, gentiles, animals, even the flies and gnats." He becomes un-Jewishly fond of the cows he tends for the peasant and of his dog. "The idea of feeding on God's creatures now repelled him," and he decides that "Jews treated animals as Cossacks treated Jews." Eventually Jacob eats no flesh, "neither meat nor fish nor anything else from a living creature, not even cheese or eggs." In the tradition of the universalizing tracts of the Old Testament, Jonah and Ruth, *The Slave* announces a widening of the limited covenant of the Law: *all* are God's chosen.

This universalist theme is implied rather than stated, but the other Old Testament revolution, the prophetic emphasis on ethics rather than ritual, is openly preached in *The Slave*. In his captivity, Jacob occupied himself with trying to recollect the 248 commandments and 365 prohibitions of the Law and incise them on a rock. After he is ransomed, Law and commentary come to seem hair-splitting and sterile, and Jacob sees the Jews around him as devoutly obeying every ritual injunction, but mistreating their fellow men. He discovers "his religion: its essence was the relation between man and his fellows."

Singer's latest parable, then, is the transcendence of law by love. The body was sin in *Satan in Goray;* in *The Slave* it comes close to being salvation. Culture and nature are both necessary. The peasant Wanda lusts for sacred learning; the pious scholar Jacob hungers for the fresh air of the fields. They complete each other, and, in a miracle at the end, Jacob and Sarah are buried in a common grave with a common tombstone reading "In their death they were not divided." Jacob fell into slavery, having been rich and lucky before the pogroms (he was a scholar supported by his wife's family); then he fell into sin with Wanda, convinced that "I am forfeiting the world to come." The rise at the end is comparable: their son becomes a prodigy and a teacher in Jerusalem; Jacob becomes a saint from whom venomous serpents turn away, and he is believed to be one of the Thirty-Six Righteous men who sustain the world.

As it denies *Satan in Goray, The Slave* reverses *The Magician of Lublin.* Conversion now is *into* the world, *into* the embrace of the nations. The highest value is human attachment rather than asceticism, ethics rather than observance. Jacob is Yasha reborn, but where Yasha suffered as Job did, to glorify God, Jacob suffers as Moses did, to prepare him to free those held in bondage.

The second half of *The Slave,* Jacob's living in Pilitz with Dumb Sarah, is less effective than the first, Jacob in slavery, which is as great as anything Singer ever wrote. The miraculous end is hard to take, and some of the characters are unconvincing. Nevertheless, *The Slave* towers over everything else being written today. Writing old-fashioned romances in an obsolescent tongue, Singer redeems the time.

LOVE AND DEATH IN A RUSSIAN NOVEL

Fyodor Kuz'mich Teternikov was born in St. Petersburg in 1863, and died in the same city, renamed Leningrad, in 1927. Although of unimpeachable working-class origins—his mother was a chambermaid—he had no use for the Revolution. Teternikov published verse and fiction over the pen name Fyodor Sologub, and was the most talented of the Russian Symbolists. Before he became a professional writer, Sologub was a teacher and school administrator. His novel *The Petty Demon* appeared in 1907. A tiny edition was reprinted early in the 1960s in the Soviet Union, in a series of "writers hostile to the state." A translation was published by Knopf in 1916, and a scholarly new translation by Andrew Field, with an introduction by Ernest J. Simmons, was published in 1962. Sologub is almost unknown in the United States, and I had never read, or seen, a book of his until this one. Now I cannot wait to read the others. *The Petty Demon* is a masterpiece.

Two actions dominate the book. In the main one, a thoroughly repulsive schoolteacher named Ardal'on Borisych Peredonov—gluttonous, rotten with superstition, cowardly, and mean—is duped into marrying his mistress Varvara by her pretense that by means of her influence on a Princess she can get him a job as a school inspector. As he waits for the appointment, he slowly sinks into madness, and ends by cutting the throat of his best friend. Peredonov is a comic figure, but it is comedy that grows increasingly monstrous, and one's laughter sours in the mouth.

In the subsidiary action, a sensual young woman named Ludmila Rutilova falls in love with and half-seduces a beautiful young schoolboy called Sasha. (His age is not given, but it is clear that he has not yet reached puberty.) The scenes in which Ludmila tears off Sasha's clothing and kisses his body, or costumes him as a girl and drenches him with perfume, or takes off most of her own clothing, lies at his feet, and pleads to be ravaged, are overpoweringly erotic, perverse and disturbing.

In another aspect, *The Petty Demon* is Gogolesque satire of Russian provincial life. The town is a vision of dirt streets, always dusty or muddy, and the people in it are fools and bores. One section of the book has Peredonov going the rounds of the town's worthies to clear his name of fancied slanders, and in the tradition of Chichikov's journey, his pilgrimage becomes a series of comic set pieces: the sententious major, the health fanatic district attorney, the pompous corseted marshal, the leading landowner with his fake peasant furniture, and so on. The quality of the town's coarseness is best imaged at Peredonov's wedding to Varvara, with a crowd of boys running alongside the carriage and hooting, and Varvara spitting at them out the window.

After Peredonov, the character who most fully embodies the general nastiness is a widow named Grushina, Varvara's crony and the writer of the spurious letters from a "Princess" that mislead Peredonov. Grushina is a lecherous sloven, her children are "shabby, dirty, stupid, and angry like scalded puppies," and she and the children communicate exclusively in screams and curses. Grushina has poor paintings of female nudes on her walls, and she drapes them to make them seem indecent. In one of Sologub's characteristically Manichaean touches, both Varvara and Grushina have lovely bodies, "slender, beautiful, and supple," but Varvara's is topped with "the head of a faded harlot," and Grushina's is marred by a wrinkled, dusty skin covered with flea bites.

The heart of the book is Peredonov, and Peredonov is manylayered. On the surface level he is a dull fool, bored and boring. He is interested in nothing outside himself; he has no opinions, and no desire to form any. On Peredonov's bloated face, even a momentary look of animation appears "dull and morose." He is childishly greedy, munching caramels as he daydreams of naked girls, gobbling jam tarts washed down with vodka as he fights with Varvara. He is terrified of drafts and of catching cold, and so cowardly that when he makes an obscene gesture at the postman he does so in the privacy of his pocket.

Beneath this ludicrous figure there is a much less laughable bully and sadist. Peredonov spits in Varvara's face, and forces her to kiss the head of his cane, which is carved in the form of a "fig." He abuses the cat, and if it shows its claws, whips it terribly. He humiliates the Rutilov girls, and encourages the brother of a poor girl to set fire to her only dress as a joke. When he steals and gobbles a pound of raisins from his own kitchen, he charges the maid with eating them, and takes their cost out of her pay. He bullies and humiliates his pupils, enjoys their tears, and tells their parents invented misdeeds to get them whipped. Peredonov's vision of happiness is: "a town where all the teachers will bow down low to me, and where all the students will be afraid and whisper in fear."

Beneath this vicious bully is Peredonov the paranoid schizophrenic. We watch his psychosis develop in the course of the book. At first it seems merely neurotic: he assumes that anyone laughing is laughing at him; he believes that everyone is hostile to him and spreading slander; he is afraid of poison in his food or drink; he is terrified of black magic and witchcraft; he fears that at any time a berserk schoolboy might bite him fatally (human saliva being poisonous). As he gets crazier, Peredonov comes to believe that the cat has gone to report him to the police, or has itself become a policeman, and that an "eyebird"—consisting of nothing but an eye and two wings—is spying on him.

In his madness, Peredonov commits a series of increasingly wild acts. He destroys a dress of Varvara's, in which a demon might be hiding; he stabs out the eyes of the court cards in his decks, "so they would not stare at him"; he inks "P" all over his body so that his friend Volodin cannot change places with him; he denounces his enemies to the police; he smears the floor with glue so that the demon will stick fast; he stabs at spies behind the wallpaper; he denounces the court cards to the police, and burns the decks; he burns down a dance hall to release the demon in the fire; he denounces a ram to the police as an impostor pretending to be Volodin; finally, he cuts Volodin's throat as one would slaughter a ram.

With impressive prescience, Sologub anticipated Freud's theory of paranoia as a defense against homosexuality. In Freud's view, the paranoid transforms and disguises his repressed homosexual attachment ("I love him") by means of projection ("He loves me") and reaction-formation ("He hates me"). Peredonov clearly has a strong latent homosexuality: he calls boy pupils by girls' names and addresses them as "sweetie pie"; he imputes lurid wickedness to them; he becomes convinced that Sasha is a girl in disguise, or both a boy *and* a girl, and he dreams of Sasha beckoning him and leading him "along dark and dirty streets." For his wedding, Peredonov puts on his wife's rouge and tries to put on her corset, rationalizing these acts as attempts to look more youthful.

The irony here is that Sasha *is* very ambivalent sexually, and that Ludmila's erotic hothouse is bringing that ambivalence to blossom. Ludmila's boldest act is to costume Sasha as a geisha for a masquerade ball, and once at the ball Sasha cooperates by flirting and coquetting shamelessly with the men, as a result of which he wins the prize. Peredonov is the principal accuser of Ludmila and Sasha, and their affair is taken to be one of his delusions. "Not everything is imagination, there's also truth in the world," he mumbles sadly at one point.

Peredonov, Sologub explains, "could not understand the spontaneous Dionysian ecstasies triumphantly calling in nature. He was blind and pitiful—like many of us." After the murder, the rumors about Ludmila and Sasha are accepted by everyone as "the ravings of a madman," and Ludmila's calm lying is accepted as the truth. "One had only to compare the mad, coarse, dirty Peredonov with the gay, delightful, well-dressed, sweet-smelling Ludmilochka." This ultimate irony seems to be Sologub's point. Ludmila, in rapport with the Dionysian ecstasies, can transfigure reality; Peredonov, a hater of life, makes any truth false.

To the extent that such things can be seen through a good translation, Sologub is a writer of great distinction. He uses short sentences to marvelous effect. Peredonov's letter to the Princess, when madness finally gives him courage to write her, is a triumph: " 'I love you,' he wrote, 'because you are cold and distant. Varvara sweats, and it is uncomfortable to sleep with her. She's like an oven. I want to have a cold and distant lover. Come to me and fulfill my need.' "

A number of scenes are masterly. One is a drunken party at which the Peredonovs invite their guests to help them soil the walls before they move, that being their spiteful custom. Another is a scene in which Peredonov and the mother of a student whip the student, secretly in the night because of the father's opposition. It is written as though they were committing adultery. The erotic tension between them crackles, and the scene is broken off as they stand together at the bedroom door, then resumed with Peredonov walking home, mumbling "It wasn't my fault. She herself wanted it." A third scene, with particular brilliance, switches from Ludmila kissing Sasha's body, "in a thrilling and mysterious worship of the blossoming Flesh," to discover her two sisters watching through the keyhole, "numb with passionate and burning excitement."

Peredonov's slaughter of Volodin has been beautifully foreshadowed by a constant identification of Volodin with sheep and rams, and by Peredonov's frequent terrified hiding of kitchen knives. The covert significance of the dual plot, I believe, is to caricature and mock the Christian mystery, the slain Lamb, and to replace it with an older joyous pagan mystery, the blossoming Flesh.

"It is of you that I have written my novel," Sologub insolently told his readers in the introduction to the second edition. And of course in his deepest meaning Peredonov is ourselves: the mindless greedy id, the cruel superego, the ego driven mad by inner war. But perhaps there is something of Sasha's beauty and Ludmila's passion in us too. With this superb book as a glass through which to see our own natures more clearly, we may not forever be blind and pitiful.

THE PRIEST WITH THE FISHNET HATBAND

"Hell is paved with the bald pates of priests!" St. Bernard thundered in the twelfth century. J. F. Powers, who used to publish sermons on that text in the form of excellent short stories, seems not to be so sure now. For many years his first novel has been almost as eagerly awaited as Katherine Anne Porter's. Unfortunately, *Morte D'Urban* is disappointing: it does not quite shape up as a novel, and it is comic in the wrong sense, meaning frivolous.

Powers has always been a very uneven writer. In the fashion of that prototype of fiction writers, when he is good he is very very good, and when he is bad he is horrid. Powers has published two volumes of short stories, *Prince of Darkness and Other Stories* in 1947, and *The Presence of Grace* in 1956. Most of the stories deal with the Roman Catholic clergy, given an intense scrutiny, although Powers has written a few early stories, and those his worst, dealing with Negro life.

There are three Negro stories in *Prince of Darkness*. "He Don't Plant Cotton" is about the firing of a Negro piano-and-drums duo for refusing to perform "Ol' Man River" often enough to satisfy a group of drunken white Mississippians. It is unconvincingly melodramatic in its central action, and ineffectively impressionist in describing the music ("Notes drew nearer, riding on ships and camels through a world of sand and water"), but it is at least a respectable try at a story. The other two are indescribably awful. In "The Trouble" the child narrator's mother is killed by a white mob in a race riot, and the bereaved family in Christian charity rescues a cowardly white rioter from a Negro mob. Here is a sample of the prose: "Daddy, I could see, was crying—the strongest man in the world was crying with tears in his big dark eyes and coming down the side of his big hard face." "The Eye" is just as bad, an absurdity about a Southern

Negro who bravely rescues a pregnant white girl from drowning and is lynched for his pains.

If Powers' weakness in *Prince of Darkness* is Negro pastoral, in *The Presence of Grace* it is pussycat whimsy. Two of the stories about priests, "Death of a Favorite" and "Defection of a Favorite," are narrated by a rectory cat, in a fashion designed to turn the strongest stomach. In the first story—it is embarrassing to have to synopsize it—the cat is conditioned by wicked priests to dread a crucifix, but is then mysteriously killed and reborn "redeemed from my previous fear." In the second the cat prays, and assists in the reform of a sinful curate by manifesting a Sign.

In his middle range, the bulk of Powers' stories consist of affectionate yet sardonic portraits of the clergy. In "The Lord's Day" a group of nuns is seen counting the Sunday collections, divided into two teams, Cubs and White Sox. The Monsignor of "The Forks" advises his earnest young curate to shave his armpits and wear "Steeple," the Cologne for Clergymen. The priest of "The Valiant Woman" and his domineering housekeeper spend their evenings playing cutthroat honeymoon bridge, in a wicked parody of a marriage. In "A Losing Game," an eccentric old pastor fires at imaginary rats in his basement and wings his presumptuous curate. In "The Presence of Grace," the same old pastor is discovered blowing out, as a fire hazard, all the vigil candles after the last Mass.

In Powers' best stories, which are among the finest of our time, he looks at the clergy, not with wry affection, but with St. Bernard's hard eye, in terms of moral absolutes. "Lions, Harts, Leaping Does" is a portrait of a saint, and is a beautiful and moving story. It shows, in a series of tiny incidents, the decline and death of an old Franciscan, Father Didymus. A devoted lay brother reads aloud to him from a volume of lives of the early popes; Didymus recalls his happiness wading in a stream with his late brother, pursued by a crayfish "clad in sable armor"; he identifies with a caged canary in his cell, and collapses in trying to free it. The story blends these symbols with consummate mastery: a thematic "Popes, Crayfish, Leaping Canaries." Didymus, sure that he is not a saint, troubled by "the grossest distractions," remembering his vocation in the imagery of "wiping the lipstick of the faithful from the image of Christ crucified," suddenly attains to a pure sanctity beyond desire, and flies into death, a freed canary indeed.

"Prince of Darkness" is a matching portrait of a sinful priest, Father Ernest Burner, a perpetual curate. In the first section of the story, as he sees through "T N T" Tracy, a disgusting Big Catholic Layman who is trying to sell him insurance, we recognize that Burner has intelligence and a degree of spiritual insight. In the later sections these disappear, and we see through Burner in turn. He is as spiritually gross as he is physically fat and gluttonous. He uses his clerical collar as a target for putting practice in his room; he daydreams of being a German war ace or an advertising copywriter; he uses a holy-water font for an ashtray; he thinks *Studs Lonigan* is the best thing since the Bible; he perceives the odor of sanctity as "body odor"; he fails as a confessor through boorish obtusity.

Powers makes some effort to identify Burner with Satan. He is nicknamed "the Prince of Darkness" because of a photographic darkroom he has set up in the rectory, and he drives his car "applying a cloven foot to the pedal." This pathetic vocationless slob is hardly Satan, merely a priest destined for hellfire (thus "Burner"). Powers' spokesmen in the story are young Father Quinlan, who quotes hard doctrine from St. Paul and mocks his fellow curate as "Saint Ernest Burner, Help of Golfers," and the archbishop, a saintly old man who quotes St. Bernard, tells Burner spiritual truths, and intends to keep him a curate until he finds "not peace but a sword" in his vocation, or forever.

Morte D'Urban is a gentler jab at the sinfulness of the clergy, with Father Burner metamorphosed into Father Urban of the Order of St. Clement, tempted by a new Big Catholic Layman. As befits his name, Urban is a worldly priest. He is a famous preacher and charmer, sporting the most liberal religious principles, interested in the salvation of only the wealthy and influential. He dines in the Pump Room on champagne and shish kebab (there is an uproarious debate with another priest over whether or not Our Lord ate shish kebab); he smokes Dunhill Monte Cristo Colorado Maduro No. 1 cigars exclusively; he plays a "near-professional"

game of golf; he wears a straw hat with a fishnet band; he identifies opposition to his ways as "puritanism and black clericalism."

The tempter, Billy Cosgrove, out of esteem for Urban gives
the Clementines the free use of a fancy office building. When
Urban is taken off the road and assigned to a primitive rural retreat house, Billy sends the house a Christmas hamper of food and
liquor, an electrified creche, and a color television set. He then
buys the order a station wagon and builds it a golf course, complete with a "shrine of Our Lady below No. 5 green."

In the course of his redemption, Father Urban commits three
ethical acts, each promptly punished. In the first, he intercedes
with a wealthy benefactor, Mrs. Thwaites, on behalf of a maid she
has cheated. Mrs. Thwaites sends him packing. In the second, he
prevents Billy, who is furious at catching no fish at a fishing camp,
from drowning a swimming deer. Billy tosses him out of the boat
and drives home without him, then spitefully abandons the station
wagon he has given the order and evicts them from the office
building. Urban's third ethical act is to refuse to go for a naked
swim with Mrs. Thwaites' married daughter or even to look at her
undressed. She hits him in the head with a shoe and leaves him
marooned on an island.

One moral of the book is openly preached by Monsignor
Renton, Father Urban's confessor, who denies the value of anything done by a priest outside his sacramental role. It is more
effectively symbolized in a few figures: an anonymous pedestrian
who stands up to Billy's Rolls Royce (as Urban does not); Father
Wilfred, who runs the retreat house in the spirit of the primitive
church; his assistant, Brother Harold, who caught 70 pounds of
fish while Billy and Urban caught none (he is the *true* fisher of
men).

The book's title, *Morte D'Urban,* introduces an obscure parallel with Malory's *Morte D'Arthur,* a work repeatedly discussed in
it. Apparently Urban is not meant to be Arthur, but Launcelot,
the worldliest and most sinful knight redeemed as the most pious
hermit and true priest. Gradually, at the retreat house, Father
Urban becomes more spiritual: filling in for a sick parish priest, he
shows something like a vocation, and develops a dimension of
honesty; finally illness transforms him. At the end he is elected

Provincial of the order because of his worldly connections, and
disappoints his backers by turning out to be a pious and unworldly director.

The problem here is that the three ethical acts are absurd,
and it is all made too easy and reassuring. Smoking Havana cigars
is not really satanic, and renouncing them is not really salvation.
The Irish Roman Catholic tradition in which Powers grew up is
puritan, with a deep distrust of the flesh. Powers has come a long
way from it, and speaks in the voice of Jansenism, the primitive
church, the Reformation and Counter-Reformation, the monastic
orders and the anchorites (at one point he refers to our seminaries
as turning out "policemen, disc jockeys, and an occasional desert
father"). But peeping through is that same Irish puritanism,
shocked by Billy's rich diet and Sally Thwaites' fine body. Powers'
Bunyanesque allegories of Father Sure-of-Hellfire and Father
Worldly lack Bunyan's quality of desperation. It is terribly funny
when Father Urban, making suburban parish calls for his own
spiritual good, is wet on by a hamster, but it is not the Dark Night
of the Soul. Powers' comedy undercuts and trivializes his drama of
redemption. When a local bishop tries to take over the Clemen-
tine retreat house for a seminary, and Urban saves it, in a trial by
combat on the links, by getting knocked unconscious by the
bishop's golf ball, we are in the world of comic strips, not of serious fiction.

Morte D'Urban makes it clear that the range of spiritual experience Powers is prepared to allow a priest is too narrow to make a
novel. The whisky priest of Graham Greene's *The Labyrinthine
Ways* (*The Power and the Glory*)—alcoholic, cowardly, weak,
the father of a bastard—dies a martyr and is perhaps a saint,
deeply sinful and deeply repentant. Powers' champagne priest,
who trims Peter's great net down to a fishnet hatband, is too chic
an image to disturb or convince imaginatively. He is a tidy
sinner, tidily redeemed.

AN EXCEPTIONAL FIRST NOVEL

How pleasant it is to welcome an excellent first novel! Bruce Jay Friedman is 32, and has published short stories in magazines, all of which I seem to have missed. His novel, *Stern*, is a delight, at once uproarious and heartbreaking, and no page of it could have been written by anyone else.

One of the hallmarks of literary excellence is the inadequacy of synopsis ("Oh, it's a play about a man who eventually kills his uncle"). In those terms, *Stern* is about a soft fat cowardly Jew of 34 named Stern, who buys a house in the suburbs and suffers from anti-Semitism. But how sociological that sounds, and how humorless. What Stern actually suffers from is internal, neurotic, and what Friedman has made of it is wild Freudian comedy.

Stern's trouble starts when a neighbor refuses to let his son play with Stern's son, calls Stern's wife and son "kikes," and shoves Stern's wife so that she falls sprawling and exposes herself. Challenged as a Jew, a father, a husband, and a man, Stern goes to fight what he calls "the kike man," and ends up doing push-ups—nine legitimate and two cheating—near the man's house. The thought of the kike man peering between his wife's legs obsesses Stern; it is agonizing but somehow exciting. He tries to get his wife to reenact it for him, and when she refuses Stern himself reenacts her fall. It is clearly a Fall, a symbolic adultery.

In his obsession, Stern develops a painful ulcer, "as though the kike man's boot had stamped through Stern's mouth, plunging downward, elevator-swift, to lodge finally in his bowels." He is sent to a rest home to heal the ulcer, and the rest home and its collection of grotesques constitute one of the funniest episodes in recent fiction: funny yet disturbing and moving, on the order of *Monsieur Verdoux*. At the home, Stern is terrified of a patient so cut away that Stern calls him "the half man," and he fears that in the night the half man will slip into bed with him. As his ulcer improves, Stern also broods about the kike man, realizing that when he gets out he will have to go back to living under that shadow and will ulcerate again. He identifies the kike man with the ulcer, dreams that the man is shrinking as the ulcer shrinks, and fancies that the rest home has guaranteed to "heal his neighborhood as well as his ulcer."

After five weeks at the home, Stern is cured by a combination of triumphs. His Jewishness is ignored. He helps win a baseball game, and a blond teen-age boy who calls him "fat ass" is enough impressed to concede: "No fooling, you get around good. I mean, for a guy with a can like yours." When the blond boy and a one-legged Greek boy get into a fight with a saloon-keeper, Stern achieves the glory of participation by pinning the arms of a spectator, a small man who wants no part of the affair. Then, to make the outing perfect, Stern goes to bed with the blond boy's girl, a beautiful passionate Puerto Rican hairdresser with literary ambitions, while his two friends wait outside. His virility reestablished by all these events, Stern fondles the Greek boy, who is crying over his lost leg, hugs and kisses the half man, suddenly revealed as Jewish too, and departs.

Back with his wife and child, Stern finds that a new aggression was committed in his absence. A boy staying at the kike man's house cut the elbow of Stern's son and called him "Matzoh." Stern's response to this is a nervous breakdown, a nightmarish period during which he clutches at strangers in the street and tells them his troubles, signs up for a six-year course at a physical culture studio, and visits a psychiatrist but flees at his price. Stern recovers miraculously after a long soothing conversation with his cracked old cleaning woman. He boasts: "I had the mildest nervous breakdown in town. I didn't miss a day of work." Finally, a year and a half after the offense, Stern fights the kike man and tells him off, then goes back triumphantly to hug his wife and son. Friedman has made sure that this is not The Coward's Redemption—Stern receives a blow that almost severs his ear and returns an ineffectual punch, and afterwards he is still afraid of the man—but it is a tiny victory nevertheless.

Stern's miseries long antedate the kike man, who is only the latest incarnation of a familiar problem. In Stern's childhood, his mother was shamelessly promiscuous, taking the boy along on her afternoon adulteries at a summer resort and letting him play outside (the role of his friends when he is with the Puerto Rican girl). When a man at the resort made an indecent remark to Stern's mother, doubling her up with laughter, Stern punched him in the stomach. She used to shame Stern in restaurants by saying, of any visible young man, "I could make him in ten seconds." When Stern's gangster Uncle Sweets broke a beggar's nose in front of Stern's mother, the boy could see her excitement. Now, with slack thighs and dyed hair, a steady drinker and self-pitier, she lets the cleaning woman perform her maternal function for Stern. (Stern is so desperate for a mother that he once spent an entire four-hour date greedily sucking a girl's breasts.)

His wife, a great-eyed, long-nosed girl, more attractively large-bottomed than he, is now the object of his intense jealousy. She takes lessons in modern dance, and after Stern sees her kissing the teacher goodbye, he imagines her going to bed with the teacher in "tangled modern dance positions," performing "endless, exhausting, intricately choreographed lovemaking." After he develops his ulcer, Stern is unable to satisfy his wife sexually ("I'm going to have to jump on a telephone pole," she says brutally after one failure), but eventually we discover that he never has been able to satisfy her. During his breakdown, while he is insane with jealousy, "the deep hot valleys of his wife's body" are particularly frightening.

Stern plays fantastic charming games with his son: "Billy One-Foot," in which they pretend that Stern's leg is a diabolical criminal; "Butterfly Hand," in which Stern's fat hand turns into a butterfly; and many others. His constant private fantasies use the same masochistic imagery of castration and mutilation, but now it is menacing and horrible to him (while comically appropriate to us). In the most complete of these visions, Stern has gone blind, and is walking with his family past the kike man's house: "The man would spot them, walk slowly forward, then gather some speed, put Stern out of commission with a judo chop, kick his child in the crotch, and then get his wife down to stab her sexually, and, worse, get her to wriggle and whimper with enjoyment beneath her conqueror while Stern thrashed blindly in the street."

Jewishness for Stern has no religious, national, or cultural content; it is merely a shameful inferiority and guilt, first learned from his father. A long flashback to Stern's college days in a boardinghouse of Jewish students consists of nothing but one sneering joke about Jewishness after another, jokes that quickly curdle friendships into hatred. This has a thematic sequel when Stern is in the air force. An intoxicated, courtly flying instructor— full of admiration for Israeli pilots he has been training—drinks with Stern and calls him "Big Jew" admiringly, as one might say "Big Swede." (Stern had called his college friend "Little Jew" nastily.) For all his joy at being "Big Jew," Stern is forced to stop the man and drive him away when people he knows overhear the conversation.

Here, as in so many places, Friedman is resolutely honest. The beautiful funny scene of Stern in bed with the Puerto Rican girl shatters just as quickly. After a quick orgasm, Stern turns against the girl and "her terrible Puerto Rican writing" and helps the boys torment her by riding her on a broomstick. (Unsatisfied by Stern, the girl can have a broomstick, as Stern's wife wanted a telephone pole.)

Stern's Oedipus complex and neurosis are classically accurate, but Friedman has digested psychoanalysis so well that only one trace of Freudian theory appears on the book's surface. The boy Stern, in the shower with his mother at the summer resort, stares "at the pathetic, gaping blackness between her legs, filled with a terrible anguish and loss." This is, a little too overtly, Freud's picture of boyhood castration-anxiety, and it makes the kike man's later genital staring just a little too pat. Nevertheless, Friedman is the most unselfconscious Freudian novelist I have ever read, and his appearance may finally herald a literary generation that can make full imaginative use of psychoanalytic insight.

Friedman's other important ancestor is Joyce, and Stern frequently suggests Leopold Bloom, without suffering in the comparison. In its lightning tempo and garish exaggeration, *Stern* will probably remind readers of Joseph Heller's *Catch-22*, but I think it is a far more serious and significant work than Heller's. *Stern* is a boldly symbolist, even allegorical, book: Stern's ulcer is rotten Jewishness, eating away at his insides; it ate away the other half of the half man; it will eat up any neurotic Jew who makes it a negative identity and uses it self-destructively.

Some of the book is amusing suburban comedy of Peter de Vries' sort: the real estate agent who plays Chopin to show prospects that he is an unworldly dreamer; the doctor whose "treatments always involved shopping bags or typewriter ribbons or old shoe polish cans"; the correct protocol for throwing up on commuting trains. The pleasure here is in recognition. But in the finest scenes in *Stern*, the pleasure is in non-recognition—we could not possibly have experienced anything so perfectly farcical. There are many of these. Perhaps a typical one is Stern's return home, after the doctor has diagnosed his ulcer. He walks across the lawn bearing his tragic news, "kicking furiously at fallen pears and crying through his nose," to find that his wife is away at a dance class, and that his parents have brought over his insane Uncle Babe to advise Stern about the stock market.

Friedman's style is uneven, and some things miss fire. I am not sure that the ending comes off, although I cannot invent any better ending. But these are minor flaws in a great success. Friedman has written a superbly funny novel about suffering and misery, somehow augmenting rather than diminishing our capacity to be moved by it. He has plunged deep into weakness and neurosis, and come up with something strong and sane. He is greatly gifted, fiercely honest, and very welcome news indeed.

LEAPING FOR GOODLY THEMIS

A book that changed my life—there are times when I think it is the most revolutionary book of the twentieth century—was reissued in 1962, marking the fiftieth anniversary of its publication. It is *Themis*, by Jane Ellen Harrison, and after being out of print for many years it is now happily available in two reprintings of the 1927 revised edition: together with a later pamphlet, as *Epilegomena to the Study of Greek Religion and Themis: A Study of the Social Origins of Greek Religion;* and as a paperback, *Themis: A Study of the Social Origins of Greek Religion.*

The year that *Themis* appeared, 1912, can now be seen to have been a watershed year, a high point of rationality and optimism which we have never since regained. Miss Harrison was 62, a fellow and lecturer in classical subjects at Newnham College, Cambridge. As early as her twenties she had been recognized as "the cleverest woman in England." (I recall that my immediate reaction to *Themis*, when I read it in *my* twenties, was to accept for the first time the existence, and thus the possibility, of an absolutely first-rate analytic mind in a woman.) Before *Themis*, Miss Harrison had published a few scholarly books on ancient art, and one bold work of theory, *Prolegomena to the Study of Greek Religion,* in 1903.

Although she was a gifted linguist (before her death she knew fourteen languages, and read cuneiform for relaxation), Miss Harrison was always a maverick classics scholar. From the first appearance of *The Golden Bough* in 1890, the work of her Cambridge contemporary, James G. Frazer, her great determination was to turn the new light of anthropology on the ancient texts. Miss Harrison was aided in this intention by a little band of the most remarkable minds working together since Darwin and his circle: Gilbert Murray at Oxford, and Francis Macdonald Cornford and Arthur Bernard Cook at Cambridge. As their senior, a geyser of energy, and a woman, Miss Harrison inspired them, collaborated with them, and set them tasks in the intellectual revolution that produced a dozen major books between 1903 and 1941.

Themis, while it is uniquely Miss Harrison's book, is at the same time a perfect collaboration. Murray, to whom the book is dedicated, contributed to it a remarkable technical "Excursus on the Ritual Forms Preserved in Greek Tragedy." Cornford wrote a brilliant chapter, "The Origin of the Olympic Games." Cook made available the materials of his forthcoming vast compendium *Zeus.* All three fed Miss Harrison ideas and information and cheered her on. We can now see how remarkable it is for Jane Harrison to stand out in this band of geniuses. Murray was a far better Greek scholar, Cornford had a much more rigorous and logical mind, and Cook was always more fertile of ideas. But Miss Harrison had the one big idea, and she had a power of imaginative understanding that went beyond any of theirs.

Themis has always seemed to me a transparently clear work. It is essentially an account of how myths arise. Myths originate, Miss Harrison insists, as "the spoken correlative of the acted rite"; in a Greek definition, they are "the things said over a ritual act." This is the *process* of mythic origins, it is the *only* process, and since 1912 it has been impossible to talk seriously about mythology in any other terms, or to use the word "myth" for anything but a narrative of known or presumed ritual origins. As they evolve, Miss Harrison shows, myths break away from their ritual bases, shift into the past tense and the third person (from "Now we do this" to "Once they did this"), and as they survive after the rite has died out, they increasingly represent misunderstanding and rationalizations of their events.

This theory was of course not new with Miss Harrison; the Greeks knew all about it, and in 1910 Arnold van Gennep had proposed just such a terminological rigor. What was new was her utterly convincing detailed demonstration that this was the fashion in which the Greek gods actually evolved, "straight out of a social custom," as the projection and concretization of their worshippers' behavior and collective feelings of awe and terror. In Miss Harrison's phrasing, "the god is the reflection, the projection of man's emotions socially reinforced."

The extension of this to *our* gods and sacred heroes, from Abraham to Jesus, is inevitable, and Miss Harrison does not neglect it. Something like the Greek rite of *omophagia*, tearing the sacrifice apart and eating the raw flesh with the divine life still quivering in it, lies buried in the Eucharist; her Greek year-god, the *eniautos-daimon*, "died for the people" as Jesus did; the Greek *boukranion*, the sacred bull's skull, equates with the horns of the altar in Exodus; Jahveh was a wonder-working ark before he was a god. If mythology is eventually the disorderly misunderstanding of ritual, so theology is the organized misunderstanding of mythology. Miss Harrison simply notes that the lies told the women and children about the men's rites are "theology."

A charming, deliberately comic consequence of this in the book is Miss Harrison's partiality toward the old dark chthonic Greek religion, rather than the later sunny Olympian gods. The mysteries of Dionysus, "utterly inhuman" to Clement of Alexandria, are "very human indeed, social and civilizing through and through" to Miss Harrison. "It is secret," she adds of a mystery rite, "not because it is indecent, but because it is intensely social, decent and entirely sacred." Thus "we must get back behind these intrusive, grasping Olympians," Olympians "only too ready to lay greedy hands on a magical rite, pervert its meaning and turn it into a 'gift-sacrifice' for themselves." Annual death and rebirth is true immortality, as against "heaven's brazen and sterile immutability." "The real true god, the Eniautos-daimon, lives and works for his people; he does more, he dies for them." The Olympian god, in a "degradation," "substitutes privilege for function," and Miss Harrison shakes a Pauline socialist finger at him: "If any will not work neither let him eat."

Themis is a better, and perhaps ultimately a more important, book than *The Golden Bough*, because it fearlessly accepts its own consequences, where Frazer drew back from his. Miss Harrison begins the book with what Kenneth Burke calls a "representative anecdote," a ritual hymn newly discovered on Crete. From that hymn, with its beautiful "leap for full jars, and leap for fleecy flocks," "leap for our young citizens and for goodly Themis," to its final implications in Olympus phosphorescent with decay, and our Bible as a liturgical romance, she never falters or retreats.

Miss Harrison gets much of her evidence from ancient

writers, mostly quoted in the original (her audience is assumed to read Greek and Latin), and from archaeology (152 text figures reproduce relevant ancient works of art). In addition she draws heavily on the field anthropology of her time: typically explaining a Cretan ritual by rites of the Wiradthuri tribe of New South Wales; or talking of ancient Greek initiation "in the bush"; or crying out, "Let us look at facts—savage facts first." One is not entirely convinced when she writes in the introduction: "Savages, save for their reverent, totemistic attitude towards animals, weary and disgust me, though perforce I spend long hours in reading of their tedious doings."

Her psychology is equally old-fashioned; it is that of William James, with an infusion of Freud in the 1927 revision (not strong enough, however, to relace James' "subconscious" with Freud's "unconscious"). Nevertheless, Miss Harrison's powerful imagination plunges far deeper than her sources. We must "think ourselves back into the primaeval fusion of things," she says, or, as she wrote in the *Prolegomena:* "It is only by a severe effort of the imagination that we can think ourselves back into an adequate mental confusion to realize all the connotations."

Her style is intensely personal. She will tell us that one tears up painful letters on receipt, or that the social silences of men are "more spacious and monumental" than those of women, or that the husband's role is "to come back with his beak full of worms." Her frankness is absolute. "This derivation I had known and from cowardice rejected," she will write, or, "my blindness seems to me now almost incredible." Her prose, as much as her spirit, is beautiful. "Because Eros is human," she writes, "there is excess and ugliness waiting to shadow and distort nature's lovely temperance." Or again: "A lonely beast in the valley, a fish in the sea, has his Dike, but it is not till man congregates together that he has his Themis." Or she writes of "the world as a living animal, a thing not to be coerced and restrained, but reverently wooed."

The revolution effected by *Themis* has not yet ended. Miss Harrison's field of classical studies was overwhelmingly converted to her views, as she notes joyously in the 1927 preface (there has since been a swing back, "reactionary" in the most literal sense, as evidenced by the *Oxford Classical Dictionary* in 1949, and by Jo-

seph Fontenrose's *Python* in 1959). Murray turned the ritual
theory on Shakespeare in 1914, Bertha Phillpotts on edda and
saga, and Jessie Weston on romance, in 1920; since then no area
of literary scholarship or criticism has been unaffected. The field
of comparative religion, really the area in which Miss Harrison
worked, will never be the same again. She called herself a "free-
thinker" and was a lifelong member of the Rationalist Association
and a lecturer for it, but she has given a truer and deeper picture
of the nature of the religious experience than even her master
William James did.

Bertrand Russell once mocked Miss Harrison's gentle spinster
manner, so incompatible with her bloody theories, by offering to
pay for a wild bull if she would rend it limb from limb. He was
deceived by appearances. She has toppled stouter temples than
has Russell himself, or Samson either. Jane Harrison is truly what
Edith Hamilton is popularly taken to be, the great lady who
found Greece marble and left it living flesh.

POETICS, DOGMATICS, AND PARABOLICS

"As readers, most of us, to some degree, are like those urchins who pencil mustaches on the faces of girls in advertisements." Only one writer in our time could have written that sentence. In its subtle conveyance of a high estimate of literature in a low image, in the underspin that "to some degree" puts on "most of *us*," in the fastidious "urchins," in the general impudence of its wit, it could only be the work of Wystan Hugh Auden. It confronts the reader on the second page of Auden's first collection of critical essays, *The Dyer's Hand,* and it promises galaxies of fireworks to come.

Auden has included none of his essays before 1946, depriving us of his Freudo-Marxist criticism as well as of such triumphs over the narrowly social criteria of the thirties as "John Skelton" (1935) and "The Public *v.* the Late Mr. William Butler Yeats" (1939). Thus we get only the criticism of Auden's Christian period, the work of a dignified man of letters past his fortieth year.

But how mean and funny that august gentleman is! Harried by the pests of poetry, he shows a trace of petulance: "No cashier writes a letter to the press complaining about the incomprehensibility of Modern Mathematics and comparing it unfavorably with the good old days when mathematicians were content to paper irregularly shaped rooms and fill bathtubs without closing the waste pipe." Of a patient cured by psychoanalysis: "And immediately come seven devils, and the last state of that man is worse than the first."

His combination of an extraordinarily well-stocked mind with a natural digressiveness makes reading Auden always an adventure. He interrupts an essay on *Henry IV* to write an essay-within-the-essay on the relationship of corpulence to alcoholism; he turns an article about *Othello* into a discourse on practical joking; his account of Byron's *Don Juan* wanders off to explore the nature of friendship.

Auden is not only knowledgeable; he is sometimes wise. This wisdom often gets disguised as a joke: "The Oracle claimed to make prophecies and give good advice about the future; it never pretended to be giving poetry readings." At other times the tone is clearly in earnest, as when Auden writes of devotional poetry: "Is there not something a little odd, to say the least, about making an admirable public object out of one's feelings of guilt and penitence before God?" Occasionally seriousness breaks through so violently that Auden writes in a voice foreign to him, as in the sudden announcement: "Today, there is only one genuine worldwide revolutionary issue, racial equality."

As he formerly used Marx and Freud, Auden now uses Christianity as a critical tool. Poetry is seen as the limited creative act possible in a world both fallen and redeemable. The traditional theological heresies are used for critical perspectives: in its denial of nature *The Tempest* is Manichaean; *The Magic Flute* is over-optimistic and Pelagian; *Don Quixote* is orthodox. As does his former tutor Nevill Coghill, to whom the book is dedicated, Auden reads *Measure for Measure* as a Christian parable of redemption, but with the important reservation that, "to my mind, the parable does not quite work." He even interprets the master-servant relationship in *Around the World in Eighty Days* and the *Jeeves* books as a parable in the comic mode of *agape*, Holy Love.

The best essay in *The Dyer's Hand* is "The Prince's Dog," an ambitious reading of *Henry IV* as Christian parable. "Parabolically" (Auden uses the archaic adjective and adverb), Falstaff "is a comic symbol for the supernatural order of Charity," a "charity that loves all neighbors without distinction." "Falstaff's neglect of the public interest in favor of private concerns," Auden adds, "is an image for the justice of charity which treats each person, not as a cipher, but as a unique person." At the end of the essay, Falstaff is equated with the second person of God, also "condemned as a Bad Companion for mankind." In turning what he calls a "fat, cowardly tosspot" into a figuration of the Christ, Auden shows a boldness in Chestertonian paradox that would have petrified Chesterton.

"The Guilty Vicarage," an inductive study of the detective story, is almost equally impressive. The voice is the voice of Aristotle: "If there is more than one murder, the subsequent victims should be more innocent than the initial victim"; "As to the murderer's end, of the three alternatives—execution, suicide, and madness—the first is preferable; for if he commits suicide he refuses to repent, and if he goes mad he cannot repent, but if he does not repent society cannot forgive." How odd that the message finally delivered in Aristotle's voice should be Kierkegaard's: "The job of detective is to restore the state of grace in which the aesthetic and the ethical are as one."

The weaknesses of *The Dyer's Hand* are the obverse of all these strengths. Pushed too far, Aristotelian induction becomes absurd dogmatism: "A young woman, dressed as a boy, can never produce a convincing image of a boy"; "In the last analysis, the saint cannot be presented aesthetically." (My sociological friends would ask on how many observations those generalizations were based.) The emphasis on brilliance and paradox tends to break the essays into strings of aphorisms, and Auden has in fact literally cut a number of them down to strings of aphorisms.

The weakness of Christian literary criticism is Christianity's inherent dualism, and it continually drives Auden into oversimple antitheses. Here are a few: "Most writers are either Alices or Mabels" (the terms come from *Alice in Wonderland*), with lists of names; "The ear tends to be lazy, craves the familiar, and is shocked by the unexpected: the eye, on the other hand, tends to be impatient, craves the novel and is bored by repetition"; "Every poem involves some degree of collaboration between Ariel and Prospero"; "Our dream pictures of the Happy Place where suffering and evil are unknown are of two kinds, the Edens and the New Jerusalems."

What we are given, in fact, is often a profound half-truth. "If *Lycidas* is read in this way, as if it were a poem by Edward Lear," Auden writes, "then it seems to me one of the most beautiful poems in the English language." "Since music is in essence immediate," he announces, "it follows that the words of a song cannot be poetry." Auden is telling us something important and serious in both cases, but a voice breaks in to remind us that *Lycidas* is oddly *not* by Edward Lear, that the words of many songs *are* poetry. Or Auden puts his assertions in language incapable of either proof or disproof, as in the remark that "our profounder amusement" in watching a clown is derived from our appreciation of the skill underlying his appearance of clumsiness. Any attempt to dispute the statement, to insist that *no*, we laugh at the clumsiness itself, walks into the trap of that "profounder"; those depths are clearly beyond us.

In Auden's stylish and witty prose there are occasional infelicities: "neither will trust one further than he can throw a grand piano"; "take them all with a strong dose of salt" (does he mean "salts?"). There is one terrible essay, a general discussion of Shakespeare called "The Globe," which makes distinctions between Shakespearian tragedy and comedy that collapse on application, denies any possibility of empathy in Greek tragedy while accepting that it arouses pity and fear, and quotes with a measure of approval D. H. Lawrence's moronic poem against Shakespeare. (A typical stanza: "Lear, the old buffer, you wonder his daughters / didn't treat him rougher, / the old chough, the old chuffer.")

In other essays, Auden is sometimes equally silly. What are we to make of the instruction that "one should only read Kafka when one is in a eupeptic state of physical and mental health and, in consequence, tempted to dismiss any scrupulous heart-searching as a morbid fuss"? Or the assertion that "Primitive cultures have little sense of humor"? Or a distinction between "boring" and "a bore" that offers Verdi, Degas, and Shakespeare as examples of the former, Beethoven, Michelangelo, and Dostoevski as examples of the latter, and gives as its final clarifying example: "The absolutely not boring but absolute bore: God"?

At his most attractive and useful, Auden the critic takes us back to Auden the poet. The essays touch repeatedly on the themes of the poetry, from the fairytale youngest son of the early verse to the questionable salvation of poets in the late verse. Sometimes the prose reminds us of the early "Journal of an Airman" in *The Orators*, as when Auden writes: "A task for the existentialist theologian: to preach a sermon on the topic *The Sleep of Christ*." The old irreverence has not quite disappeared, we realize, brought up sharply by: "It is morally less confusing to be goosed by a traveling salesman than by a bishop." What has happened is that new butts have joined that fleshly bishop: the lying, greedy psychoanalyst; the forward-looking Utopian, sometimes named Hitler.

In a fine essay, "Translating Opera Libretti," written in collaboration with Chester Kallman, Auden writes technically of metrics: "When a composer sets verses to a slow tempo, verse dactyls and anapaests turn into molossoi, its trochees and iambs into spondees." In "Writing," explaining that by the time Goethe had converted his contemporaries to Wertherism he had "gotten the poison out of his system," Auden indirectly defends his own departure from Marxism and his retitling of his Marxist poems as jokes. In that range from the small technical to the largest ideological, and particularly in the autobiographical Inaugural Lecture at Oxford, "Making, Knowing and Judging," these essays constantly enlighten us about Auden the poet. *The Dyer's Hand* makes it clear that Auden, in the tradition of Shaw, is not really interested in any writers but Shakespeare and himself. On both topics he is sometimes profound and sometimes silly, but he is never boring or a bore.

JOHN STEINBECK AND THE NOBEL PRIZE

Almost the first criticism I published dealt with John Steinbeck. I reviewed *Sea of Cortez* in 1942, finding the book's ecological perspective a key to Steinbeck's earlier works. In an article in *The Antioch Review*, June 1942, I went over all his books up to that time, finding the two novels that are like stage plays, *Of Mice and Men* and *The Moon Is Down,* to be the pivots of his shifts in social commitment.

These pieces were not the beginning of my interest in Steinbeck as a serious writer, but almost its end. His next book was a war quickie called *Bombs Away,* followed by *Cannery Row,* which struck me as merely an insipid watering-down of Steinbeck's engaging earlier book *Tortilla Flat.* I stopped reading him, thus missing what I gather is the further dilution of *Cannery Row* in *Sweet Thursday.* It seemed to me that, away from his roots in the Salinas valley, Steinbeck had nothing to say, and that, perhaps, he had nothing further to say in any event.

When *The Winter of Our Discontent* was published in 1961, I had returned to the curious profession of book reviewing, and I read it for review. It seemed far too trivial and dishonest a book to waste space on, and I put it aside. Later in the year, because my review and article were now in anthologies, the editor of a pamphlet series on American writers invited me to do a pamphlet on Steinbeck. I said that I was no longer interested in Steinbeck, and chose instead one of the few fiction writers of the thirties to hold out against the social trend, Nathanael West.

Then, in 1962, to my amazement (and not mine alone), John Steinbeck was awarded the Nobel Prize for Literature. In a radio broadcast, Dr. Anders Osterling, the secretary of the Swedish Academy, announced that the prize was principally for *The Winter of Our Discontent,* which the Academy saw as a return to the "towering standard" of *The Grapes of Wrath.* With *The Winter of*

Our Discontent, Osterling said, Steinbeck "has resumed his position as an independent expounder of the truth."

"Steinbeck more than holds his own," the Academy announced in its official statement, with the five previous American winners: Sinclair Lewis, Eugene O'Neill, Pearl Buck, William Faulkner, and Ernest Hemingway. Spotty as that list is, the Academy's announcement was not a truth universally acknowledged. Swedish papers mocked the choice, and the Academy revealed that criticism of the award that year had been "heavier than usual." The *New York Times* observed delicately in an editorial: "We think it interesting that the laurel was not awarded to a writer—perhaps a poet or critic or historian—whose significance, influence and sheer body of work had already made a more profound impression on the literature of our age." Among the contenders Steinbeck had edged out, it was stated, were Lawrence Durrell, Jean Anouilh, Pablo Neruda, and Robert Graves.

Well, it could have been worse. Steinbeck has been a serious writer, perhaps even an important one. The choice might have been (and may yet be) Herman Wouk. But to single out *The Winter of Our Discontent* as the occasion for it is incredible. I went back and reread the book. It is the purest soap opera, a work of almost inconceivable badness. The hero and narrator, Ethan Allen Hawley, is descended from the first family of his Long Island whaling town; he is fallen on hard times and working in what he calls a "wop" grocery. In the first pages, he addresses his wife as "bugflower" and has a long dialogue on the street with the banker's dog, so that the reader is fairly warned that before long he will be up to the armpits in whimsy.

The liveliest character in the book is a woman named Margie Young-Hunt (I wouldn't like to turn a Freudian loose on that name), a friend of Ethan's wife, Mary. Margie has had two husbands; she is "pert-breasted" and possesses a "proud fanny." At first sight, Ethan recognizes in her eyes that "This was a predator, a huntress, Artemis for pants. Old Cap'n Hawley called it a 'roving eye.' It was in her voice too, a velvet growl that changed to a thin, mellow confidence for wives." Margie promptly vamps him, then starts the plot going by telling Mary's fortune with a French Tarot deck, prophesying wealth and success for Ethan.

Margie next reappears at the grocery store as a vulgarian's vision of delight: "Her behind stuck out nice and round and bounced slowly, one up and one down with each step. She was well enough stacked in front so she didn't have to emphasize them. They were there." As Ethan hands Margie a can of coffee, "every part of her body moved, shifted, announced itself quietly. 'I'm here, the leg. Me, the thigh. Not better than me, the soft belly." Eventually she leaves, "her neat buttocks jumping like live rubber." That evening, when Margie visits *both* Hawleys, she is transformed. "If her behind bounced, I couldn't see it. If anything was under her neat suit, it was hiding."

In the course of the action, Margie is revealed to be the great-grand-daughter of a witch. Her list of lovers includes the town's chief of police and Ethan's Italian employer. She challenges Ethan provocatively: "You've never had a quick jump in the hay in your life." When he finally comes to visit her, she changes into something flimsy and scented, and assures him: "Don't worry. It's a cologne Mary has never smelled on me." Then she reveals her knowledge of all his crooked business secrets. As Ethan stands up to go, she says: "Don't you want to go to bed with me? I'm good. That's what they tell me." Either terrified of her witchcraft or faithful to his bugflower, Ethan flees.

Margie Young-Hunt is not even the most preposterous part of *The Winter of Our Discontent*. The prose is. Sometimes it is Mickey Spillane ("A flare of searing red pain formed in my bowels and moved upward until it speared and tore at the place just under my ribs") and sometimes it is hollandaise sauce ("July is brass where June is gold, and lead where June is silver").

The plot involves a series of shady efforts by Ethan to better himself financially, in response to Margie's Tarot fortune. He takes bribes; he reports Murullo, his employer, to the Immigration Service for illegal entry; he encourages an alcoholic friend to drink himself to death. In ways too complicated and absurd to explain, these result in Ethan's inheriting the store and acquiring the alcoholic friend's property, on which an airport will be built. Ethan prepares a loony holdup of the bank across the street, in which he will be disguised by a Mickey Mouse mask, but is luckily prevented from bringing it off. He then holds up the bank in another fashion, when he confronts the crooked bank manager with his deed to the land and insists that he be cut in for 51% of the syndicate. This is handled in a melodramatic and ridiculous scene that would disgrace a soap opera writer ("You'll feel better, sir, when you have got used to the fact that I am not a pleasant fool").

At the end of the novel, Ethan gets his comeuppance. The "I Love America" essay with which his son Ethan Allen Hawley II won a television contest turns out to have been cribbed from a speech by Henry Clay. The boy is shameless. "Who cares?" he says. "Everybody does it. It's the way the cookie crumbles." His father goes off to cut his wrists in the bay, but does not. The end.

The final thing that should be noted about *The Winter of Our Discontent* is its soupy picture of married love. (The book ran as a serial in *McCall's*.) The coyness of the Hawleys' love talk is thoroughly disgusting. Here is an account of their dalliance at a motel: "We dined in greasy dignity on broiled Maine lobsters sloshed down with white wine—lots of white wine to make my Mary's eyes to shine, and I plied her with cognac seductively until my own head was buzzing. *She* remembered the number of our doll house and *she* could find the keyhole. I wasn't too buzzed to have my way with her, but I think she could have escaped if she had wanted to." The next morning Ethan brings Mary's breakfast on a tray, with "a bouquet of microscopic field flowers to grace the royal breakfast of my dear."

The Nobel Prize committee was not alone in taking this ludicrous marshmallow seriously. The jacket of the book carries three blurbs. Lewis Gannett announced: "The finest thing Steinbeck has written since *The Grapes of Wrath*." "One of his best," said Edward Weeks, noting specifically: "The women in it are particularly appealing." (Ah, that proud fanny!) As for Saul Bellow, he not only puffed *The Winter of Our Discontent*, but he defied anyone else not to do so. "In this book," Bellow wrote, "John Steinbeck returns to the high standards of *The Grapes of Wrath* and to the social themes that made his early work so impressive, and so powerful. Critics who said of him that he had seen his best days had better tie on their napkins and prepare to eat crow."

I wish that I could understand the minds of such people. I cannot, and to assume their honesty I must disparage their intelligence. I have since read *Travels with Charley in Search of America,* a series of travel articles from *Holiday* that became a leading best-seller. It is a hodge-podge of superficial social criticism, ripe sentimentality, one endless joke about the urination of Steinbeck's dog, bad prose, encounters that surely must have been invented, and factual inaccuracies. There are streaks of honesty and insight in the book, and one chilling and effective look at New Orleans racism. *Travels with Charley* and *The Winter of Our Discontent* are clearly the work of a writer who, if he was not always a lightweight, is a lightweight now.

One concurrence with my opinion is interesting, honest, and impressive. The reporters asked John Steinbeck if he really thought he deserved the Nobel Prize. "Frankly, no," he said.

THE EXTREMES OF E. E. CUMMINGS

The death of Edward Estlin Cummings at the age of 67 was peculiarly disturbing. I had never met him, but we had mutual friends, and he and I had exchanged a few letters. In college, I had read his poetry over and over, until I knew a considerable amount of it by heart. Where the effect of other exciting contemporary poets—Stevens and Eliot particularly—had been to teach me a respect for craft, Cummings, although he had plenty of craft, had had an opposite effect, and one that was truly liberating. In all that owlish scowling, his work seemed to say, never forget that making a poem is humping the old cow. It is that perpetually irreverent voice that we have lost.

A posthumous publication allows us to hear some of Cummings' last remarks. It is *Adventures in Value,* a book of 50 photographs by Marion Morehouse, Cummings' widow, with text by Cummings. I am not competent to review anything pictorial, and I will make no remarks about the photographs beyond saying that they look handsome to me. Cummings' text has the visual gimmicks of his poetry: spaces are not skipped after punctuation within the sentence; one caption is, in its entirely, "&"; another is like a Cummings verse line: "a wave . . . beginning–e-x-p-a-n-d-i-n-g–UpRe-ArInG–to:"

The title of *Adventures in Value* is a pun, on pictorial values, the relationship of light to shade, as well as on human values. At their best, Cummings' captions are as ingenious and beautiful as his best poetry. Who but our non-lecturer would describe a photograph of a zucchini squash standing against a well as "a pleasing cross between porpoise & penguin, who is obviously listening with his nose"? As for beauty, here is his caption for a photograph of a rock that appears to have a face and lichen eyes:

> can any thing or vision touch the strangestness of such a timidly
> ferocious(with its crazily lopsided hypergrin)not quite imag-

inable anonymity:nameless a dazedly upgazing predeity of ogre-
like benevolence;yearningly a primordial(& still with chaos
clumsy)universal cauchemar—a sorrowing horror,bigly whose
(boosted from all mysteries of earth's unconsciousness)both
eyes are flowers?

Many of the captions, unfortunately, have only the sentimentality and bitterness of the late poetry. A photograph of a stuffed
plush elephant, "a darling personage," floats bravely on a sea of
gush. Other captions complain bitterly that the times are out of
joint: "muckers don morningcoats,masters become their servants'
servants,thieves are acclaimed & liars applauded,unchildren
murder their nonparents,& politicians inherit the earth"; Cummings dreams of an earlier time "when loafing wasn't mankind's
sole aim," or grumbles about the "UNamerican vice of softhead-
edness."

"When a writer who has been important to you dies," I wrote
in connection with the death of Hemingway, "the thing to do is to
go back and read his best work." When Cummings died, I took
my own advice and went back to the most complete edition of his
verse, *Poems 1923-1954*.

Reading almost 600 poems from ten earlier volumes, one first
sees the faults. Of course Cummings published too much, never
able to tell which of his diamonds were paste. As R. P. Blackmur
once charged, the poetry shuffles monotonous vague counters:
"death," "flower," "rain," "spring," and others. Cummings was terribly sentimental, although he learned to disguise his early girlish
tone ("there fell upon the night, like angel's tears, / the syllables
of that mysterious prayer,") with typographic and other facades.
He never again published anything quite so corny as the sonnet
(few of his poems have titles) in which the poet takes the hands
of his beloved's new love, "saying, Accept all happiness from me."

Cummings was often childish, writing tired spoonerisms
("absitively posolutely," "Rish and Foses") or labored schoolboy
humor ("and the hitler lies down with the cohn"). His fake tough
guy style, running to "will youse dearie?," "let on to / the bulls
he'd bumped a bloke," or "buncha hardboil guys," tends to fall
away and reveal a bunch of violets.

In the thirties Cummings discovered that he was not an anarchist, but a Republican who hated the New Deal. His bitterness against the times becomes pervasive and almost hysterical in poems like the ballade "Jehovah buried, Satan dead," or "flotsam and jetsam," with its ingenious rhyming of "three cheers for labor" with "bugger thy nabor." At any time Cummings might fall into jargon ("extemporise the innovation of muscularity") or pointless anagrams, such as turning "grasshopper" into "PPEGORHRASS."

Finally, there are plain failures of craft: the ruinous pun ending the monologue by the mother all of whose sons were "kilt" ("They called them the kilties") or the equally ruinous last line of the lovely poem that begins: "so standing, our eyes filled with wind, and the / whining rigging over us." Sometimes Cummings wrote with the most extraordinary clumsiness, producing a line such as "ere with the dirt death shall him vastly gird," or the inept "no liar looked him in the head" (to rhyme with "bread") that mars the beautiful tribute to his father, "my father moved through dooms of love."

All this has to be said, but it is of no importance. A writer survives in his best work, not in his worst, and at his best Cummings has written at least a dozen poems that seem to me matchless. Three are among the great love poems of our time or any time: the sonnet "who's most afraid of death? thou"; the sonnet "if i have made,my lady,intricate"; and "somewhere i have never travelled,gladly beyond," with its magnificent and justly famous last line, "nobody,not even the rain, has such small hands."

The best two of Cummings' funny poems generate their humor out of bitter melancholy, as do the great clowns and the finest blues. One is the early sonnet that reminds "the Cambridge ladies who live in furnished souls" that sometimes above Cambridge the "moon rattles like a fragment of angry candy." The others is the late sonnet that begins "pity this busy monster,manunkind," and ends:

> We doctors know
>
> a hopeless case if—listen:there's a hell
> of a good universe next door;let's go

A few of Cummings' mean poems are mean in a fashion that is lifegiving and humane. One is his protest against the martial spirit of the First World War, "i sing of Olaf glad and big," with its heroic martyred conscientious objector. Another, equally disaffected with our mission in the Second World War, is the moron's patriotic speech that concludes:

> *dem*
> *gud*
> *am*
>
> *lidl yelluh bas*
> *tuds weer goin*
>
> *duhSIVILEYEzum*

One neither Republican nor anti-literary, the savage obituary for President Harding, is short enough to quote entire. It reads:

> *the first president to be loved by his*
> *bitterest enemies" is dead*
>
> *the only man woman or child who wrote*
> *a simple declarative sentence with seven grammatical*
> *errors "is dead"*
> *beautiful Warren Gamaliel Harding*
> *"is" dead*
> *he's*
> *"dead"*
> *if he wouldn't have eaten them Yapanese Craps*
>
> *somebody might hardly never not have been*
> *unsorry,perhaps*

At the other extreme, two of Cummings' finest poems can only be called joyous. One is the lyric "in Just- / spring," where everything is "mud-luscious" and "puddle-wonderful." The other fine poem that seems to me truly joyous is on that most unpromising of subjects, a whore's orgasm. It begins "her careful distinct sex whose sharp lips comb," and it seems to me one of the most remarkable poetic celebrations of the sex act that I have ever read.

Finally, there are three poems that cannot be neatly categorized but are uniquely Cummings. One is the endlessly-anthologized, but still fresh and glistening, "Buffalo Bill's / defunct." Another is the wonderful poem about apples, and perhaps about

Eden, "it's over a (see just / over this) wall." The third is the lovely and mysterious "this is a rubbish of human rind," which ends:

> *this is a dog of no known kind*
> *with one white eye*
> *and one black eye*
> *and the eyes of his eyes*
> *are as lost as you'll find*

The first book of critical essays on Cummings, edited by S. V. Baum, has the worst title of the year: $E\Sigma TI:$ *e e c.* It includes some fine analyses of Cummings' poems, the best by Laura Riding and Robert Graves, and some useful placings of Cummings in the literary tradition. The unsympathetic articles show that all the charges we make now have been made tirelessly for forty years, and several enthusiastic pieces show that it is just as hard to be original in praising Cummings ("The wonder of the wide-eyed child," said Paul Rosenfeld; "Cummings waves his gay delightful banner of individual joy," said Theodore Spencer).

At his best, Cummings had a superb eye, seeing a waiter drifting between cafe tables "like an old leaf / between toad-stools," or offering as the only caption for a still life in *Adventures in Value*, "note the nail" (in reference to a nail sticking out half an inch from the wall behind). He sometimes displayed an equally good ear, as in the message from the "muffhunter" that concludes one poem: "daze nutn like it." When E. E. Cummings died, something equally unduplicatable went out of the world.

J. D. SALINGER'S HOUSE OF GLASS

With the publication of *Raise High the Roof Beam, Carpenters, and Seymour: An Introduction,* all of J. D. Salinger's seven stories about the Glass family are finally in book form. The book should of course have been called *Seymour,* to match *Franny and Zooey,* but the shapeless title is typical of Salinger's new rough-hewn look.

The three earliest stories about the Glasses appeared in *Nine Stories* in 1953. The first and still the best of them is "A Perfect Day for Bananafish" (1948). It is about a neurotic young man, Seymour Glass, on vacation in Florida with his empty-headed wife, Muriel. The story strongly suggests that Seymour's marital difficulties are sexual. In the first paragraph, Muriel is shown reading an article called "Sex is Fun—or Hell." When the bananafish appear, in Seymour's improvisation to entertain a little girl named Sybil, they are terribly Freudian bananafish, who swim into a hole and gorge themselves on bananas, then die.

"A Perfect Day for Bananafish" is a tight and economical masterpiece. Every touch is masterly. Sybil's mother is fully defined when she goes off for a Martini and promises Sybil "I'll bring you the olive." Muriel is as perfectly defined when Seymour says that she may be out "having her hair dyed mink." All of Seymour's shy tenderness comes out in his delightful conversation with Sybil, climaxed by his kissing the arch of her foot. The sudden end of the story, Seymour's blowing out his brains while Muriel lies asleep on the other bed, has the shock of perfection.

"Uncle Wiggily in Connecticut" (1948) is a long carouse by two former college roommates, Eloise and Mary Jane. Eloise reveals that she is unhappily married, and that her true love was Walt, killed in an absurd accident during the war. Walt is not identified as a Glass, but the nonsense for which Eloise loves him is very Glassy (he called her wobbly ankle "Uncle Wiggily"), and

Salinger later adopted him into the family. The story is slighter than "Bananafish," but the conversation of the girls in unfinished sentences is a triumph of craft, and the end, with Eloise crying over her daughter's myopia and her own loss and corruption, is deeply moving.

The third of these stories, "Down at the Dinghy" (1949), shows Boo Boo Glass Tannenbaum, sister of the dead Seymour, attempting to placate her small son Lionel. He has been upset by the maid's reference to his father as a "big sloppy kike," which he innocently understands to mean "kite." Boo Boo charms him out of it with typical Glass loving banter, and at the end of the story the united household is about to go sailing off in the dinghy, happy kites all.

"Franny" (1955) is a transition to the later stories. Although it is as tight and economical as the first three, it is vastly longer and more ambitious. A college girl named Franny is visiting her date, Lane Coutell, at a college like Princeton on the day of the Yale game. The scene is their lunch at a fashionable campus restaurant. Lane wants what he thinks Franny is, "an unimpeachably right-looking girl" and familiar bedmate. Franny is undergoing a religious crisis, and wants what Lane is certainly not, a *guru*.

As Lane eats his frogs' legs and talks conventionalities, Franny rails against the vanity of the world, warily preaches a Way of incessant prayer, cries in the washroom, and finally faints, presumably as a result of fasting. The non-meshing conversation shows Salinger at his most brilliant, and the story's ending, with Franny revived and mouthing silent prayer, is extraordinarily powerful. The only flaws in "Franny" are the first appearances in Salinger's work of "fancy" writing: the ladies' room at the restaurant "appeared to be hardly less commodious" than the dining room; Franny sits down on a toilet "without any apparent regard to the suchness of her environment."

Between the writing of "Franny" and the next story, "Raise High the Roof Beam, Carpenters," which appeared later in 1955, Salinger seems to have created the Glass family of seven wonderful grown-up Quiz Kids. For Salinger, who has only one sib, an elder sister, and who disguises himself thinly as Buddy Glass, the writer of the later stories, the Glasses seem to be wishful imagi-

nary playmates on the order of Eloise's daughter's "Jimmy Jimme-
reeno" in "Uncle Wiggily." For the reader, the Glasses are a
comparable wishful fantasy, everyone's ideal family of loving
geniuses.

"Raise High" is 104 pages long, for most of its length a funny
and charming account of Seymour's marriage to Muriel; he fails to
appear at the wedding, then elopes with the bride. The problem is
that Seymour's ghastly mismatch and suicide, originally no more
than the sort of fictional symbolic action by means of which a
writer kills off a failed marriage, must now be justified in terms of
a new saintly and all-wise Seymour. As a consequence, the story is
interrupted, in fact severed, while Buddy leaves a group of wedding guests in his living room and sits in the bathroom reading
Seymour's diary, which is quoted for twelve pages. (Salinger likes
those Lutherish bathroom revelations, we notice, as this one is
preceded by Franny on the toilet and followed by Zooey in the
tub, while the letters and memos the characters read grow to
scriptural proportions.)

The diary tells us that Seymour married Muriel because "I
love and need her undiscriminating heart," and that her middle-
class vision of marriage is "human-size and beautiful." He committed suicide, apparently, out of the fullness of his joy; before
the marriage he had the scars of an earlier suicide attempt on his
wrists; as a child he found the sight of his friend Charlotte petting
Boo Boo's cat so beautiful that he threw a stone at her, resulting in
nine stitches and partial facial paralysis. We could not care less.
Meanwhile, the story, with Buddy's deserted guests, sits awk-
wardly in the living room, and eventually departs.

"Zooey" (1957) is a mawkish account of the cure of Franny
by family love two days after her agony in the ladies' room. A
long introduction by Buddy, in which he says that he is offering
not a short story but "a sort of prose home movie," is ruinous, as
are his later apologies for his style, which is limp beyond belief
(Zooey's beauty, we are told, is vulnerable to "glibly undaunted
and usually specious evaluations"). Eventually Franny is cured
when Zooey, after his own preaching fails, performs rites of incu-
bation in Seymour's old room, and brings her a religious message
from Seymour. Instead of the redemptive pre-sexual young girl

(Sybil, Esmé in "For Esmé—with Love and Squalor," Phoebe in *The Catcher in the Rye*) we have the redemptive dead brother, Holden Caulfield's Allie inflated to monstrous size.

Salinger's Big Religious Package is offered in "Zooey": the Upanishads, the Diamond Sutra, Meister Eckhart, Dr. Suzuki on *satori*, saints, *arhats, bodhisvattas, jivanmuktas,* Jesus, Gautama, Lao-tse, Shankaracharya, Hui-neng, Sri Ramakrishna, the Four Great Vows of Buddhism, God's grace, the Jesus Prayer, *japam,* Chuang-tzu, Epictetus, and the Bible. Unfortunately, these make an indigestible mixture, and Franny should be sicker at the end than she was at the start. Sometimes Zooey preaches the hard mystic religion of attaining to the divine by withdrawal and detachment from the world; on other occasions he preaches the soft humanitarian religion of loving mankind, in which their mother Bessie's chicken soup is "consecrated."

Finally, then, we have "Seymour: an Introduction" (1959), the last of the Glass stories to date. Without plot or action, it is a rambling monologue of 137 pages about Seymour by Buddy, studded with apologies for the digressions, or interpolated protests by Buddy against his own prose, or challenges that readers who want the "restrained" or the "classical" leave now. Its subject, I suppose, is hero worship, or brother fixation. Buddy calls Seymour his "liege lord," his "Davega bicycle." The chief impression the piece makes is of Buddy's self-indulgent whimsy: offering the reader a "bouquet of very early-blooming parentheses," chatting about the earlier Seymour stories, and apostrophizing his "infuriatingly uncommunicative" readers.

Moreover, the Seymour of all this turgid hagiography is preposterous. He is "a *mukta,* a ringding enlightened man, a God-knower"; his great poems are in a double-*haiku* form and are, from Buddy's prose paraphrases, hogwash; he gives his brother soft and sentimental misadvice about writing; he buys his ill-fitting clothes "like a young *brahmacharya* . . . picking out his first loincloth"; he is a master of Zen and the art of marbles. One wonders how Muriel lived with him for six years without blowing *her* brains out first.

I think that Jerome David Salinger is the most talented fiction writer in America. The progress of his Glass series in a little more than a decade from one of the finest short stories of our time, "A Perfect Day for Bananafish," to one of the most boring ever written, "Seymour: an Introduction," is appalling. One can understand Salinger's rebellion as another example of the impatience of the ablest *New Yorker* writers with the form of the well-made story they have so fully mastered (one sees the same impatience with form in the recent stories of John Updike). But a writer breaks through limiting forms into fuller and deeper forms, such as those of *Moby-Dick* or *Ulysses,* not into anarchy and incoherence.

Salinger has a marvelous sensitivity to the young, to the language, to the fraudulence of contemporary America, to the *Zeitgeist.* He can bring characters wonderfully to life even in unsuccessful wholes: the Matron of Honor cursing Seymour in "Raise High," Bessie clanking with hardware in "Zooey," Waker giving away his bicycle in "Seymour." *Life* called Salinger the most influential man of letters in the United States today, and I am sure that he is and will continue to be even after this new book. But his highway has turned into a dirt road, then into wagon ruts, finally into a squirrel track and climbed a tree. Salinger must come down and get about his business.

CHIRON AT OLINGER HIGH

When a volume of John Updike's stories appeared in 1962, I concluded a review of it with what is, I hope, quite uncharacteristic gush: "One awaits his next novel as a child awaits Christmas morning. This may be the year when every wish comes true." I am embarrassed by the sugarplummy tone, and I wish that my typewriter had been somewhat less unshackled at the time, but the great expectation is accurate. I cannot imagine a serious reviewer who is not awed by Updike's talents and by his potential for greatness.

That anticipated novel, *The Centaur,* is not a complete success, and some of it does not work at all, but it is a bold and ambitious break with the naturalistic limits of *Rabbit, Run,* and it marks a big step forward. *The Centaur* tells Updike's familiar autobiographical story of the sensitive homely boy in Olinger High School, pulled in various directions by his parents, his girl, and his ambitions, but it tells it in new dimensions. Now the boy's father, a general science teacher at the school, is the central figure, and there is an elaborate parallel with Greek mythology, in which the father is Chiron, the noblest and wisest of the centaurs, and the son (and narrator) is Prometheus, whose theft of fire for mankind Chiron dies to atone.

The first chapter of the book, culminating in the father's virtuoso mad lecture on the history of the universe, is superb. I can think of nothing in fiction to surpass it since the Nighttown scene in *Ulysses.* At first the reader is confused by the double nature of the protagonist, who is simultaneously George Caldwell, a man wearing trousers and driving a 1936 Buick, and Chiron, a great gray-dappled centaur, wounded by a poisoned arrow shot by one of the boys in his class. Thus on one level, in a flashback, he has surprised Vera Hummel, the girls' gym teacher, showering in the basement locker room; on the other he is gazing on Aphrodite naked in a woodland pool.

Soon the reader discovers that the Chiron image is meta-phoric, a wishful fantasy of idealized teaching, of a life spent gravely discoursing to Achilles and Heracles, Jason and Asclepius, beneath a great chestnut tree on Olympus. The arrow tipped with hydra venom is similarly metaphoric for the hate George feels em-anating from his pupils, clotted in his bowels and, he believes, turned to cancer. These metaphors are nevertheless presented with great realism. George is enough of a centaur to drop a steam-ing horseturd in the school hallway near the trophy case; the arrow is real enough so that the local garageman, Al Hummel (Hephaestus), has to cut the steel shaft with an acetylene torch to remove it.

As George lectures to his class for a brilliant twenty minutes on the origin of the universe in a primeval explosion, the condensa-tion of the earth, the development of life on it, and the evolution of species, the classroom turns surrealistic and nightmarish. As George talks of primitive marine organisms, the piece of chalk in his hand turns into a large warm wet larva, and a paper airplane thrown by one of the boys becomes a white flower, which yowls like a baby. When George gets to multicellular forms, Mark Youngerman's acne leaps to the wall and starts blistering the paint. At the mention of extinct trilobites, a boy spills a paper bag full of living trilobites onto the floor, and as they scutter between the seats or curl into balls, the boys drop textbooks on them, and one girl becomes a parrot and starts eating them.

All the latent sexuality George feels in the classroom erupts. Louis Zimmerman (Zeus), the school principal visiting the class, sits down beside a plump girl named Iris Osgood (Io) and un-dresses her. Ray Deifendorf tickles the neck of Becky Davis, then turns into a centaur and mounts her. Meanwhile George's elo-quent marvelous rhetoric goes on desperately, until at the chap-ter's end everything comes together in a symphonic climax. George strikes the centaur covering Becky; the centaur turns back into a boy, now crying; George arrives at his conclusion, the ap-pearance of a tragic, death-foreseeing animal "called Man"; and the buzzer sounds for the end of the hour.

Some parts of this episode suggest the *Alice* books, some parts *The Circus of Dr. Lao,* some parts the work of Nathanael West. Everywhere it proclaims the influence of *Ulysses,* from the largest mythological correspondence down to the smallest mad transformation. Despite this, the chapter is at no point derivative or stale; it is a pyrotechnical display of unique originality and power.

The rest of *The Centaur*, despite many felicities, is not up to the first chapter. Most of the mythological parallels (neatly indexed for the reader) seem arbitrary and pointless. Johnny Dedman, a high school junior with a mastery of pinball machines, incarnates Daedalus. Hummel's three mechanics are Cyclopes, so that George can think of them as "one-eyed morons." Medusa keeps the study-hall with "yellow pencils thrusting from her tangled hair." The knee hammer of Doc Appleton (Apollo) is Omphalos, the navel of the world. Even the identification of George's 15-year-old son Peter with Prometheus adds little. Peter's dream of being chained to a rock in the Caucasus, while the world of adult sexuality and shame torments him, is an effective metaphor for adolescence, but the Prometheus who incurred the punishment, the implacable rebel, has little to do with the shy groping Peter of the novel.

In a few cases, the correspondences work beautifully. A drunk who, in an uproarious scene, accuses George of picking up Peter for immoral purposes, refusing to believe that they are father and son, turns out to be the god Dionysus. The parallel gives the scene the sort of resonance we get when Polyphemus and his club loom behind the Citizen and Bloom's "knockmedown" cigar in *Ulysses*. The Depression turns out to have been caused by the rape of Persephone, and the pomegranate seeds that she ate in Hades' kingdom appear mysteriously in the high school hallway, perhaps out of Chiron's droppings. Most of all, the Chiron-Caldwell correspondence is successful, and Chiron deepens and enriches Caldwell, as an emblem of the nobility of spirit that Caldwell conceals.

Peter's girl, Penny Fogleman (Pandora), is the familiar loyal, loving, not-so-bright girl of Updike's stories, best embodied in Molly Bingaman of "Flight." Peter realizes that "young as she was, recent as our touching was, little as I gave her; she would sacrifice for me." Peter has a severe case of psoriasis, a disfiguring skin condition, and Updike describes his crusts and scabs far too lovingly. Psoriasis is of course another symbol for the adolescent condition, disfigured and shameful, but it is a little too pat, another study-hall Medusa.

Then, in a touching and wonderful love scene, Peter tells Penny about his ailment and shows her the scabs on his belly. With her calm inclusion of them within the arc of her love, the symbol suddenly justifies itself, and works profoundly. Then Peter rests his head against Penny's groin, the "Pandora's box" from which all the world's woe will someday emerge, and for the present at least finds only innocence and peace.

There is another innocent and beautiful love scene in the book, this one between George and Hester Appleton (Artemis), a spinster schoolteacher devoted to him. They achieve a symbolic communion when she confesses to him the sentence she lives by—*"Dieu est très fin"*—and he recites for her the beginning of a poem he learned as a child. It is George's only lyric moment in a period otherwise devoted to failure and proclaiming failure. He aspires to be known as "Caldwell, the Kid-Killer"; he sees teaching as a war to the death with his pupils; he ceaselessly denigrates himself for his ugliness, ignorance, and stupidity, his inadequacy as a father and a man. Except for Peter, no one but Hester sees George's Chiron spirit shining through his addled bitterness.

Some of the weaknesses in *The Centaur* are familiar from Updike's other writings. The narrator's present keeps climbing onstage with his past, in the peculiarly unconvincing form of "an authentic second-rate abstract expressionist living in an East Twenty-third Street loft with a Negro mistress." A two-page digression on this present, with its "worthless" paintings, Peter's inability to "make that scene" as a Negro, and his relationship to his mistress, with "its rather wistful half-Freudian half-Oriental sex-mysticism," seems either irrelevant to the story of the father's redemptive death, or makes it pointless.

Updike's young men have a nervousness about sex, a guilty preoccupation with the perverse, that led to an unintentionally ludicrous scene in *Rabbit, Run,* and in this book leads to some absurd meditations by Peter on the esthetic beauty of postures on obscene playing cards. The moving love scenes are inhibited and tentative: the shapeless love of an adolescent, the mute love of a spinster for a married colleague. Updike's compulsive preoccupation with his adolescence is a questing back to innocence, and it is this that gives Peter's narrative its Ancient Mariner tone. He must assure his mistress, to whom he is narrating the story, that the Caldwell life together, "for all its mutual frustration," was *good*. The albatross is of course the Oedipal father, obsessive throughout Updike's writing, and one may hope that, in Chiron's sacrificial acceptance of death on the book's last page, this heavy bird has finally been cut loose.

Updike's baroque metaphors and similes sparkle on the page. Chiron recalls his infancy as "a half-furred and half-membranous squid of fear"; the classroom air is filled "with a hovering honey of insolence"; ducks are "the color of old piano keys"; middle-aged lovers mesh with one fat shopworn sigh"; young lovers clutch and bump heads "like a pair of doped rams." Everywhere the language is magical, incandescent: the language of poetry. John Updike, barely past thirty, has every gift the novelist needs. If *The Centaur* succeeds only partially, it is a partial success in a realm inhabited only by great writers.

SIN IN PORTUGAL

José Maria Eça de Queiroz (1843-1900) is said to be the greatest Portuguese novelist. I have no opinion on the matter, since I have never read any other. He is certainly very impressive. *The Relic* was published by Knopf in 1925, in a translation by Aubrey F.G. Bell (the title page says from the *Spanish*). A decade ago Noonday reprinted *The Relic* in Bell's translation and published *Cousin Bazilio* in a clotted translation by Roy Campbell. Now we have *The Sin of Father Amaro,* translated by Nan Flanagan. The rest of Eça de Queiroz's books, so far as I know, are at present unavailable in English—the familiar fate of a major writer in a minor literature.

The Relic is an outrageously funny satire about a religious hypocrite, who makes a pilgrimage to the Holy Land in order to inherit his aunt's fortune, and ruins it all by the old parcel switch. The book is criminally marred by one chapter in which Eça gets earnest and gives his hero a reverent rationalist vision of Christ's Passion. It is as though Kingsley Amis had published a novel with one chapter by General Lew Wallace. *The Relic* is a joy to read if one skips the third chapter, and the threadbare plot merely adds to the fun.

The other two books are tragic novels, and it is their themes that I intend to discuss here. *Cousin Bazilio* tells of the seduction of an innocent Lisbon housewife, Luiza, by her sophisticated cousin, and its fearful consequences in blackmail by a servant, and Luiza's illness and death. The blackmail scenes approach melodrama ("I give the orders now!" says Juliana, the servant) and at one point things fall into farce (when word gets out about how well Juliana is living, hordes of governesses, cooks, gardeners, coachmen, postillions, footmen, porters, commissionaires, and cook's helpers apply for positions). Nevertheless, the book has great power and beauty, and its pictures of the bored seducer

(clearly a cruel self-potrait) and of the spiteful servant are masterpieces.

The Sin of Father Amaro is about the seduction of a virgin by
a priest in a Portuguese provincial town, and *its* fearful consequences in her death in childbirth and his arranging the murder of
their child. This time it is not a simple matter of villain and victim.
The priest was as desperately infatuate as the virgin, and is as
much seduced. Their names, Amaro and Amelia, seem to suggest
that it is *amor* that has conquered. In common with the Euripides
of *Hippolytus* and *The Bacchae,* Eça does not appear to like the
god, but he never underestimates the god's power. *The Sin of
Father Amaro* is extraordinarily compelling, despite one big defect: the erotic tease is one of the longest since *Pamela,* and well
before p. 206, when the priest and the girl finally go to bed together, the tension has snapped.

Both novels share a pattern. A figure of perfect goodness puts
things right (recovers Luiza's letters, brings Amelia to confession
and repentance) but the woman must nevertheless expiate her sin
by death; the discoverer or witness of the sin also dies; the guilty
man eventually laughs it off. In a sense, these novels are tracts:
Father Amaro warns that the wages of sin is childbirth, and
Cousin Bazilio that the wages of sin is insolence from the servants;
Father Amaro is a sermon against clerical celibacy, and both
novels are demonstrations that one deadly sin rapidly begets the
other six. In a deeper sense, the novels do not really warn or
preach; they evoke pity and terror, and purge them in catharsis.

The Sin of Father Amaro takes full advantage of the tensions
inherent in a Roman Catholic culture. Its image of the clergy is
devastating. One priest dies of apoplexy from gluttony; another
takes his siestas with a mistress; a third spends *his* siestas brutally
raping the peasant girls on, fittingly, the threshing floor; another is
an unprincipled scoundrel; and, loveliest touch of all, one is interested in nothing but cooking, so that his Sunday sermons consist
entirely of recipes.

The portrait of the Roman Catholic Church is quite as devastating. Clerical celibacy is shown to be repulsive in principle and
almost non-existent in practice. ("It's the one thing in life worth
living for" is a priestly opinion about sex.) The Church's God is "a

Being who only knew how to deal out suffering and death"; its rule is tyrannical and aimed at breaking the spirit; its teaching is obscurantist and absurd. Scapulars, rosaries, images, and relics are elaborately mocked. Devout old women are shown to be rotten with psychotic fantasies, and the one devout layman in the book, a bringer of grace to the troops, is caught in a homosexual act with a sergeant. Father Amaro himself dreams of a return of the Inquisition to punish his enemies, and his chief weapon in the seduction of Amelia is *The Canticles of Jesus,* a work of pious pornography.

Context somewhat softens this. If the priests in the book are villains, the anti-clericals and radicals are just as unprincipled and almost as detestable. True Christianity is represented by one decent layman, João, Amelia's fiancé, who hates the clergy but admires Jesus, and by the saintly Abbot Ferrão, Amelia's salvation, who dismisses the wicked priests as "Pharisees." Abbot Ferrão preaches the author's message, a religion of Christian love and charity, in which "one tear shed in sincerity was sufficient for the remission of a life of sin."

The symbols of Christianity give an erotic *frisson* to the seduction. In the seminary, Amaro had visions of the Virgin as a beautiful naked girl, and he later dresses Amelia in a cloak presented to the Virgin and embraces her; Amaro talks of the Mass while squeezing Amelia's knee between his; the confessional is a place for lewd whispers; the sense of sin is a powerful aphrodisiac in the book.

In his introduction to *Cousin Bazilio,* Frederico de Onis speaks of Eça as "the introducer of French realism and naturalism into Portugal." These terms do not really convey the quality of the books. "Realistic" and "naturalistic" were banners in nineteenth-century French literature against vapid romances and tales of glamorous highlife. In the twentieth century, "realism" has come to mean listless English family chronicles and "naturalism" to mean grimy slices of American life. The best realism has always been poetic and symbolist.

Eça is this sort of symbolist-realist, and his work shimmers with image and metaphor. The foreshadowings of later events in the first fifty pages of *Cousin Bazilio* make an impressive list. A

cuckoo clock strikes in the first sentence; a friend of Luiza's husband Jorge reads from a play about the punishment of an adulterous wife; Jorge's study contains a "plaster statue, very much the
worse for wear, of a bacchante in delirium"; a photograph of
Jorge has crossed swords mounted over it; a cigarette holder is
carved in the shape of "Venus mounted voluptuously over a
tamed lion"; "a pure white moth" flutters around the candle
flames.

Freud credited writers with discovering the truths of psychoanalysis before he did, and in that sense Eça de Queiroz is a very
knowing pre-Freudian. *Father Amaro* is full of deliberate sex
symbols. Amelia is ashamed to write a love letter to the priest
with the same pen, "wet with the same ink," with which she has
just accepted João's proposal of marriage. Amaro says that as her
confessor he will "govern her with a rod of iron." A doctor prettily
explains displacement: "The heart is a term which usually serves
us, for decency's sake, to designate another organ." (In *Cousin
Bazilio,* Eça has some fun with what I assume is the same Portuguese word. Bazilio sings to Luiza, and an old fool in the room
praises his voice, remarking: "You possess a most powerful and
excellent organ. I should say the finest organ in all our Lisbonese
society.")

The novels of Eça de Queiroz made me realize how much
more sensual nineteenth-century fiction is than current fiction.
Eça can render smouldering passion in a detail: Amelia's saving
the hair out of Father Amaro's comb; Luiza stroking her own soft
body after Bazilio pays his first call. Everything is done by understatement and suggestion. Whether the restraint is imposed by
censorship and the times, or is self-imposed, it is essential. Our
novelists, who put everything on the page relentlessly, soon come
to produce no more effect than a seed catalogue. At one ugly
point in *Cousin Bazilio,* Bazilio tries to convince a friend of
Luiza's attractiveness "by adducing lascivious episodes and giving
a detailed physiological description of her person." We can
readily imagine the episodes and the details. *Our* novelists would
have given a blow-by-blow account of Luiza's habits and cata-
logued all her plumbing.

The other thing that contributes to the sensuality of these

novels is a sense, lost in our time, of the possibility of sordidity and degradation. Father Amaro, "breathing like a bull," deflowers Amelia while an old procuress crouches in the cellar; he continues their affair in the sexton's house, with Toto, the sexton's paralyzed daughter, listening and screaming: "The dogs are getting on each other!" Bazilio takes Luzia to a house of assignation that smells of damp and mildew, and seduces her on a bed with a patched mattress and dirty sheets. To the novelists of our time, these details would be indifferent or mildly interesting. Only to the extent that we can feel Amelia's horror as Toto screams, or blush for shame with Luiza, do their acts acquire significance.

Eça de Queiroz had the luck to live in a culture with a sense of sin, the brains to know that the realistic and the symbolic enhance one another, and the talent to produce richness with great economy. He is not the equal of Flaubert; he is sometimes soft whereas Flaubert is always hard. But he is a very considerable novelist, and one should probably learn Portuguese to read the rest of his work.

THE GODDESS AND THE SCHLEMIEL

A new sort of American novel seems to be emerging in the sixties. I am led to that conclusion by the appearance of a first novel, V., by Thomas Pynchon. It strikingly resembles another recent first novel, Joseph Heller's *Catch-22*, and it has a number of things in common with other first novels of the decade, including two excellent ones, Walker Percy's *The Moviegoer*, and Bruce J. Friedman's *Stern*. V. is raw and formless in comparison with those two, but it is powerful, ambitious, full of gusto, and overflowing with rich comic invention. Pynchon is a writer of enormous talent and potential, and before making some observations about the new sort of fiction that I think V. represents, I will discuss some features of his remarkable novel.

V. is almost impossible to synopsize, or even to describe. It has an interwoven double plot: in one action, an ex-Navy Italian-Jewish drifter named Benny Profane pursues the good life with little success; in the other, a friend of his, named Herbert Stencil, dredges up the history of a fabulous adventuress and secret agent named "V." (Stencil discovers, or invents, everything about her except the important fact, which the reader eventually figures out, that she was Stencil's mother.) The relationship between these two plots is a subtle and complex one. The international hi-jinks of the chapters involving V., with their grand amours and exotic wickedness, oddly serve to make the random lechery and low carousing of Profane's world seem not sordid but human and sympathetic. At the same time, V., as a Platonic myth of the passions, enlarges the significance of the contemporary action.

Pynchon takes advantage of his international melodrama for all sorts of fine mean parody. Sometimes he writes specimens of E. Phillips Oppenheim or the Baroness Orczy; at other times, Lawrence Durrell or the French New Wave. The international incidents are deliberately preposterous, from the first armed assassin disabled by a kick from a well-shod boot, to the last double agent going numb at the threat of exposure and fiendish retribution.

Pynchon is even more wildly imaginative, high-spirited, and funny in the Profane episodes. A Brazilian salad man at a *borscht* resort acquires a machine gun, camouflages it with watercress and endive, and sits through meals pretending to strafe the guests, dreaming that they are Arabs and that he is an Israeli soldier. "Yibble, yibble, yibble," he says, pointing at one well-fed Jew after another, "got you dead center, Abdul Sayid. Yibble, yibble, Muslim pig." A Jesuit priest, Father Fairing, convinced that the rats are about to take over New York City, moves down to the sewers to convert the rats to Roman Catholicism, and by blessing and exorcising all the sewer water between Lexington and the East River, and between 79th and 86th, he creates Fairing's Parish. One friend of Profane's smokes fine quality string from Bloomingdale's; another reads an avant-garde western called *Existentialist Sheriff*.

At other times Pynchon seems principally interested in harrowing the reader. A nose-lifting operation is described in detail for five pages, a young ballerina is horribly impaled during a performance, and one chapter is devoted to the sadistic atrocities against natives committed by the Germans in German South-West Africa in 1904 and later. Only the last of these episodes has any revelance that I could see. It soon becomes clear that Pynchon is indirectly commenting on the Nazi crimes against the Jews, one of the things that have created Profane's numbed world.

The least successful feature of *V.* is Pynchon's whimsy. As in musical comedy, his characters sometimes interrupt their conversation to break into duets. The juvenile names resemble those of *Catch-22*: Dewey Gland, Baby Face Falange, and such. New York is usually referred to as "Nueva York." The comical behavior of drunken sailors gets to be a bore. When Pynchon's invention flags he flogs it, and the reader may be reminded of *Mad*.

The garish fantasy of *V.* dominates the book. We see her first as a 19-year-old Yorkshire girl named Victoria Wren, deflowered by a British agent in Cairo during the Fashoda crisis in 1898; then in Florence in 1899, seducing Stencil's father on a couch in the

British consulate; after that, nameless in Paris in 1913, a lesbian fetishist in love with a young ballerina she dresses as a boy; then as Veronica Manganese in Malta in 1919, by which time she has a star sapphire sewn into her navel and a glass eye with a clock for a pupil; then as Vera Meroving of Munich in German South-West Africa in 1922, punctuating a garden conversation by braining a goldfish; finally, disguised as a nameless priest on Malta in 1939, dying in an air raid, during which some children find her unconscious and despoil her, killing her in their efforts to dig out her star sapphire.

These are only the few of V.'s impersonations that we see. Stencil reports that she spent a year disguised as an old fisherman in Mallorca, that she was a partisan in Asia, and that she crashed a stolen airplane in Spain. Beyond that, V. is some great female principle, embodied even in the rat Veronica, who was either Father Fairing's saintly nun-to-be or his mistress, "depending which story you listened to." She is the goddess Venus and the planet Venus, the Virgin, the town of Valetta in Malta, and the imaginary land of Vheissu with its iridescent spider monkeys and Volcanoes. She is Vesuvius, Venezuela, the Violet of a vulgar mnemonic; ultimately, she is the V of spread thighs and the mons veneris, vagina, and vulva.

None of the real characters in the book can quite come up to this fertility goddess. Profane is a self-identified *schlemiel* who works at such jobs as hunting alligators in the New York sewers, or being night watchman in a laboratory that mutilates plastic human dummies. Women throw themselves at him, but something always goes wrong: if he is not interrupted by a comic intruder, he is repelled by the girl's eagerness and changes his mind. Profane finally manages an affair with Rachel Owlglass, a Bennington alumna who loves him and wants to transform him. There are several beautiful and moving love scenes between them, written with power and honesty. Profane turns out to be incapable of accepting the responsibility that Rachel represents, and when last seen he is on Malta, with a new girl, looking for sewer work.

Surrounding Benny and Rachel are a group of young eccentrics who call themselves the Whole Sick Crew. Slab devotes his life to painting a series of Cheese Danish canvases; Esther Harvitz is the mistress of her plastic surgeon; Roony Winsome tapes street fights; his wife Mafia plays Musical Blankets with male roomers named Charisma and Fu; and so on. Just outside the Crew are two sympathetic characters: Paola Maijstral, a Maltese who disguises herself as a Negro whore named Ruby; and McClintic Sphere, a Negro jazz musician and a parody of Ornette Coleman, who plays a hand-carved ivory alto saxophone. In a wider circle are two truly grotesque figures: Shale Schoenmaker, Esther's nose surgeon and lover, who cannot control his impulse to remodel the rest of her; and Dudley Eigenvalue, a "psychodontist," who diagnoses his patients' emotional difficulties as "malocclusion," "deciduous dentition," or "heterodont configuration."

Along with *Catch-22* and other recent first novels, *V.* represents a deliberate return to old-fashioned literary conventions. It has the long chapter subtitles of older comic fiction ("In which Rachel gets her yo-yo back, Roony sings a song, and Stencil calls on Bloody Chiclitz"), the comic capitals of George Ade ("a ghetto for Drunken Sailors nobody knew what to Do With"), and an omniscient narrator who explains things to the reader. The British Angry Young Men derive from the tradition of Fielding, Smollett, and the picaresque novel; *Catch-22, V.,* and the others derive principally from Sterne's *Tristram Shandy,* Twain, and the conventions of digressive oral narrative. What has been lost is the earlier innocence. If Pynchon has been influenced by Sterne, he has also been visibly influenced by our bitter symbolists of the thirties, Nathanael West and Djuna Barnes.

These new novelists also delight in impure forms. The doomed love between Profane and Rachel is the material of tragedy, and Pynchon handles it with a great purity of feeling, but jostling their scenes in the book are wild comedy, outlandish melodrama, and bloated caricature. The hero of the modern novel has been unheroic for a long time—one has only to think of Swann and Leopold Bloom—but rarely so unheroic as these protagonists. Benny Profane is as soft and fat as Friedman's Stern, as cowardly as Heller's Yossarian, as addicted to "yo-yoing" (traveling aimlessly back and forth on subways and ferries) as Percy's Jack Bolling is to escapist moviegoing. Hemingway's Lieutenant

Henry in *A Farewell to Arms* made a separate peace and deserted the war after he had fought bravely; Benny Profane, who never fought in any war, has made a separate peace in every human struggle, even the one against mice (pro-mouse, Benny springs traps).

These heroes are in neurotic withdrawal and thermonuclear shock. They suffer from meagerness of aim, asking only to be physically gratified and otherwise to be left alone. Pynchon wants more of life than Benny does, and his message is delivered as a series of slogans by the book's sympathetic characters. "Love with your mouth shut," McClintic tells us, "keep cool, but care." (How treacherously that last appears to resemble Krishna's message to Arjuna in the *Bhagavad Gita:* Do your duty without attachment.) "You have to con each other a little," Rachel tells Profane, trying to prevent a quarrel.

What Pynchon and his fellows are really offering us are the slogans of revisionist psychoanalysis: kindness, consideration, mutuality, unselfish love. But outside and beyond this world of moderate adjustment is V., who wants more of life than Pynchon does. She wants passion, power, total immersion in the destructive element, and rebirth in the artifice of eternity. It is a sign of Thomas Pynchon's intelligence and imagination that he knows that too.

THE ENGLISH ILIAD

In our day of courtly and chivalric warfare, the adventures of King Arthur and his knights of the Round Table have a particular relevance. The appearance of two new editions of Sir Thomas Malory's book suggests an increasing popularity. One reissue is *Le Morte Darthur*, two volumes in one, with modern spelling by A. W. Pollard and a glossary. The other is *Le Morte d'Arthur*, a paraphrase in modern idiom, condensed to less than half, by Keith Baines, with decorations by Enrico Arno. Malory was himself no verray perfight gentil knight, but a brawler, rapist, and cattle thief, who wrote the book in Newgate Prison in 1470. Wherever Malory is now, I hope that he is pleased at the survival and success of his fantasy life.

Le Morte Darthur is not quite the English *Iliad*. E. K. Chambers, in a pamphlet on Malory, quotes an unnamed poet's characterization of the book as "the dim Arthuriad," and that comes closer to accuracy. Malory compiled romances, but he did not try to integrate them into an epic. *Le Morte Darthur* does resemble the *Iliad* in some respects. It is quite as savage, for example. When Sir Gaheris catches his mother Queen Margawse in bed with Sir Lamorak, he cuts off her head with his sword, so that her hot blood spurts all over Sir Lamorak, hot blood "the which he loved passing well" in another fashion. In the style of Diomedes or the enraged Achilles, these heroes fight as ghouls: in battle their horses are "in blood up to the fetlocks"; as for the happy victor, "all was blood and brains on his sword."

The *Iliad* has the marvelous eloquence that Malory's book lacks. Examples are Sarpedon's speech, as he goes into battle, acknowledging human mortality, or Achilles reproving Lycaon before killing him. The Arthurian knights tend to fight first and talk afterwards, and their talk is almost always conventional address. The chief of them, Launcelot, is much inferior to Achilles as a character. He lacks Achilles' range of feeling, his flawed and complex personality, his tragic purchase of glory at the cost of early death. The quest for the Grail does not unify *Le Morte Darthur* as the war against Troy unifies the *Iliad,* and, in fact, by the end of the book the Grail has been forgotten.

Perhaps it is best to get all of *Le Morte Darthur's* failings out of the way at once. The book consists of eight separate tales, with little beyond the concept of the Round Table to integrate them, and great inconsistencies between them. For example, Sir Gawaine is chivalric and heroic in some tales, and a jealous, treacherous, and inadequate knight in the Tristram section. There are all sorts of loose ends. Sir Breuse Saunce Pité, "the falsest knight of the world now living," appears periodically to kill a defenseless damosel or to trample a fallen knight, but no one ever catches him, and halfway through the book he quietly disappears. Two knights, first Sir Pellinore, and then Sir Palamides, pursue the Questing Beast, and King Arthur and Sir Tristram at different times see the Beast and hear its stomach rumble "like unto the questing of thirty couple hounds," but the Beast is never captured and never explained.

In some respects *Le Morte Darthur* is childish. One of its units, "The Tale of King Arthur and the Emperor Lucius," is a preposterous saga in which Arthur's Knights defeat the Roman army of 60,000 and get Arthur anointed Emperor of Rome. There are stretches where only the adulteries reassure the reader that he has not strayed into a Junior Classic. Finally, many of the characters are conventional. King Mark, for example, is a tormented, ambivalent, and complex human being in Gottfried von Strassburg's *Tristan and Iseult;* in Malory he is a cardboard villain: faithless, treacherous, cowardly, and weak.

Once that all that is said—and it must be said—we arrive at the wonders and delights of *Le Morte Darthur.* If it is not the English *Iliad,* it comes closer to it than any other work in the language. True, Launcelot does not get to choose glory and a short life, but we know that he would have if given the choice. When Sir Balin is told that the sword he has acquired will cause the deaths of his brother and himself, he says only, "I shall take the adventure that God will ordain me," and keeps the sword.

When one compares Malory, not with Homer, but with what Tennyson or T. H. White made of King Arthur and the Round Table, one comes to appreciate *Le Morte Darthur* more. Elaine, the Maid of Astolat, dying for love of Launcelot and ordering her corpse to be floated down the Thames to him on a barge, is stale caramel in Tennyson, but in Malory the episode is fresh, touching, and beautiful. We snicker at White's portrayal of the Round Table knights as a group of chaps good at games, but no one snickers, reading Malory, when the traitor Sir Meliagraunce reveals the adultery between Sir Launcelot and Queen Guenever by throwing back her bed curtains and showing the sheets and pillows all "bebled" with Launcelot's blood.

Perhaps the finest touch of all is one that Malory inherits from the ancient rites underlying his myths. The tragic final events, kin to the Robin Hood contests, occur in May, when, as Malory reminds us, "every lusty heart flourisheth and burgeoneth, for as the season is lusty to behold and comfortable, so man and woman rejoice and gladden of summer coming with his fresh flowers." What flourisheth and burgeoneth, of course, is Sir Modred's treachery, King Arthur's death, and the dissolution of the fellowship of the Round Table.

Given characters that are really no more than ritual roles, Malory manages to produce a considerable complexity in them. As a true knight, Sir Launcelot may not lie, but he may not acknowledge his affair with the Queen either. When a lady charges him with it, he answers unhappily: "I may not warn people to speak of me what it pleaseth them"; when a knight charges him with it, he challenges the knight to prove it at combat. Launcelot's mortal sin keeps him from success in the Grail quest, but after Arthur's death he forsakes the world and dies repentant, a pilgrim and a hermit, and his bishop has a vision in which a great band of angels heave Sir Launcelot into heaven—that "heave" gives a wonderful sense of the knightly muscles under the hermit's gown.

Sir Gawaine becomes most human near the end of the book, when he lies on the ground wounded and conquered by Launcelot, and tries to provoke Launcelot into killing him. Sir Palamides, the Saracen knight, is a contradictory figure: he is brave and courteous, but he fights unethically; he is frantic with jealousy toward superior knights, and when he is bested in a tourney he weeps and wails all night. Palamides turns out to be not a hysteric but a lovesick Byronic hero somewhat in advance of his time, even composing ballads about his hopeless love. Finally there is Sir Dinadan, whose cynical realism about the likelihood of pain and defeat in fighting comes out of the real world in which Malory lived, and is never understood by any other character.

The other male figures, including King Arthur, are conventional. The women are similarly flat, with two exceptions. Queen Guenever is a real woman: terrified of pain, passionate, cynical, and hot-tempered. The other is an unnamed gentlewoman (Artemis?) who shoots an arrow at a deer and manages to hit Sir Launcelot "in the thick of the buttock"; when he protests, she airily dismisses the incident.

The great glory of *Le Morte Darthur* is its language. When two knights fight, "either smote other so that horse and man went to the earth, and so they lay long astonied, and their horses' knees brast to the hard bone." Here is the genesis of a royal bastard: "The king had ado with her, and gat on her a child." A wicked king has "purfled" (embroidered) a mantle with the beards of kings he has overcome; when he demands Arthur's beard, Arthur answers: "Thou mayest see my beard is full young yet to make a purfle of it." Sir Launcelot, on an adventure, rides "overthwart and endlong in a wild forest." In his sin he hears a voice curse him as "more harder than is the stone, and more bitter than is the wood, and more naked and barer than is the leaf of the fig tree." King Arthur, running to his death at the hands of his traitorous son Sir Mordred, cries out: "Tide me death, betide me life."

The Baines rendition is in this respect an unmitigated disaster, comparable to making Howard Pyle out of the Robin Hood ballads. "How sad that I broke my magic sword!" says Baines' King Arthur ("I have no sword," says Malory's). Baines' Arthur calls a cannibal giant "You murderous freak!" (Malory's calls him only "glutton"). "Certainly we will teach him a much-needed lesson," says Baines' Sir Launcelot, in the voice of a scoutmaster ("I shall be your rescue and learn him to be ruled as a knight," says Malory's). Dame Liones calls Gareth "cockroach" in Baines (it is "kitchen knave" in Malory). "If that is what your conscience dictates, you must go," says Tristram's father in Baines ("I will well," he says in Malory, "that ye be ruled as your courage will rule you"). And so on.

Robert Graves contributes a characteristic introduction praising Baines' travesty as a "workmanlike task" that improves the book by "removing all of the idle rhetoric." It is about time that someone protested Graves' misuse of his great imaginative gifts in muddying every scholarly water he touches. His introduction also tells the innocent reader that the historical existence of Arthur, as a Roman general named Arturius, has been "proved beyond reasonable doubt," and that "Arthur had long been converted into a counter-Christ, with twelve knights of the Round Table to suggest the Twelve Apostles, and with a Second Coming."

It seems hardly worth saying that there were 150 knights of the Round Table. As for the Second Coming, Malory, who (unlike Graves) could tell his own fantasies from reality, observed that many believe that King Arthur will return, "but for myself I do not believe this." King Arthur achieved his true immortality in *Le Morte Darthur,* and so, for that matter, did bad Sir Thomas Malory.

FRUITCAKE AT TIFFANY'S

I knew Truman Capote when he was an office boy at *The New Yorker*, faintly comic in the intensity of his ambition to become a writer. Well, he has made it. Capote has published two novels, two collections of stories, and two books of reporting. Despite this meager output over 20 years, he is taken very seriously, as the result of a complex combination of talent and shrewd promotion. In 1963 Capote reached an apotheosis in *Selected Writings of Truman Capote*. It contains selections, chosen by the author, from all the books except the novels, along with three new pieces.

The *Selected Writings* makes it clear that Capote has a real talent, however flawed and limited it may be. Over the years his work has changed markedly. Such early stories as "A Tree of Night" (1943) and "Miriam" (1944) are in the tradition of Djuna Barnes' short fiction: bizarre, gothic, and nightmarish. Such recent fiction as "Breakfast at Tiffany's" (1958) and "Among the Paths to Eden" (1960) is more like the work of Christopher Isherwood: wryly comic, perceptive, and oddly impersonal. This is not improvement—the early stories are as effective in their own terms as the late ones—so much as a psychological transformation of the author, a shift from a preoccupation with an inner world to a concern with the outer world, sometimes almost sociological.

At its best, Capote's fiction produces the terror and pity that Aristotle distinguished as the emotions proper to tragedy. The ending of "A Tree of Night," with Kay catatonic under her raincoat as the horrible woman robs her, is truly chilling. The ending of "Miriam," Miriam's return, is equally fine, and if its terror is less, its pity is considerably more. Sometimes Capote gets his effect with beautifully chosen detail, as when Vincent in "The Headless Hawk" gives the girl, D. J., forty-odd dollars to buy clothes, and she spends it on a leather windbreaker, a set of military brushes, a raincoat, and a cigarette lighter. Mary O'Meaghan's perfect imitation of Helen Morgan in "Among the Paths to Eden" is one of those moments that seize the heart.

Capote has a mastery of the world of fantasy. The dreams in his stories are powerful and convincing: Vincent's dream of the headless hawk in the story of that name, Walter's dream of an old castle where only old turkeys live in "Shut a Final Door." Capote is just as effective when he uses fantasy for comic purposes, as in the old drunk's delusion in "Children on Their Birthdays" that the girls are midgets in the walls trying to get at his supply of toilet paper. It is this capacity that Capote uses to evoke the special imaginative world of childhood in his novels. In the stories, it is often a world of adults become childlike and innocent: in "Master Misery," Oreilly's song about loveberry pie, and the playing-house weekend that Sylvia and Oreilly spend together, "like the most beautiful party Sylvia could remember."

"A Christmas Memory" (1946) is the best of the early stories, and the one that most fully displays these features of Capote's talent. The narrator is seven, and his elderly female cousin is sixty-something, but they are two children together, and the Christmas fruitcakes they bake contain all the magical world of childhood. The details have an absolute rightness. The cousin's reason for never seeing a movie is: "When the Lord comes, let me see him clear." After she and the narrator are separated, she sends him a dime wadded in toilet paper in every letter, with the instructions: "See a picture show and write me the story." Their Christmas gifts —for the third year each has built a kite to surprise the other—are as corny and pat as the gifts in O. Henry's "The Gift of the Magi," *and* as apt to move the reader nevertheless.

Mark Schorer, whose blurbing account must be considerably overdrawn by now, says of Capote's prose in his introduction: "perhaps its single constant quality is the unerring sense of style." Is it? Let us look at some examples. Capote loves to say everything twice: "an enormous, really huge head." He evades the responsibility to describe precisely: "like a child aged abruptly by some uncanny method"; "in an undefinably obscene manner"; "somewhat naked children." He muddles syntax dreadfully: "he could no more dispossess it than could, for example, a dead man rid his legendary eyes of the last image seen"—here Capote doesn't mean that the eyes are legendary, but that the inability is.

Capote has a terrible ear. For example, he hears the question, "After all, *where* are we going to gossip?" with the emphasis on the "where" instead of the "are." Here is an entry in the Limp Second Clause Sweepstakes: "A competitive spirit had pervaded the purchasing of these outfits, of which more than several had a certain Eskimo-look." His metaphors and similes are often wildly inept: *Porgy and Bess*, "when slipped under the dialectical microscope, proves a test tube brimming with the kind of bacteria to which the present Russian regime is most allergic"; something stops "like the hands of a dropped watch"; of Marlon Brando: "how superbly, like a guileful salamander, he slithered into the part."

When Capote tries fancy writing, the results are sometimes catastrophic. At one point he challenges comparison with James Joyce by rewriting the famous ending of "The Dead." Capote writes: "A snowstorm moving across Colorado, across the West, falling upon all the small towns, yellowing every light, filling every footfall, falling now and here: but how quickly it had come, the snowstorm: the roofs, the vacant lot, the distance deep in white and deepening, like sleep." But the comparison is fatal to Capote, and when last seen he was blowing across Colorado.

Bad prose is not Capote's only defect. Leaden whimsy weighs down a good half of his stories, and at least once, in the case of "Children on Their Birthdays," the story sinks under the weight and drowns. Some of the reporting is smothered in chic; witness a sentence from "A House on the Heights": "Not that this is the Heights' sole *maison de luxe:* we are blessed with several exponents of limousine life—but unarguably, Mrs. O is *la regina di tutti.*" The one thoroughly bad story in the book, "House of Flowers," is a pastoral fantasy of happy amorous Haitian peasants, all moulded out of milk chocolate. One story, "The Headless Hawk," suffers from what I have come to call the Albertine Strategy. As in the case of Tennessee Williams' "Rubio y Morena," which it somewhat resembles, it would have been better had its boyish female consort been frankly a boy.

More important than these defects are two major failings:

Capote has no subject to write about and no interest in ideas. The best example of this is "Master Misery." It is about a Mr. A. F. Revercomb, who buys people's dreams, generally at the rate of five dollars a dream; when he has acquired all their dreams, he has stolen their souls. Unless this is a satire on psychoanalysis, which seems highly unlikely, it is not *about* anything; it is a free-floating image of deprivation, with no reference. It does not specifically symbolize any malaise of the modern world, or any special condition of life, or even any universal human condition. It is just a pointless fable in which dreams are imagined as commodities.

It is, I think, Capote's recognition that he has a creative imagination, but no subject on which to exercise it, that has increasingly turned him toward reporting. But here too the lack of interest in ideas, along with the tin ear, handicaps him. The best-known of Capote's pieces, "The Muses Are Heard," tells us everything about the Soviet Union except what we want to know: what Russian life was like for *Russians* in 1956. We hear characters use language that we know from the stories is Capote's own (orange "hulls" for "peels," for example); it then becomes much less likely that Capote really met a hip Russian who said: "So a lot of squares don't dig it. They don't flip. So is that big news?"

Again, Capote's imagination sometimes saves him. If "The Muses Are Heard" is a failure as a whole, one character, Mrs. Gershwin, is brought magnificently to life. A single image, of four men silently beating a fifth on a Leningrad street, says more than all the rest of the article. There are similarly powerful images throughout the reporting: Marlon Brando as a boy, running away from home every Sunday, rain or shine; Capote himself running from a gang at the end of "A House on the Heights." But these are flashes, and we never get any sustained revelation.

The novella, "Breakfast at Tiffany's," although it is not free of Capote's faults, seems to me the best thing that he has yet done. The plot is wildly improbable. It is absurd that Holly Golightly should be arrested for transmitting coded messages that enable a convict named Sally Tomato to control his worldwide drug syndicate. It is absurd that the narrator's horse should run away with him up Fifth Avenue. But these two absurdities are necessary contrivances for one beautiful and touching scene. Holly is arrested in the narrator's bathroom, waiting for the bruised narrator to finish a bath so that she may rub him with liniment; the liniment bottle is broken in the scuffle; when the narrator jumps out of the tub he cuts his feet; "Nude and bleeding a path of bloody footprints," he follows Holly and the detectives helplessly to the door.

The comedy in "Breakfast at Tiffany's" is always slightly tinged with melancholy. Holly herself is a reincarnation of Isherwood's Sally Bowles, and an improvement on her. Holly is done in wonderful brush strokes: her oral parentheses, her doing in a rival with the gentlest hint of venereal disease, her inability to cook anything not exotic, her training herself, as a call girl, to get excited only by men over forty-two; her desire for a "quite coony baby." Holly's quarrel with the narrator while he is rubbing her back with suntan oil is a marvelous scene, perfectly rendered. The end of the novella, Holly's cat finding a home, is absolutely right. For all its absurdities and awkwardnesses, "Breakfast at Tiffany's" is a triumph. There is a lot more to Truman Capote than that checked weskit that the ads used to show.

DR. CHEKHOV'S DIAGNOSIS

Whatever else he is, if anything, the reviewer in one of his functions is a shopping service. In those terms, the shopper's best buy
is *Seven Short Novels by Chekhov* in paperback for 95 cents,
seven novellas of the highest quality at less than 14 cents apiece.
Gleb Struve contributes an introduction, prefaces to each novella,
a chronology, and a bibliography. The new translation by Barbara
Makanowitzky, despite her weakness for split infinitives, is read-
able and vigorous, rescuing Chekhov from the musty, stilted language of Constance Garnett. Five separate footnotes explain that
kasha is a porridge, and three more explain that *kvass* is a fer-
mented beverage—I do not know why.

The seven novellas are: *The Duel, Ward No. 6, A Woman's
Kingdom, Three Years, My Life, Peasants,* and *In the Ravine.*
They show the range of Chekhov's command of Russian life, from
the fashionable highlife of *A Woman's Kingdom,* in which Lyse-
vich tells Anna that she must marry to experience "the sweetness
of the first infidelity," to the brutish world of *Peasants,* where marriage is a fist in the face. They also show Chekhov at the height of
his fictional powers, in the 1890s, in the novella form that, as the
four-act play form did, gave him more space for his architecture
of the emotions than the short story form did. I have space to
discuss only the three novellas that I like best: *The Duel, My Life,*
and *In the Ravine.*

The Duel, which Chekhov mockingly characterized to A. S.
Suvorin as "What a Russian salad!," is a remarkable ironic structure. In the main plot, Laevsky, a Turgenev "superfluous man"
and wastrel, resolves to desert his mistress, Nadezhda, mainly out
of boredom and self-disgust. When he catches her in bed with a
lover, he changes his mind. In the subplot, Laevsky is despised
and hated by a social-Darwinian zoologist, von Koren, who eventually provokes him into a duel and tries to kill him. Laevsky is

providentially saved—the bullet grazes his neck—and this escape and Nadezhda's sin combine to fill him with joy, and to regenerate him. At the novella's end he is married to Nadezhda, and is hard-working and frugal.

The Duel is thus a fable of good growing out of evil—Nadezhda's infidelities, von Koren's murderous hatred—but it is an ironic fable. Von Koren had called the unregenerate Laevsky a "cholera microbe," but Laevsky the drudge has not become a man, merely a harmless microbe.

The strength of the work lies in the eloquence of its rhetoric, the verbal duel between Laevsky and von Koren, which is more important than their duel with pistols. Von Koren indicts Laevsky as a parasitic voluptuary in three pages of blistering, brilliant rhetoric, concluding with Laevsky's typical dreams: "First he dreams he is married to the moon, then he imagines he is summoned by the police and sentenced to cohabit with a guitar." Laevsky is equally eloquent about von Koren as a power-mad despot, but most of his eloquence is reserved for his own worthlessness, which he describes more cruelly than von Koren does. The result of this verbal duel and suicide is to leave both parties lying dead, and to create by negation a powerful humanistic ideal, a man who would be as responsive as Laevsky, without his weakness, as responsible as von Koren, without his ruthlessness.

My Life is an equally complex novella about a narrator named Missail Poloznev, who deserts his class, the provincial intelligentsia, to become a housepainter. It begins in the manner of a novel by one of the British Angry Young Men, with an alienated and cynical young hero's cheeking his boss and getting fired from his ninth boring clerical job. It soon turns out to be much more than that, however, and it ends as a powerful Chekhovian vision of love's victimage. The narrator is deserted by his wife, Marya, a wonderful portrait of one of those emancipated Russian women, —Lou Andreas-Salomé comes to mind—who habitually drove a man for two years and then traded him in. Missail remains hope-lessly in love with Marya. His sister, Cleopatra, dies bearing an illegitimate child by her married lover, Dr. Blagovo, who (as did Marya) goes calmly on his way. In the novella's final irony, Bla-govo's sister Anyuta turns out to love and worship Missail, but is unable to acknowledge her love because of the class barrier between them. The last scene is deeply moving. Anyuta walks with Missail and Cleopatra's child; then, as they enter the town, she walks on ahead and pretends not to know them.

These dramas of betrayal and cowardice are enacted in a scene of great ugliness, Russian provincial life at its most repulsive. The father of Missail and Cleopatra is the town architect, who designs deformed and ugly houses that become the town's style, and takes bribes in the serene belief that "they were given him out of respect for his spiritual qualities." The townspeople occupy themselves with torturing dogs, eating flies, hooting at Missail for becoming a worker, cheating and insulting the workers they employ, and plucking live sparrows bare. "Gogolesque pig-snouts," Dr. Blagovo calls them, and he should know because he is one himself.

In the Ravine chronicles the terrible destruction of a contented and prosperous village storekeeper named Grigory Tsybukin. One of his sons is sentenced to Siberia for counterfeiting; the other is spineless in character and deaf. The deaf son's wife, Aksinya, is an adulterous monster. She seizes the business, drives away her sister-in-law Lipa, and brutally kills Lipa's child, Tsybukin's only grandchild, then mistreats and starves the old man.

The power of these calamities lies to a great extent in the heavy, fated quality of their foreshadowing, very like the prophesied dooms of Greek tragedy. In the first paragraph we are told that the village is famed only as the place where a deacon once ate up all the caviar at a funeral. Then the days are "oppressive, gloomy"; the samovar drones "predictions of misfortune"; the telephone stops working because of "the bugs and cockroaches breeding in it." Lipa appears and is discovered to have been frightened for life when an employer once stamped his foot at her. At Lipa's wedding, the groom cries and prays to God to avert "the inevitable misfortune," and the peasants the Tsybukins have cheated gather outside to curse the wedding party. Aksinya looks "the way a little snake looks." When Lipa's child is born, he is so small, thin, and pitiful that it seems unnecessary to give him a name. The most powerful symbolic foreshadowing is the novella's title, which represents the ravine in which the village lies. This ravine is human depravity, the gaping pit, Aksinya's maw, even her voracious and barren sexuality. When, at the novella's beautiful end, Lipa feeds the starving old man, we climb out of the ravine for the first time.

The other new book of Chekhov fiction, *The Image of Chekhov*, consists of forty short stories selected and newly translated by Robert Payne. It is not so good a buy as the paperback volume (although forty stories at $5.95 come to less than 15 cents apiece) because many of the stories are not worth having. Payne's translation is even more fluent and readable than Miss Makanowitzky's, but he is a better translator than editor. His introduction attacks the familiar portrait of Chekhov in pince-nez, insists that Chekhov was "quite astonishingly handsome," and explains that these forty stories were chosen and printed in chronological order to give us a better portrait or image, to show us "the autobiographical thread running through them."

As though we cared. What we want from stories is not a picture of their author, but a vision of life. When Payne quotes Chekhov's notebook entry, "Perhaps the universe is suspended on the tooth of some monster," we have all the biographical facts we need. Many of the early slight stories that Payne includes are not worth the space. This is not to say that all of Chekhov's stories of the 1880s are inadequate. "The Ninny" has real bite, "The Huntsman" is a moving love sketch, and the end of "The Princess," the Princess' self-satisfaction at her own Christian forgiveness, is masterly. Best of all is "Anyuta," written in 1886, and less than five pages long. The scene in which the medical student studies the location of the ribs by having Anyuta sit naked in the cold, with her ribs marked in charcoal, is overwhelming—one of the most disturbing images in literature for that ultimate crime, treating people as things.

However, the longer stories written after 1890 gave Chekhov the room he needed for greatness. The three best of them—"Big Volodya and Little Volodya," "Anna Round the Neck," and "The Lady with the Pet Dog"—make Payne's book worth buying. "Big Volodya and Little Volodya" tells of silly Sophia Lvovna. Married to one Volodya, she has an affair with the other, a singer of "Tara-ra-boom-dee-ay," and is thrown over by him the next week. It is not of the slightest importance, except that it breaks her heart, and ours.

"Anna Round the Neck," for a change, is about a woman's triumph. This Anyuta marries for money, is taken up by society for her beauty and the roundness of her heels, and then treats her husband as a servant. The story carefully plants material that is harvested in a superb ending. Anna's husband is awarded the order of St. Anna, second class, by His Excellency, who then makes the title joke, that the husband now has two Annas round his neck. A final tableau shows us Anna herself, round the neck of the world.

"The Lady with the Pet Dog" is about an affair between two people, Gurov and Anna, unhappily married to others. Their affair starts as vacation dalliance and ends as a passion that dominates their lives. The story is strengthened by a series of powerful and resonant symbols: Gurov's vision of beautiful cold women with the lace on their lingerie like fish scales; the eternal constancy of the sea, as Gurov and Anna watch it at Yalta; a beggar who enters the gates of Anna's house and is attacked by dogs. The last pages, in which Gurov realizes that love is a burden, almost a doom, have the bitter realism of the greatest love poetry.

"Medicine is my lawful wife and literature my mistress," Chekhov once wrote to Suvorin. As a writer, Chekhov was always very much the doctor: compassionate but detached. Near the end of his life, he wrote to Vladimir Tikhonov, "I only wished to tell people honestly: 'Look at yourselves, see how badly and boringly you live!' " It is a diagnosis, but he is careful not to prescribe. The disease is the human condition, and Dr. Chekhov knew that it is incurable.

A DYING LIFE

"Italo Svevo" (Italus the Swabian) is the unlikely pen name taken by Ettore Schmitz, born in 1861, a prosperous Jewish businessman in Trieste. He is best known as the original of Leopold Bloom in *Ulysses;* this is a partial truth, since Bloom takes some traits from Schmitz, but takes many more from Joyce himself. The Freudian novel Svevo wrote late in life, *La Coscienze di Zeno (Confessions of Zeno),* has a deserved popularity. In 1963, Svevo's first and favorite novel, *Una Vita (A Life)* achieved its first American publication, translated from the Italian by Archibald Colquhoun. It is amazingly good, and, for a book that appeared in 1892, amazingly contemporary and relevant.

A Life is the story of Alfonso Nitti, a doctor's son from the provinces, who works as a correspondence clerk in a Trieste bank. After the fashion of an Alger hero, Alfonso rises in the bank and wins the friendship of Annetta Maller, the boss' beautiful daughter. One night he goes to bed with her and they arrange to marry; then everything suddenly disintegrates. Disgusted by Annetta's unchastity, Alfonso goes back to his village, where his mother dies. Deserted by Alfonso, Annetta turns against him, and agrees to marry her cousin. Alfonso is transferred to the bank's "Siberia"; he is challenged to a duel by Annetta's brother; he kills himself.

Annetta is shallow and foolish, but I think that we are meant to see her love for Alfonso as real, and his denial of it as reprehensible. The demand on Alfonso is made most poignantly in a letter to him from Francesca, Annetta's confidante. "Only your presence here can save you, save us," she writes. But Alfonso stays in the country with his mother, and all is lost. We can best judge Alfonso's misconception of Annetta by his reiterated conviction of her coldness: "he could not imagine an expression of affection or desire on her calm marmoreal face"; "calculation marked the limits of the tiny whiffs of passion which the young lady allowed herself." When they go to bed together, he is disconcerted to find her "an obliging, passionate lover," and when he leaves her in the morning she is laughing with happy sensuality and promising many more such nights.

The pathos of failure and betrayal does not keep *A Life* from being wryly funny throughout. Details are grotesquely inconsistent: Alfonso becomes the friend of Annetta's cousin because "he was so small and insignificant that Macario felt fine beside him"; at other times he is "tall and quite well set up." Svevo constantly mocks the poignancy of his story by a style of cynical aphorism. A remark about Alfonso is a typical example: "He knew from his reading that women always forgive a homage to their beauty in any, even criminal, form."

A Life is an exploration of something we had thought the monopoly of our own dispirited age: the intellectual's self-doubt, self-pity, tired blood, and neurosis. Alfonso daydreams of "self-mastery, wealth, and happiness," but when wealth and happiness are offered him he flees from them (Francesca calls it "escaping from the consequences of your good luck"), and the only self-mastery he attains is in the act of taking his own life.

In one aspect, Alfonso's *Angst* is very Jewish, and his blood is tired because his creator's blood is tired, after eighteen centuries of dispersion. In one of those perfect typographic errors that tell all, Colquhoun's *A Life* misprints Trieste as "Triste," and truly it is the land of Triste that Alfonso inhabits. He sometimes dreams of going back to his village to work in the fields, but his true ideal is the Diaspora Jewish ideal of a life of culture wholly divorced from nature, a life of books and the mind, not acts and the body. In this aspect, Annetta is nature, an opulent body, and Alfonso samples it and flees.

In another aspect, Alfonso embodies the death wish. "Where there is no blood," Svevo reminds us, "it cannot be made to flow." If Annetta appears marble but is really full of passion, Alfonso is the reverse. "You've found a way of calling your own coldness 'dignity,'" Francesca, his severest critic, tells him. Alfonso dreams of an old age in which "he would be able to describe having 'lived' in the sense that word was used by others." His ideal state is "renunciation and quiet," and after various inadequate tries at re-

nunciation (he gives away money and passes up an available
girl), he discovers "the renunciation of which he had dreamed"
—it is the renunciation of his life in suicide. In these terms, Annetta symbolizes life, and when Alfonso sees her after his return to
Trieste, "it seemed impossible that he had ever possessed such a
splendid creature."

Underlying the *Angst* and the death wish there is a model
Oedipus complex. Alfonso is in love with his widowed mother, as
she is with him. The book begins with Alfonso's letter to her, asking permission to give up his job and come home to live. When he
does come home to find her dying, she can only go to sleep if he
holds her hands; he promises that "they would always be together
for the rest of their lives"; she jealously warns him against the love
of women, including Annetta; after her death he dreams of "his
mother, still young, and humming as she worked for him." The
revulsion and disgust Alfonso feels at Annetta's "fall," we realize,
has been displaced from his feelings toward his mother.

In common with all the great works of realism, *A Life* shows
a mastery of symbolism too. A number of strong ironic foreshadowings frame its dramatic action. As they watch some gulls, Macario tells Alfonso that one must be a seagull and "drop like lead
on prey at the right second by instinct." Alfonso takes this advice
with Annetta, and decides that Macario was wrong in thinking
him "incapable of fighting and seizing his prey." In a deeper
sense, however, Macario was prophetic: Alfonso can seize his prey
but he is incapable of holding on to it.

One of Alfonso's fellows in the bank, Miceni, early in the
book foreshadows Alfonso's eventual fall from grace and exile to
the Siberia of the countinghouse; a rival, Fumigi, whose proposal
to Annetta is rejected, ends in business failure and madness, as
Alfonso will end comparably. When Alfonso is returning to Trieste from the country, he sees a man thrown off the train because
he cannot pay the fare; this man too foreshadows Alfonso's fate.
Most ironically, Alfonso seduces Annetta in the Maller library,
redolent of "a strong smell of glue"—but even the strong glue of
sexuality cannot hold these lovers together.

The ancestry of *A Life* is the tradition of French psychological realism about *l'amour* that runs from Madame de la Fayette

and Constant, to Flaubert and Proust. If the book's ancestry is French, its progeny are Italian: the early Moravia of *The Time of Indifference* and the Pavese of *The House on the Hill*. Alfonso's "state of boredom, of grayness and monotony," his world in which "everything bored him," is Moravia's; the Alfonso who weeps as he declares his love to Annetta, not out of love but out of self-pity, might be an inadequate Pavese hero.

What *A Life* most closely resembles is the new American novel of our time, the fiction of the sixties, which I tried to characterize in a review of Thomas Pynchon's *V.*, How familiar we have become with the despairing cry in *A Life:* "To be treated decently? Is that too much?" Svevo observes that in his self-description Alfonso "seemed to be suffering from some world-wide disease." Svevo was prescient to notice it then; now it is epidemic. It is the sickness of Yossarian in *Catch-22*, of the protagonist in *David Knudsen*, of Jack Bolling for most of *The Moviegoer*, of Benny Profane in *V.*, of Gabe Wallach at the end of *Letting Go;* a sickness of the moral will, asking gratifications without responsibilities.

Svevo published *A Life* at his own expense in 1892; it was a resounding failure. In 1898 he similarly published a second novel, *Senilità* (translated, at Joyce's suggestion, *As a Man Grows Older*); it was similarly unsuccessful. *As a Man Grows Older* tells the same Oedipal story in broader comic terms. The autobiographical hero is now 35-year-old Emilio Brentani, who works for an Insurance Society and has published an ignored novel. Instead of a dying mother, he is burdened with a dying virgin sister.

The greatest change is in the life symbol. She is now Angiolini Zarri, a big, healthy, beautiful blonde who is having simultaneous affairs with Emilio and with most of the male population of Trieste, so that she generally comes running to him warm and flushed from someone else's bed. Emilio feels senile at 35, and Angiolina represents youth and life to him. But what he really wants, it becomes clear, is a mother, not Miss Trieste 1896, and after Angiolina has left him and his sister has died, he synthesizes the two into a happy memory of an idealized female figure.

In 1907, James Joyce, who supported himself by giving private English lessons in Trieste, acquired Ettore Schmitz and his wife as pupils. Schmitz confessed that he had once been a writer, and showed Joyce his two novels. Joyce praised them highly, and encouraged his pupil to return to writing. Schmitz, become Svevo again, took his time about it, and in 1923 he published *Confessions of Zeno*, once more at his own expense (Stanislaus Joyce claims that it was written in a fortnight). *Zeno* is a bitterly honest and wonderfully funny treatment of the same Oedipal story, this time fully aware of psychoanalysis. It is told as a series of autobiographical essays written by Zeno—a compulsive smoker and adulterer—for his psychoanalyst.

Tirelessly promoted by Joyce, *Zeno* was a great success; reviews and articles everywhere proclaimed Svevo's mastery. He acknowledged that Joyce had "renewed the miracle of Lazarus." From 1926 on, Svevo was one of the most acclaimed writers in Europe. He had little time to enjoy his fame, however, since he was killed in an automobile accident in 1928. For an author who had killed himself off symbolically at 30, and had passed into imaginary senility at 35, how ironically apt.

ANTIQUE HARVESTER, LOVELY RITUALIST

In 1950, when he was awarded the Bollingen Prize in poetry, John Crowe Ransom was asked for comment by a *Times* reporter. "I am surprised," he said. "There is nothing recent of mine for the committee to have considered, and my old work is small in volume when the inferior things are screened out. I know now that when I was writing it I had no sound education in poetry, and was in torture trying to escape from the stilted and sentimental verbal habits which conditioned me. My stuff came out of the academy, I am sure that is apparent."

In honor of Ransom's 75th birthday, his publisher brought out a revised and enlarged edition of *Selected Poems*. It enables us to refute in detail Ransom's fantastic self-estimate. His poetry is quite the reverse of unsound, tortured, stilted, sentimental, or academic. With the possible exception of 76-year-old Marianne Moore, Ransom is the finest poet in the United States today. His mastery is unmistakable from the first stanza of the first poem in the book, "Winter Remembered," the earliest work included:

> *Two evils, monstrous either one apart,*
> *Possessed me, and were long and loath at going:*
> *A cry of Absence, Absence, in the heart,*
> *And in the wood the furious winter blowing.*

The reasons for Ransom's comparative lack of fame as a poet are many. Ironically, his great prestige as a teacher, critic, and founding editor of *The Kenyon Review* has helped to obscure his stature as a poet. Other factors are his extraordinary modesty, typified by his reaction to the Bollingen Prize, and his fastidious refusal to engage in any form of self-promotion.

More important, perhaps, has been Ransom's limited and brief output. "The total volume of my verse is not very large," he observes ruefully in the preface to *Selected Poems*. The book includes 53 poems, averaging one a year for Ransom's adult life. All but five were published many years ago, in *Chills and Fever* (1924) and *Two Gentlemen in Bonds* (1927); the remaining five were published before 1945; for the new volume Ransom has extensively rewritten two of the earlier poems, one with a commentary explaining and justifying the revisions. Thus the bulk of his work was written in a single marvelous decade, from 1916 to 1926.

Ransom judges himself by the highest standard conceivable. The 1945 *Selected Poems* includes only 42 poems, less than half of those in the two volumes drawn on. In *Poems and Essays* in 1955, Ransom weakened to the extent of including two more from the earlier volumes; now there are nine more plus the two revisions. These nine poems are not as good as Ransom's best, but anyone else would be proud of them. They include "Vision by Sweetwater," a magnificent creation and destruction of the innocence of childhood, and "Hilda," in which the bereft poet would follow Hilda's ghost: "But what I wear is flesh; it weighs like stone." Ransom still has not relented to the point of including such fine poems as "Miss Euphemia," "In Mr. Minnit's House," "Inland City," or anything at all from his first book, *Poems About God* (1919).

Other factors that have kept Ransom's poetry from the widest recognition are intrinsic to the verse itself. It seems old-fashioned in its tone of ironic detachment, so much so that a reviewer welcomed Ransom in 1920 as "an American Georgian." A stanza from "Necrological," a poem about a medieval friar's visit to a battlefield, provides an example:

> *Close by the sable stream that purged the plain*
> *Lay the white stallion and his rider thrown,*
> *The great beast had spilled there his little brain,*
> *And the little groin of the knight was spilled by a stone.*

The "little" for the knight's groin, associating it with the horse's brain, at first seems cold; actually, it is deeply compassionate in its irony. Together with "spilled" and "stone," it pleads the terrible precariousness and vulnerability of human life.

A second quality that has limited Ransom's audience, but that is, with his tone of ironic detachment, an important factor in his

excellence, is the quality that **F. R.** Higgins called, in reference to
W. B. Yeats, verse "tuned, as it were, slightly off the note." A good
example here, in its off-rhyme and eccentric-cam metrics, is a
stanza from the beautiful "Janet Waking":

> *One kiss she gave her mother.*
> *Only a small one gave she to her daddy*
> *Who would have kissed each curl of his shining baby;*
> *No kiss at all for her brother.*

"Probably the most of my poems are about familiar and familial situations; domestic and homely things," Ransom writes in
the commentary on his revision in *Selected Poems*. This is as mis-
leading as his Bollingen statement. "Janet Waking" is ostensibly
domestic and homely, about the death of a child's pet hen. But its
true subject is mortality, and the tragic discovery of mortality.
Beneath his familiar and familial subjects, Ransom's themes are
the great themes of poetry: love and death.

Many of Ransom's best poems are written about the point of
tension between life and death: "Dead Boy," a lament for "the old
tree's late branch wrenched away"; "Necrological"; "Bells for John
Whiteside's Daughter," in its poignant understatement seeing the
dead child as wrapped in a "brown study"; "Blue Girls," which
threatens the young and beautiful with a terrible vision of old age
and "Blear eyes fallen from blue"; "Hilda"; and "Janet Waking,"
with its magnificent conclusion:

> *And weeping fast as she had breath*
> *Janet implored us, "Wake her from her sleep!"*
> *And would not be instructed in how deep*
> *Was the forgetful kingdom of death.*

Ransom finds the vanity of human aspiration neatly symbolized in the alternation of chills and fever, the title of his second
book of verse. "Here Lies a Lady" is about a highborn lady's
death, "After six little spaces of chill, and six of burning." "Judith
of Bethulia" ends with Judith triumphant after she has killed Ho-
lofernes, as a result of which "a madness fevers our young men,"
and the poet asks, "Inflamed by the thought of her naked beauty
with desire? / Yes, and chilled with fear and despair." "Parting,
without a Sequel" shows us a girl who has permanently dismissed

her lover: "And all the time she stood there hot as fever / And cold as any icicle."

Ransom's other great theme is the tension of ungratified sexuality. This is the subject of "Spectral Lovers," where the girl's unexpressed willingness and the man's scruples turn them into spectral lovers, their unconsummated love "a bird / Whose songs shall never be heard." The finest of all of Ransom's poems, "The Equilibrists," treats the same subject with even greater richness, seeing unconsummating lovers as orbiting in an equilibrium, held in orbit by the equal pulls of honor and lust. The poem is too long to quote entire, but I must quote the stanzas in which honor and lust are translated into otherwordly alternatives:

> *In Heaven you have heard no marriage is,*
> *No white flesh tinder to your lecheries,*
> *Your male and female tissue sweetly shaped*
> *Sublimed away, and furious blood escaped.*
>
> *Great lovers lie in Hell, the stubborn ones*
> *Infatuate of the flesh upon the bones;*
> *Stuprate, they rend each other when they kiss,*
> *The pieces kiss again, no end to this.*

(Note the pun of "tinder" and "tender," the double meanings of "sublimed" and "infatuate," the powerful internal rhyme of "rend" and "end.")

A number of Ransom's poems concern themselves with knightly combat, an amusing metaphor for the intellectual jousting of literary life. He makes mocking use of such archaic and scholarly words as "ogive" (pointed arch), "thole" (endure), "pernoctated" (passed the night), and "diuturnity" (something lasting). Other poems are as far from the domestic and the homely as one can get. "Armageddon" is an amazing account of the final battle between Christ and Antichrist, seen as an odd kind of chivalric ballet. "Antique Harvesters" harvests history, in what appears to be a corner of Kentucky, with everything so numinous that even the fox pursued by spectral hunters becomes a "lovely ritualist." "Painted Head" starts as a description of a portrait and in the course of nine quatrains manages to create an aesthetics, a metaphysics, and an ethics.

The two revised poems in the book, "Master's in the Garden Again" and "Prelude to an Evening," show that after more than twenty years of poetic inactivity, Ransom has lost little of his mastery; and the modest and engaging commentary on the latter poem shows how effectively his fine critical intelligence serves his creative imagination.

As a poet, Ransom remains an original. One can see the faint influence of John Skelton in such a poem as "Somewhere Is Such a Kingdom," of John Donne in "The Equilibrists," of Thomas Hardy in "Puncture" and "Master's in the Garden Again" (the latter dedicated to him), of Wallace Stevens in "Prometheus in Straits" and "Prelude to an Evening." One can see other poems from which Robert Graves has learned, or Robert Lowell, or Howard Nemerov. But in a deeper sense, John Crowe Ransom's poetry seems to be without ancestry and descendants, to spring up timeless and beautiful like Indian pipes in deep woods, to delight our minds and refresh our hearts.

AN INEPT SYMBOLIST

I missed Guenter Grass' *The Tin Drum* when it was published in this country in a translation by Ralph Manheim. The chorus of praise for it, some from people whose judgment I respect, convinced me that I had been mistaken to pass it by. When Grass' second novel, *Cat and Mouse,* appeared, also translated by Ralph Manheim, I took advantage of the event to read both books.

My original impulse appears to have been right. I found *The Tin Drum,* despite some virtues, quite disappointing; much of it is repellent and, fatally, repellent in a boring fashion. As everyone must know by now, *The Tin Drum* is the story of Oskar Matzerath, a Danzig dwarf born in 1924, who narrates the first 30 years of his life while incarcerated in a mental hospital following his conviction for a murder he did not commit. Oskar resembles a three-year-old and often plays a child's tin drum; he had the power of shattering glass with his voice, but lost it and grew a hump instead; he believes himself to be the son of his mother's lover, and the father of his half-brother Kurt. Oskar has worked as a tombstone carver and a life model; most recently he has been a commercial success as a concert drummer, enormously popular with the elderly for the regressive fantasies that his drumming produces in them.

The book has a great deal of raw power, and many scenes are quite upsetting. These include: an encounter with an eel fisherman, lovingly shown pulling his catch out of the horse's head he uses for bait; the consequent suicide of Oskar's pregnant mother, by forcing herself to eat eels and other fish and then vomit them up; a neighbor's killing of his four tomcats with a poker when he could not stand their smell; a card game in which a dying man is forced to participate, with a poke in the ribs every time he sags; the blithe machinegunning of five nuns gathering crabs on a Normandy beach in front of a German pillbox; the mercy shooting of young sailors stuck in the portholes of a burning submarine.

Some of Grass' language is eloquent and effective. Oskar does fantasias on words; he will create an eel prayer, or a loving dialogue between two radishes. Here is Oskar meditating on his love for his stepmother Maria: "I might have my eyes vaccinated and find tears again. At the nearest butcher shop Oskar would put his heart through the meat-grinder if you would do the same with your soul. We might buy a stuffed animal to have something quiet between us." Grass' language is sometimes a little forced and spurious, as German jazz is: Oskar coughs in church, and the cough climbs into the choir and organizes a Bach society; when Oskar feels an impulse, "hedgehogs mated under the soles of my feet."

The other great strength of the book is its mockery of German hypocrisy. When a dwarf friend of Oskar's becomes Goebbels' jester, the friend describes himself as the "inward emigration." After the war, little Kurt becomes a black market businessman, specializing in lighter flints. The most successful nightclub in Duesseldorf is the Onion Cellar, serving nothing but onions, which the patrons cut up to have a good public cry. In two mad postwar vignettes, the lieutenant who ordered the machinegunning of the nuns in 1945 reappears a decade later for a military inspection of the ruined pillbox, and two German soldiers ordered to execute a Polish partisan in 1939 are seen as civilian businessmen in 1954, still obediently trying to execute him.

Some of the book is authentically funny, although the humor is always on the edge of the macabre. Oskar says of a friend that he lay in bed for days, urinating into beer bottles, when "with a little spirit of enterprise he might have urinated in the washbasin." There is an uproarious love affair between a sadist and a masochist, rising to passion each time he tramples her big toes and turns the nails black, ending sadly when new nails will no longer grow.

Having dutifully listed all the things that I can find to praise, I must now confess that they do not seem to me to add up to anything. The meaninglessness of the symbols is the major defect. Oskar's tin drum, marked as central by the book's title, at first seems to have a clear significance, when Oskar hides under rostrums and breaks up Nazi meetings by turning the marches into waltzes and Charlestons. Ah, the reader thinks, Oskar is Thoreau's different drummer, a symbol for the Other Germans. But Oskar

denies this, and says that he similarly broke up meetings of Boy
Scouts and Vegetarians. The reader soon discovers that the important feature of the drumming is hiding under the stand, as Oskar
similarly hides under the family table and under his grandmother's skirts. Eventually the drum comes to symbolize so many
things that it symbolizes nothing.

So with the other symbols. A great deal is made of an identification with Jesus. At one point a plaster statue of the boy Jesus
miraculously drums for Oskar, and at another point Oskar calls
himself "Jesus." It is all hokum, however, and Oskar is more
nearly Judas: he betrays both his legal father and his true father
to their deaths, the former in a genuinely horrifying scene. Similarly, Oskar's ability to shatter glass with his voice seems at first as
though it will turn out to be a meaningful symbol, perhaps for the
power of art. By the time Oskar sings a heart-shaped opening in a
water glass, with an engraved inscription under it, as a souvenir
for a girl midget, this too is hokum.

The Tin Drum's vision of sex is not as distasteful as *Naked
Lunch*'s only because it is less sadistic. Oskar's mother and her
lover play a kind of footsie under the card table, in which his sock-
clad foot gropes between her thighs. A married woman who tries
to take her pleasure with a live eel is bitten and maimed. Oskar is
seduced by Maria after they make a fizz drink, from fruit-flavored
powder and his saliva, in her navel; later he fights with her and
punches and bites her genitals. And so on, and so on.

Much of Grass' style is pointless mannerism. He switches at
random from the first person to the third; he retells one chapter
endlessly, beginning it again and again with slight changes. He
describes Oskar's conquest of one lady in a military metaphor,
then switches to metaphors from poetry and music; other coy
metaphors add salacity to other sexual adventures. Sometimes a
nasty detail becomes a political metaphor: the ghastly disintegra-
tion of an exhumed female corpse is a comment on the disman-
tling of industrial plants in the Ruhr and Rhineland; the inability
of two drunken lesbians to copulate makes Oskar despair of the
reunification of Germany.

It is all shapeless and random. Oskar meets a girl named Ulla
at a party and helps her throw up by putting a finger down her

throat; she soon joins him as a life model, and they are painted surrealistically, with Ulla cut open in the middle and Oskar sitting reading between her spleen and liver. What is the relationship of these details to each other? None, except that they are equally disgusting. But Swift, in *Gulliver's Travels, ordered* the disgusting and nauseating to produce a meaningful work of art. The comparable details in *The Tin Drum* seem chosen only to produce their individual *frissons*. In one scene, Oskar and his employer Korneff stand in a cemetery during a funeral, and Oskar squeezes the boils on Korneff's neck; the squeezing is described between lines of the Lord's Prayer. Why? Why not? If the eel-fishing scene is revolting, as it truly is, why not repeat it later in the book? And so Grass does. The reviews announced him as the German Joyce or Faulkner, but I am afraid that he is only the German Gregory Corso.

Grass' second novel, *Cat and Mouse,* is even more disappointing than *The Tin Drum. Cat and Mouse* is about the fixation that the adolescent narrator, Pilenz, has on a schoolfellow, Joachim Mahlke. Mahlke is a loner with a protuberant Adam's apple, a wizard at diving for salvage. In the course of the novel Mahlke outgrows his anti-war sentiments to become a heroic tank commander. When he is not allowed to make a speech at his old school, which had expelled him for stealing a veteran's Iron Cross, Mahlke kills himself. The "mouse" of the title is Mahlke's Adam's apple—I do not know why, and I do not know what the "cat" stands for—and everything Mahlke does is to distract attention from it or to conceal it.

Cat and Mouse suggests Alain-Fournier's *The Wanderer* rescored for a German brass band. It is as obsessed with the bladder as is *The Tin Drum,* and merely adds an obsession with the Adam's apple. Grass' style is even more self-conscious than it is in his first novel. Pilenz refers to Grass as "the fellow who invented us because it's his business to invent people." He starts to tell a story and breaks off with the remark: "a dismal, complicated story, which deserves to be written, but somewhere else, not by me." He wonders "who is writing this in the first place," and asks at the conclusion, "Who will supply me with a good ending?"

A little fellow pounding on a tin drum wanders through *Cat*

and Mouse, and seagulls emit "glass-cutting screams." The narrator switches pointlessly from the first person to a second-person
address to Mahlke. The symbols—cat, mouse, Adam's apple, Iron
Cross, the absurd salvaging—are again meaningless. A kind of
foreshadowing that we might call "shotgun foreshadowing" is
used to foretell Mahlke's eventual suicide: the boys predict
"Someday he's going to hang himself, or he'll get to be something
real big, or invent something terrific."

One perfect detail in *The Tin Drum* convinces me that Grass
has talent. A band of SA men wreck the toystore of a Jew named
Markus; they then go after Markus and find him slumped over his
desk, a suicide. "One of the SA men with puppets on his fingers
poked him with Kasperl's wooden grandmother." I do not think
that this gem of bitter irony justifies almost 800 pages, but it
shows that if Grass ever learns his craft, he might be quite a
writer.

IN DEFENSE OF PORNOGRAPHY

When John Cleland's *Fanny Hill* was openly published in 1963, as *Memoirs of a Woman of Pleasure*, I decided not to review it. The occasion was serious, but the book was not. Although written as a first-person memoir by a courtesan, it makes little effort to be convincing as female sexual psychology (as, say, Doris Lessing's *The Golden Notebook* is). When the New York State Supreme Court declared Cleland's book to be obscene and forbade its sale and distribution in the state, I changed my mind about reviewing it. If it does nothing else, a review gives me a chance to congratulate Walter J. Minton, the president of Putnam's, on his courage in publishing *Memoirs of a Woman of Pleasure* and fighting in the courts for his right to do so. I support him unequivocally in those actions. (Putnam's venture, I should add, would have been unlikely without the prior heroism of Barney Rosset and Grove Press in publishing *Lady Chatterley's Lover* and *Tropic of Cancer* and defending them in the courts.)

The same year, the fourth number of Ralph Ginzburg's hardbound quarterly *Eros* was declared obscene by the United States District Court in Philadelphia, along with another of Ginzburg's publications, *The Housewife's Handbook on Selective Promiscuity*, by "Rey Anthony." *Eros* seems to have been banned for a series of color photographs of embraces between a naked Negro man and a naked white girl. Since the embraces are of the most decorous sort, on the order of studying together, I can only conclude that integrated education is the issue, which makes it the responsibility of other specialists. *The Housewife's Handbook*, however, with the Cleland book, raises important questions about censorship.

Memoirs of a Woman of Pleasure seems a good example of pornography according to Judge Woolsey's distinction in the *Ulysses* case: the exploitation of obscenity with salacious intent.

Written in 1749, it tells of the sexual adventures of Fanny Hill, which increase in imaginative variety from page to page. The book has set pieces appealing to various deviant impulses: female and male homosexuality (the latter probably added by a later hand), sadism and masochism, necrophilia, voyeurism, and so forth.

The tone of the sexual descriptions is usually rapturous, particularly in regard to orgasm. Cleland's people might be squirting hot fudge sundaes into one another; "the titillating inspersion of balsamic sweets" is a typical description. Otherwise, in contrast to that of later pornography, the book's style is attractive, with an eighteenth-century distinction of language. Cleland uses no vulgar words, preferring glamorous euphemisms: sex organs are "his mighty machine" and "that luscious mouth of nature"; a rear view of a naked girl "gave somewhat the idea of a pink slash in the glossiest white satin."

Ultimately, I think, *Memoirs of a Woman of Pleasure* becomes boring to adults because of the limited possibilities of variation in these events (a fact for which Cleland several times apologizes in the book). When Fanny copulates standing on her head, *Memoirs* becomes ludicrous. The same ludicrous point is reached in *Jou Pu Tuan* (The Prayer Mat of Flesh), a Chinese seventeenth-century pornographic classic by Li Yü, when the hero progresses from going to bed with three women to going to bed with four. (In contemporary pornography, the absurdity of posture and numbers increases alarmingly.)

As *Memoirs* is a good example of pornography, *The Housewife's Handbook on Selective Promiscuity* seems a good example of obscenity, indecent material *without* salacious intent. I think this despite the offensive title, which Mrs. Anthony says she chose herself, and despite the possibility that the book is a fake. I believe it to be honest and authentic, for reasons soon to be given. It is the frank sexual autobiography or case history of a woman in her late thirties. Its revelation, says Albert Ellis in his introduction, is "that sex can actually be fun." I cannot imagine a wilder misstatement. The bald sex scenes are alternated with similarly bald accounts of the author's whitish vaginal discharge when she had a venereal disease, her dropped and protruding uterus in pregnancy, her self-disgust at not knowing whether any given child is husband's or lover's, her constant money trouble, and her inability to get up the payments for a daughter at the Plucky Poodle School (that Plucky Poodle School is one of the details that lead me to think the book authentic). The *Handbook's* true revelation is that sex can often be a pain and a mess.

What the book is most like is those dreary monologues about their troubles that one gets from hotel chambermaids as the penalty for being in the room when they come to clean it. Mrs. Anthony's main trouble is that she discovered clitoral masturbation at nine and has been fixated on it ever since; she has taught her various husbands and lovers to "massage" (her word) her clitoris to bring her to orgasm, and, since she is not much of a lubricator either, they massage her with Vaseline (I wonder how much the Chesebrough Manufacturing Company will appreciate the plug). This is surely of some interest, but any adult reader sexually excited by it must get his kicks oddly.

What makes me think the book authentic is that the language takes sad little stabs at gentility, unduplicatable by any hack or ghost writer. I italicize: "Clint had found the tips of my breasts *anew*"; simultaneous orgasm proved impractical because "it left no one *at the helm, so to speak*"; "he read a *piercingly* lovely poem to me" (it is by Irwin Edman). The book's lengthy recital of the author's opinions about sex in its emotional, institutional, and legal aspects is as inauthentic as her slightly prissy language is authentic; I assume that she got the opinions from the pile of marriage manuals that one of her lovers presented to her.

I am, then, not a very good witness for the defense, since I believe that both books are suppressible under the law. But the law is wrong. Neither book should be banned; in fact no publication should be banned. I realize that this is the quixotic position of Justice Black, who finds censorship of any kind unconstitutional according to the first amendment's clear statement: "Congress shall make no law . . . abridging the freedom of speech, or of the press." With him, I believe that this means exactly what it says, not the more reasonable and limited thing that we have taken it to mean (as we have similarly corrected those Gospel absolutes about turning the other cheek and loving our enemies).

The argument for the censorship of pornography and obscenity is based on the harmful consequences, to the reader and to society, that are alleged to follow from such reading: masturbation, loss of chastity, fornication, perversion and homosexuality, rape and child violation. In regard to masturbation, I do not believe that it requires any such stimulus. As for loss of chastity, I share Jimmy Walker's doubt that anyone ever got seduced by a book, but if two pure young people *were* to read a book and pop into bed as a consequence, I would answer with D. H. Lawrence, "One up to them!" These books may teach and encourage a wider range of heterosexual activity, oral and anal as well as genital, and should be welcomed if they do. I do not believe that they encourage homosexuality or crimes of sexual violence; I think that they discourage the former by assuaging Oedipal guilts, and make the latter less likely through cathartic release.

All this is hypothetical, since no one knows the effects of such reading on behavior. In 1943, Dr. Glenn V. Ramsey published a list in the *American Journal of Psychology* of what had actually proven sexually exciting to 291 young boys. It included sitting in class, taking a shower, sitting in church, urinating, taking tests, finding money, and hearing the national anthem. None of these seem bannable, except perhaps the national anthem.

While John Cleland is not legally allowed to stimulate sexual desire, whole industries—fashion and advertising, perfume and cosmetics—work at it full time. Mrs. Anthony is not allowed to tell our youngsters what it feels like when a woman is sexually satisfied, but a whole literature tells them with impunity what it feels like when a woman is beaten, kicked, burned, stabbed, or shot. The real corrupter of our youth is sadism, not sex, as that pioneer G. Legman argued in *Love & Death* in 1949, but even here censorship seems inadvisable.

If there were bad consequences of the abolition of censorship, they might be outweighed by the good consequences. Ruth Benedict's classic study, "Continuities and Discontinuities in Cultural Conditioning," in *Psychiatry* in 1938, shows that adolescence is so great a crisis in our culture because our culture is discontinuous, and the adolescent must painfully unlearn one set of standards and learn their opposite. In regard to sex, we expect a sexless child and a sexually uninhibited adult. As Mrs. Benedict shows, many of our adults cannot "unlearn the wickedness or the danger-ousness of sex." "It is not surprising," she adds, "that in such a society many individuals fear to use behavior which has up to that time been under a ban and trust instead, though at great psychic cost, to attitudes that have been exercised with approval during their formative years." The greatest single advantage of the aboli-tion of censorship, it seems to me, would be to make our culture more continuous, helping to free child and adult from fear, inhibi-tion, and guilt.

The open distribution of pornography and obscenity would thus encourage heterosexuality, and discourage impotence and frigidity. As such, it is life-giving, a stimulous to joy and a source of socially harmless pleasure. Despite the forces of censorship, sexual intercourse is not a depraved and shameful vice. It is a normal body function, habitual to the judge's parents, George Washington, and many leaders of the Girl Scouts. It will become habitual to our innocent daughters, or we should hope that it will.

The true defense of pornography and obscenity, as they en-courage sexuality, is that they are harmless or beneficial. I agree with the bawd in *Memoirs,* who "considered pleasure, of one sort or another, as the universal port of destination, and every wind that blew thither a good one, provided it blew nobody any harm." In regard to censorship, the argument from literary merit is ab-surd and irrelevant. Of course no work of serious literature should ever be banned, but Anthony Lewis, in his article "Sex—and the Supreme Court" in *Esquire,* June 1963, is probably right in saying that after the Supreme Court's Roth decision "no serious literary work can now be termed constitutionally obscene."

Despite such temporary setbacks as the recent ruling by the New York State Court of Appeals that *Tropic of Cancer* is ob-scene, that battle appears to be won. It is the works "without the slightest redeeming social importance" that must be freed from censorship, or, rather, that sexual stimulation by symbol and im-age be recognized, in our time of bad marriages and worse non-marriages, as having redeeming social importance. I am aware that, the conditions of legislative reelection being what they are,

obscenity laws are effectively unalterable at present. Then, judi-
cial appointment being what *it* is, let them not be enforced.

As for the fact that so much pornography and obscenity is
dreadful, that the *Memoirs* and the *Handbook* are not the worst
of it but more nearly the best of it, that is a problem for literary
criticism, not for jurisprudence. Leave them to the strangler's
hands of the critic. It is his responsibility to say that Rechy's *City
of Night* is illiterate trash, or Burroughs' *Naked Lunch* sadistic
slop. But let them be published, and let those who want them buy
them and read them. Experience and taste will save us, those of us
who want to be saved.

A JAPANESE MASTER

My favorite painting in all the world is one that I have never seen. It is "Portrait of Taira Shigemori" by the medieval Japanese painter Takanobu, and it is in a private collection in Tokyo. I know it from a color reproduction in André Malraux's *The Voices of Silence,* and every time I look at it again I am left breathless with wonder and delight. I feel (as Malraux meant me to feel) that this painting communicates perfectly to me across great barriers of time and culture.

Some Japanese prints, less powerfully, give me the same experience, but Japanese literature does not. The poetry seems to me entirely untranslatable, reading in English as faint rubbings of vanished poems. The few Japanese novels that I have read tended to leave me with a vague feeling of having missed the point. When she dyes a syllable of his name on her kimono, or he gives her the smaller segments of the tangerine, it is enormously significant, is it not? But significant of what, exactly?

In 1963 I picked up Junichiro Tanizaki's *Seven Japanese Tales,* translated by Howard Hibbett. Before I had finished the first tale, "A Portrait of Shunkin," I knew that I was in the presence of a master, and that, however native Tanizaki's fiction might be, it is also securely within the tradition of European literature. I had the sense of immediate communication that the Takanobu portrait gives me.

I was a little late coming to him. Tanizaki (now dead) was then 77; he had been publishing for more than 50 years; he was said to be Japan's greatest living writer; and he was a strong candidate for the Nobel Prize. Three of his novels have been published in this country: *Some Prefer Nettles* in 1955, *The Makioka Sisters* in 1957, and *The Key* in 1961. After reading all except the first, I am lost in admiration for Tanizaki's talents and variety.

Two of the novellas in *Seven Japanese Tales* are master-

pieces. My favorite, "A Portrait of Shunkin" (1933), is like nothing else I have ever read. It is the story of a female monster and
her devoted slave. Shunkin is a blind samisen virtuoso and Sasuke
is a former servant of her family and pupil of hers, who himself
becomes a samisen master. He cares for her, runs her school, and
they live together and have children. She will not marry him because of his social inferiority, however, and the children are sent
out for adoption.

The novella rises to two related horrors. In the first, Shunkin,
probably in revenge for her sadistic and rapacious treatment of
pupils, is disfigured by an unknown attacker, who throws a kettle-
ful of boiling water on her face as she sleeps. Shunkin makes Sasuke promise never to look at her ravaged face, and he keeps his
promise by blinding himself with a sewing needle. These awful
deeds, which arouse the sort of pity and terror that the self-
discovery and self-blinding of King Oedipus do, result in a love of
serene beauty. When Sasuke tells Shunkin of his act, she for the
first time feels respect and love for him, and they embrace, weeping. "I am inclined to think," the narrator comments, "that the
destruction of her beauty had its compensations for Shunkin in
various ways. Both in love and in art she must have discovered
undreamed-of ecstasies."

There are a number of exotic Japanese customs in the novella, but Tanizaki's craft makes the details of nightingale singing
or lark soaring, Shunkin's hobbies, seem as reasonable and familiar as my own pursuits. They are not put in for local color; they
function symbolically in the story. The nightingales, which must
be taken from the nest in infancy and carefully trained to sing
artificial calls, perfectly symbolize the exactions of art; and Shunkin's prized lark, which soars up and never returns, bears with it
her sight, her beauty, and her life.

The horror and ecstasy of the novella are kept in perfect tension by a narrator, a masterly creation, who endlessly questions,
speculates, and doubts. Thus we see Sasuke's fanatic joy in sacrifice through the eyes of a man who cannot comprehend it (Melville uses the same device in "Bartleby the Scrivener" and "Benito
Cereno"). The narrator's skepticism at the end of the story is perfect: "It seems that when the priest Gazan of the Tenryu Temple

heard the story of Sasuke's self-immolation, he praised him for the
Zen spirit with which he changed his whole life in an instant,
turning the ugly into the beautiful, and said that it was very
nearly the act of a saint. I wonder how many of us would agree
with him."

The other superb novella in the book is "The Bridge of
Dreams" (1959). It is another disturbing and perverse study of
devotion, now in a recurring chain. The narrator's father is so devoted to his first wife that he gives his second wife her name and
turns the second into a facsimile of the first; the second wife loves
her husband so devotedly that when she has a child by him she
sends it out for adoption, so that her predecessor's son may retain
all her maternal love. The narrator, Tadasu, loves his stepmother
(who has entirely merged with his mother in his mind) to the
point of marrying, after his father's death, in order to have someone to take care of his stepmother; after she dies he divorces his
wife and takes his half-brother, who "looks exactly like Mother,"
to live with him.

The story is thus a succession of ingrown triangles. These
relationships are perverse and symbolically incestuous: Tadasu
suckled at his mother's breasts until he was four; his stepmother
encourages him to continue the habit, and he suckles at her dry
breasts until he is 13; when her baby is sent away, Tadasu, then
19, sucks the milk from her breasts. He suffers "an agony of
shame" until he realizes that his father must have arranged it all.
In this perversity, again, there is great beauty. The various trios sit
by the garden pond to enjoy the cool of the evening, with one
mother or another dangling her feet in the water while father or
son drinks beer, happy and at peace in their web of ties.

The symbolic resonance that birdsong brings to "A Portrait of
Shunkin" is obtained here by poetry and one odd symbol. The
novella begins on a poem, "On reading the last chapter of *The
Tale of Genji*," written by one or the other of Tadasu's mothers.
Other poems are quoted about the stream, or are inscribed on the
gates of Heron's Nest (their house), or are mounted on the transom, or come to the narrator's mind in connection with some feature of the house. The effect is to cover Heron's Nest with a patina
of order and beauty, so that the perverse attachments of the mem-

bers of the family can be recognized as the corruption of traditional virtues.

The odd symbol is a "water mortar," a hollow bamboo tube under the pond's inlet, designed to clack regularly as it fills and empties. As an infant sleeping at his mother's breast, Tadasu heard the clack of the water mortar in his dreams; it is disconnected when his father is dying, and is started up again after the funeral. It seems to symbolize the security and reassurance that are the goals of the characters' neurotic attachments.

Ultimately, though, the water mortar remains mysterious, a voice not quite explainable by either hydraulics or psychoanalysis. All the mysteries of this uncanny novella remain: we never learn what the real reason is for anything, or which mother wrote the poem, or even whether Tadasu's wife killed his stepmother, as he suspects that she did. The title symbol, the bridge of dreams, is at once the title of the last chapter of *Genji* (where it represents Life), the footbridge over the pond at Heron's Nest, and Father's dying words (which well represent his Faustian ambition, handed on to the others, to bridge love across death).

The best of the other stories, "A Blind Man's Tale" (1931) is a historical novella about the warlord civil wars of the sixteenth century; its theme is likewise devotion, the lifelong loyalty of the narrator, a blind minstrel and masseur, to his noble lady. The other four are short, and much less impressive. They are: "The Tattooer" (1910), "Terror" (1913), "The Thief" (1921), and "Aguri" (1922). I think that, as was the case with Chekhov, Tanizaki needs the roominess of the larger form for his highest artistry.

The two novels that I have read further display Tanizaki's range. *The Makioka Sisters* is an excellent novel of a sort that does not very much interest me, the long realistic family chronicle. Its action is the struggle to get the third sister, Yukiko, properly married; when that is achieved the novel ends. Meanwhile Tanizaki has taken us through "the most disastrous flood in the history of the Kobe-Osaka district," "the worst typhoon" to hit Tokyo "in over ten years," and the China Incident. The book communicates the very texture of Japanese life, and that is the trouble. When, on their honeymoon, Teinosuke asks his wife Sachiko to name her favorite fish, and she names sea bream, this is not some powerful symbol of her aspirations, as are Shunkin's nightingale or Tadasu's water mortar; it is just her taste in fish.

The Key is something else again. Hardly longer than a novella, it is a sensual and melodramatic story, told in His and Hers diaries, of a professor's debauching of his innocent wife, so successfully that she kills him to live with her lover, who will be married for convenience to her daughter. Ikuko is another monster, another Shunkin, but here we watch the process of manufacture.

Tanizaki's theme is not really devotion, but devotion curdled into neurotic fixation. In the fashion of Japanese culture, he is very matter-of-fact about the body. What is quite remarkable is the way Tanizaki combines this with a sense of the body's mystery. There is no matter-of-factness, but a burning sensuality, in the professor's photographing his wife naked in *The Key*, published when the author was 70, or in Tadasu at his stepmother's breasts in "The Bridge of Dreams," published when the author was 73.

In this respect, as in many others, Tanizaki reminds me of the Leskov of "Lady Macbeth of the Mtensk District." If one cannot be Tolstoi or Dostoevsky, it is not too bad to be Leskov.

NABOKOV'S GIFT

"I have no desire to twist and batter an unambiguous *apparatus criticus* into the monstrous semblance of a novel," says the mad critic Charles Kinbote in *Pale Fire*. He succeeded in producing the most ambiguous *apparatus criticus* imaginable, and his maniacal creator, Vladimir Nabokov, twisted and battered that into the finest comic novel since *Ulysses*. 1963 marks the first English publication of Nabokov's last novel written in Russian, *The Gift* (1937), translated by Michael Scammell with the collaboration of the author. It is as marvelous in its own way as *Pale Fire*, and it displays another variety of the same fantastic form: the novel as both literary criticism and the spoof of literary criticism.

One would have to know a great deal more than I do about Russian literature to get all the references and parodies in *The Gift*. (This neatly reverses *Pale Fire*, where poor Kinbote didn't know enough about America to realize that Chapman's Homer was a home run hit by Sam Chapman.) The story itself, told alternately in the first and third person, is simple and delightful. Two young émigré Russians, Fyodor Godunov-Cherdyntsev and Zina Mertz, fall in love in Berlin about 1925. Fyodor is a poet and a *schlemiel:* when he goes swimming in the park, his clothes are inevitably stolen; when he spends his last coin to telephone Zina, of course he gets the wrong number. This figure of fun is nevertheless brilliant, talented, and good. Zina, the landlady's daughter, has "burning, melting, sorrowing lips," and is one of the two admirers of Fyodor's verse in the world. She is the principal "gift" of the title, and the tricks of fate that bring the two together are the novel's subject, or at least its plot.

We get glimpses of this chaste and tender love story, as though it were a lovely meadow, through periodic gaps in a fantastically elaborate topiary hedge, the literary criticism. Nabokov writes of the book, in his foreword: "Its heroine is not Zina, but

Russian literature. The plot of Chapter One centers in Fyodor's poems. Chapter Two is a surge toward Pushkin in Fyodor's literary progress and contains his attempt to describe his father's zoological explorations. Chapter Three shifts to Gogol, but its real hub is the love poem dedicated to Zina. Fyodor's book on Chernyshevski, a spiral within a sonnet, takes care of Chapter Four. The last chapter combines all the preceding themes and adumbrates the book Fyodor dreams of writing some day: *The Gift*."

Nor is this the half of it. There are long literary discussions, of the greatest brilliance, that Fyodor has with another poet, Koncheyev, in his imagination. The metrical theories of Andrey Bely are explained and illustrated. Fyodor endlessly meditates on earlier Russian writers, and his biography continually measures Chernyshevski against them. Fyodor quotes Marx in blank verse, "so it would be less boring." Chapter Four, the biography, is framed between the sestet and octave of a sonnet to Chernyshevski, making what Nabokov calls "a spiral within a sonnet." The last paragraph of the book conceals a parody Pushkin stanza.

As passionately as Fyodor loves Zina, Nabokov loves Words. The book's language dances and sparkles. An oil slick on the pavement is "asphalt's parakeet." After he has been writing poetry, Fyodor is unable to sleep because "discarded word-shells obstructed and chafed his brain and prickled his temples." A streetcar is "rare, almost legendary," and a lawyer is "repulsively small, almost portable." Of a symbiotic caterpillar-ant relationship, Nabokov writes: "It was as if cows gave us Chartreuse and we gave them our infants to eat." Sentences in *The Gift*, in the complexity of their syntax and the thrust of their images and metaphors, are poems. Here is a typical one:

> He was walking along streets that had already long since insinuated themselves into his acquaintance—and as if that were not enough, they expected affection; they had even purchased in advance, in his future memories, space next to St. Petersburg, an adjacent grave; he walked along these dark, glossy streets and the blind houses retreated, backing or sidling into the brown sky of the Berlin night, which, nevertheless, had its soft spots here and there, spots that would melt under one's gaze, allowing it to obtain a few stars.

Nabokov writes in the foreword: "I am not, and never was, Fyodor Godunov-Cherdyntsev; my father is not the explorer of Central Asia that I still may become some day; I never wooed Zina Mertz, and never worried about the poet Koncheyev or any other writer. In fact, it is rather in Koncheyev, as well as in another incidental character, the novelist Vladimirov, that I distinguish odds and ends of myself as I was circa 1925." Reading this characteristic disclaimer, one is immediately reminded of the Freudian negative: The patient said the person in his dream was not his mother; so, then, it was his mother.

Of course Fyodor Godunov-Cherdyntsev is Vladimir Nabokov, and Zina Mertz is the wife Véra to whom he has dedicated a number of his books, including this one. Fyodor's childhood experiences repeat again and again those Nabokov recalls in his memoir, *Conclusive Evidence;* Fyodor's poems parody Nabokov's poems; in fact, in the 1920s, Nabokov published his verse in émigré journals over the name "Godunov-Cherdyntsev." My consultant in Russian literature, to whom I am indebted for that last fact, also tells me that Koncheyev is the poet Vladislav Khodasevich, described with apparent irrelevance in *The Gift's* foreword as "the greatest Russian poet that the twentieth century has yet produced."

The book, then, is Nabokov's mockery of himself, his writing, and his courtship of his wife, but it is a gentle and affectionate mockery. In similarly denying that the book is autobiographical in a recent BBC interview, Nabokov made the interesting statement: "I am very careful to keep my characters beyond the limits of my own identity." The truth behind this remark is that Nabokov inflates his self-portraits beyond the limits of his own identity. Fyodor is only one in a series of grotesque and wonderful self-caricatures—Humbert Humbert, Timofey Pnin, Charles Kinbote —and is the least grotesque and most engaging of them. In disguise in *The Gift,* Nabokov is able to parody and criticize his own work. A description of Fyodor's faults as a writer, given by Koncheyev in a dialogue Fyodor imagines, is, with Mary McCarthy's admirable review of *Pale Fire* in *The New Republic,* the best Nabokov criticism we have.

Along with Nabokov's passion for language, as great as that

of Joyce, is a preoccupation with the-past-recalled-by-memory, comparable to that of Proust. "Strange, strange are the mishaps of memory," Fyodor writes, dredging up an American dentist with a French mistress from his St. Petersburg childhood. Fyodor's poems are reminiscences of childhood, his individual memories; his book on Chernyshevski is something like a national or collective memory. This nineteenth-century Russian revolutionary seems at first the least likely person for Nabokov to write about; he clearly, with Fyodor, detests him. But the detestation and mockery combine with a deep human sympathy and compassion, and the result is a biography that is frequently uproarious and ultimately heartbreaking.

But Chernyshevski, too, images—mirrors, really—Nabokov. His dreadful twenty years of Siberian exile are an ironic commentary on Nabokov's own exile from Russia, caused by men claiming to be Chernyshevski's heirs. The Minister of Justice who finally freed Chernyshevski was Nabokov's paternal grandfather, Dmitri, after whom Nabokov's son is named. And Chernyshevski, as a rebel against the Little Father, must obscurely speak for impulses deep in Nabokov, who loves and worships his wonderful father in *Conclusive Evidence*, as Fyodor loves and worships *his* wonderful father in *The Gift*.

Without pages of quotation it is hard to convey the brilliance and verbal corruscation of *The Gift*. Nabokov invents a painter and a whole series of loony paintings to go with him. When a foolish playwright stands up to read from his work, Nabokov writes a foolish play for him. Fyodor's father teaching him about butterflies and moths becomes a little lepidopteral treatise; Fyodor's father on an expedition to Central Asia becomes an article out of the *National Geographic*. To greet Fyodor's book on Chernyshevski, Nabokov writes a series of parody reviews, including one charging that Fyodor invented a biographer (as I do not doubt that he did). A meeting of the Society of Russian Writers in Germany is the funniest scene I can recall since the Marx brothers split up.

The earliest of Nabokov's Russian novels available in English is *Camera Obscura* (published here as *Laughter in the Dark*), written in 1925, when he was 26. It is a sour and cruel comedy about the torments of a blind man. By the time of *The Gift,* 12 years later, Nabokov had become genial and benign. The mockery in *The Gift* is kindly, and, if everyone gets sandpapered a little, no one gets flayed. (No Russians, anyway. Fyodor detests the Germans, and they are consistently portrayed in the book as fat, ugly, stupid, cruel, authoritarian, and swinish.)

One of the nicest inventions in *Pale Fire* is the Zemblan word *alfear,* defined as "uncontrollable fear caused by elves." We need a word (*nablaf?*) for uncontrollable laughter caused by Nabokov. He is wonderfully funny, while at the same time he is wonderfully serious. His books are intricate puzzles, Chinese ivories, Fabergé eggs; they represent the triumph of artifice. But his themes are profound: the interpenetration of illusion and reality in *Pale Fire;* the interpenetration of art and life in *The Gift.* Nabokov is a unique phenomenon in our literature (no one has yet had the temerity to imitate him except Thomas Pynchon in *V.*), as he was a unique phenomenon in Russian literature. *Pale Fire* and *The Gift,* which continually threaten to shatter the novel form, turn out finally to be enlargements of it, as *Ulysses* and *Finnegans Wake* are. It is about time we recognized that Vladimir Nabokov is a novelist of major importance.

THE GREAT FITZGERALD

In 1922, after he had published *This Side of Paradise, The Beautiful and Damned,* and two volumes of short stories, all in two years, F. Scott Fitzgerald was somewhat in the position of J. D. Salinger today. He was accepted as the spokesman for a generation, the flappers and their hip-flask escorts; he had a vast personal following that would buy anything he wrote; he was himself a legendary figure. Fitzgerald was 26 years of age, and things would never again be as good.

By 1925, Fitzgerald was writing to a friend, "I want to be extravagantly admired again," but *The Great Gatsby* disappointed Fitzgerald's jazz-age public, and his reputation began its slow decline. His next novel, *Tender Is the Night,* did not appear until nine years later. It was neither a critical nor a popular success, and the decline became precipitous. In 1939, *The Great Gatsby* was dropped from the Modern Library because it sold too slowly, leaving not one of Fitzgerald's books in print. When Fitzgerald died in December, 1940, his reputation was at the lowest point it could reach.

The slow recovery began in 1941, with the posthumous publication of the unfinished *The Last Tycoon.* Rehabilitation was greatly accelerated in 1945, when Edmund Wilson edited a respectful miscellany, *The Crack-Up.* By 1951, there was a Fitzgerald boom going, and that year there were four books: Budd Schulberg's "novel," Arthur Mizener's biography, a collection of essays on Fitzgerald edited by Alfred Kazin, and a collection of stories edited by Malcolm Cowley. By 1958, when Sheilah Graham's *Beloved Infidel* revived Fitzgerald-the-legendary-figure, all the novels were back in print. In 1961 *Tender Is the Night* alone sold more than half a million copies, in four editions. In 1962, a letter from Fitzgerald to Maxwell Perkins, his editor at Scribners, sold at auction in London for 7,000 pounds, almost

$20,000. In 1963 there were at least six books on Fitzgerald, and he has visibly become an industry. If only Fitzgerald could have lived to see it—how he might have laughed.

Fitzgerald's early idolators adored him for the wrong reasons; in the years of scorn he was neglected for the wrong reasons; perhaps now he is again being celebrated for the wrong reasons. Two books, Andrew Turnbull's editing of *The Letters of F. Scott Fitzgerald* and Arthur Mizener's editing of *The Fitzgerald Reader,* give us a look at quite a lot of the evidence. What was he really like, this fallen and risen idol, and how good was he really?

The Letters, which includes the more interesting half of all of Fitzgerald's surviving letters, gives us rather a blurred image. The letters to his daughter Scottie are warm, moving, and—really—those of a terrible father. The effect of all his love and responsibility was to impose an identification on her ("because you are so much like me"), and to nag her most cruelly (*"you* have spent two years doing no useful work at all, improving neither your body nor your mind, but only writing reams and reams of dreary letters to dreary people").

The letters to Perkins and to Harold Ober, Fitzgerald's agent, show the dirty underbelly of the literary life. Fitzgerald complains to Perkins in 1921 that his novel has not been advertised in Montgomery, Alabama, although Floyd Dell's has; in 1933 he sends Perkins a snapshot "which enlarges to a nice 6 x 10 glossy suitable for rotogravures." The letters to Ober progress from boasting to whining, from begging to abusing.

Where we can see Fitzgerald most clearly, the image is still blurred, because *he* was blurred. There is one particularly revealing letter, written in 1920 to an aunt and uncle. Fitzgerald writes: "I'd rather live on less and preserve the one duty of a sincere writer—to set down life as he sees it." A few paragraphs later he adds, with no sense of contradiction: "But I am not averse to taking all the shekels I can garner from the movies. I'll roll them joy pills (the literary habit) till doomsday."

Intermixed with all the marks of weakness, marks of woe, are passages of profound self-understanding and truth. Fitzgerald writes to his daughter with great insight: "I am too much of a moralist at heart and really want to preach at people in some acceptable form rather than to entertain them." "Writing is a sheer paring away of oneself leaving always something thinner, barer, more meager," he writes to Scottie. To his wife, Zelda, varying the metaphor: "I'm digging it out of myself like uranium—one ounce to the cubic ton of rejected ideas." "I am his [Hemingway's] alcoholic just like Ring is mine," he writes to Perkins, and, some years later, "In a *small* way I was an original."

The Fitzgerald Reader seeks "to give the reader a representative selection" of Fitzgerald's work, by which Mizener means a selection of the best, as the jacket more accurately acknowledges. Included are the whole of *The Great Gatsby*, the first seven chapters of *Tender Is the Night*, three chapters from *The Last Tycoon*, 15 stories, and four articles. Everything that Fitzgerald wrote was autobiographical, surely, but Mizener, whose interest in Fitzgerald seems largely biographical, has chosen the most self-revealing stories and articles. He has then presumptuously grouped his selections into four biographical sections, which are called "Winter Dreams," "The Crack-Up," "Pasting It Together," and "Handling It with Care," as though Fitzgerald's primary importance to literature were that he had had a breakdown.

Fitzgerald's primary importance to literature is that at his best he was a marvelous writer. Even his poor stories show flashes of brilliance. A preposterous story called "May Day" has one fine moment, when Edith says: "I think it's a perfect insult to call anyone a good woman in that way. It's a slam. You've been drinking, Gordon." "Winter Dreams" becomes weak and evasive at the end, but it begins with absolute authority: "Some of the caddies were poor as sin and lived in one-room houses with a neurasthenic cow in the front yard, but Dexter Green's father owned the second best grocery-store in Black Bear—the best one was 'The Hub,' patronized by the wealthy people from Sherry Island—and Dexter caddied only for pocket-money."

As nothing in Fitzgerald is hopeless, so nothing is quite flawless either. *Gatsby* is almost a perfect novel, but it has one scene as bad as anything Fitzgerald ever wrote (the drunks in the wrecked car) and it presents seriously one of his silliest aphorisms ("There are only the pursued, the pursuing, the busy and the tired"). An otherwise good and effective story, "The Rich Boy," is fatally injured by the false and cowardly scene where Anson declines to ravish Dolly because a picture of his true love appears before his eyes. A very funny self-mockery, "Financing Finnegan," goes suddenly flat at the end.

The best of Fitzgerald is matchless. "Absolution," which I consider his one completely successful short story, in its beginning and end rises to an intensity of vision almost Blakean. Scene after scene in *The Great Gatsby* shows absolute mastery: Gatsby's stretching out his arms to the green light at the end of Daisy's dock; the reunion of Gatsby and Daisy, with Daisy crying into the heap of his beautiful shirts; Daisy and Tom sitting over cold fried chicken and ale, after Daisy has killed Tom's mistress; Nick's final thoughts. *The Last Tycoon* has such miracles too: Kathleen's first appearance, floating on a head of Siva; the telephone call from the orang-outang; Stahr and Kathleen, after their carnal congress, sitting with the soles of their shoes touching; the Emersonian Negro on the beach.

Most of the stories in *The Fitzgerald Reader* are terrible. The earlier ones are mainly wishful fantasies. Fitzgerald sees himself rich and "black with tan" in "'The Sensible Thing,'" or quarterbacking the freshman team to victory in "Basil and Cleopatra," or giving up the bottle to care for the little girl in "Family in the Wind." The later ones are contrived and gimmicky, such as "'I Didn't Get Over,'" or self-pitying, such as "The Lost Decade."

Fitzgerald was a writer with only one story to tell: the story of his life. In his inferior work he told it transparently, with gossamer disguises. His young heroes get rich and win their Zeldas, not by writing, but by engineering in Peru; when he goes to Hollywood, his older heroes are "lucky in the market"; his forgotten celebrity, who has been on a ten-year binge, was once a famous architect.

In his superior work, on the other hand, Fitzgerald managed to get some aesthetic distance from himself as subject, by feats of splitting, dissociation, and combination. Gatsby was based on a man Fitzgerald knew, combined with the romantic half of Fitzgerald (the realist half became Nick Carroway, the narrator). In just the seven chapters of *Tender Is the Night* included in the

Reader: Tommy Barban has Fitzgerald's good looks; Abe North is a composite of Ring Lardner's wit and Fitzgerald's pranks and lack of productivity; Rosemary, awed and gushy at Dick Diver, is Fitzgerald awed and gushy at Gerald Murphy; Diver himself combines Murphy's strengths and Fitzgerald's weaknesses.

The splittings and combinations of Fitzgerald in *The Last Tycoon* are even more astonishing. The narrator, Cecilia Brady, is Fitzgerald himself, all swoony at the thought of Irving Thalberg; turned into young Budd Schulberg to have a narrator who grew up in Hollywood; then, turned into a girl because Scottie's father knows how she would see certain things. The part of himself that was involved with Sheilah Graham, Fitzgerald blends with Thalberg to make Monroe Stahr; the wry, failed writer part becomes Wylie White. And so on.

Lunatic as this process sounds, it was necessary to enable Fitzgerald to write his finest work, and his finest work—"Absolution," *Gatsby*, parts of *Tender* and *Tycoon*—is small in quantity but just as great as they say. Gatsby is Great because he transforms himself into a work of art, and Fitzgerald was great only when he was able to accomplish the same thing.

SEEING FITZGERALD PLAIN

In the last essay I tried to construct an image and estimate of F. Scott Fitzgerald from a volume of his letters and a selection of his writings. The image came out a little blurry, because the man contained multitudes, and the estimate found him variously the best writer and the worst writer of our time. Since these feats of construction, in an effort to compare my opinions with those of my peers, I have read four more 1963 books dealing with Fitzgerald.

Kenneth Eble's *F. Scott Fitzgerald*, a volume in the United States Authors series, is a short introductory study. Eble gives a lot of critical attention to the stories: because they have been relatively neglected, he says in the introduction; but really because he likes them, as the book makes clear. Eble has some impressive insights. He calls attention to "Fitzgerald's singular ability to dignify the trivial while remaining faintly ironic toward it"; he says that Gatsby's death, "mean as it is, affects a reader in a tragic way"; he points out "the hard core of morality" that Fitzgerald has in common with Melville, Hawthorne, and James.

In general, Eble's estimate of Fitzgerald's work seems to me just, even his suggestion that *The Great Gatsby* may be the greatest novel between *Huckleberry Finn* and *The Catcher in the Rye*. He consistently overpraises the stories: the Basil Duke Lee yarns are "excellent in craftsmanship." "The Ice Palace" is "as good a story as Fitzgerald ever wrote," and so on. Eble even finds the novels "often weaker in total effect than the stories of which they are made." Except for this overestimate, and such whimsies as describing Fitzgerald's three essays on his crack-up as "one of the superb short stories in American literature," Eble's book is a sensible and good one.

So much cannot be said for William Goldhurst's *F. Scott Fitzgerald and His Contemporaries*, which comes jacketed with high praise from Harry Levin. Goldhurst's book is the product of a wonderful idea—to present a writer as a series of interactions with other writers—but Goldhurst is not up to it. (The other writers are Edmund Wilson, H. L. Mencken, Ring Lardner, and Ernest Hemingway.) Instead of delicate interactions, Goldhurst creates iron shackles: Fitzgerald "dare not" give a character anti-German sentiments "for fear of including himself among the super-patriots against whom Mencken fulminated"; Lardner "contributed important elements to *The Great Gatsby*"; Hemingway's style "left an indelible impression" on *Tender Is the Night*.

Goldhurst writes the limpest imaginable language. What is Myrtle Wilson doing in *The Great Gatsby?* She is having "an adulterous affair" with Tom Buchanan. Who is Tom Buchanan? He is "the unscrupulous and well-to-do representative of Fitzgerald's American 'aristocracy.' " How does his wife, Daisy, occupy herself? "She indulges in an adulterous liaison with Jay Gatsby." To pursue another line of questioning, did Fitzgerald attend Princeton? No, he went to the "tree-shaded campus of Princeton." What did he have when he got out? He had "a plenitude of youth, ideas, and promise." What happened when Scribners accepted his first novel? "The youthful author who a few months earlier had tasted the sobering drafts of defeat now found himself intoxicated on the wine of his achievement." What did Wilson's opinions of that novel do? They "left a lasting impression." Who gave *The Last Tycoon* "a memorable reception"? "American critics and fictionists."

This Alger language fittingly clothes Goldhurst's ideas. He is a great dispeller of notions that no one ever held for a moment. My favorite passage in his book, for its true graduate school whiff, contrasts Fitzgerald and Lardner in their "treatment of Florida," and has a footnote beginning: "Others writers of the period also left impressions of Florida." My favorite fact is: "But it was not until *The Great Gatsby* that Fitzgerald introduced the game of baseball into his fiction." For utter insensitivity, there is an account of Wolfsheim in *Gatsby* as a type of "alien outsider" similar to Cohn in *The Sun Also Rises;* for perfect owlishness, there is Goldhurst quoting "La Belle Dame Sans Merci" to characterize the Divers' marriage in *Tender*.

One turns with relief to Matthew J. Bruccoli's *The Composition of* Tender Is the Night. Bruccoli's book is a pioneer technical study, and he has wrestled for years (as Fitzgerald wrestled before him) with 3,500 pages of manuscript, representing three different versions of the novel in 17 drafts. In the first few pages one is put off by Bruccoli's inept writing. He misuses "fulsomely" to mean something like "handsomely"; he refers to "J. B. Priestly"; he isn't content to call something "balderdash," it must be "lugubrious balderdash"; and he uses such pointless poetic inversions as "This key to the understanding of Dick Diver, Fitzgerald in the end has failed to give."

But Bruccoli is a real scholar and critic, his book is a useful and important one, and his prose is not all that bad. Sometimes he puts an insight beautifully, as in his statement that Dick does not seduce Rosemary "so much as he accepts her pity in the form of her body." Bruccoli not only shows what Fitzgerald changed in rewriting, but he makes sensible conjectures about the reasons for the changes, even where he has to contradict Fitzgerald's own explanations in the process. In the course of his study Bruccoli explodes a number of fallacies generally believed by the Fitzgeraldines: that *Tender* was killed by social-conscious reviews, that its flashback structure was an afterthought, that it was cut down from a much larger novel, and so on. The reader finishes Bruccoli's book with an enormous admiration for Fitzgerald's painstaking craftsmanship, and for Bruccoli's skilled archaeology in reconstructing it.

Arthur Mizener's collection of critical essays, *F. Scott Fitzgerald,* is a volume in the Twentieth Century Views series. Its 17 essays give us a look at the whole spectrum of Fitzgerald criticism. Two of the essays are first-rate, perhaps the best things yet written on Fitzgerald. One is Lionel Trilling's "F. Scott Fitzgerald," published in 1945. Trilling is bold enough to compare Fitzgerald with Goethe, perceptive enough to see that the technique of *The Great Gatsby* is essentially ideographic, with that of *The Waste Land* (and Pound's *Cantos*), and eloquent enough to say that, with his remark that if Daisy ever loved Tom "it was just personal," Gatsby "achieves an insane greatness." The other essay is William Troy's "Scott Fitzgerald—the Authority of Failure," also published in 1945. This brilliant piece shows that *failure* is the consistent theme of Fitzgerald's work, with "Absolution" and *The Great Gatsby* as the most adequate "objective correlatives" for it.

Most of the essays in *F. Scott Fitzgerald* have something useful to say. Wright Morris tells us that Fitzgerald "let his line out deeper than Hemingway and Twain." Edwin Fussell calls attention to Fitzgerald's "subtly paradoxical prose style" and "deep-seated integrity as a writer." Charles E. Shain observes that Fitzgerald "writes from so near his own bones." John Henry Raleigh points out that although Nick knows "that the content of Gatsby's dream is corrupt, he senses that its form is pristine," and Raleigh contrasts Nick and Gatsby in terms of the difference between Wordworth and Blake. A. E. Dyson remarks that Daisy "turns out to be literally nothing, and vanishes from the novel," and he calls *The Great Gatsby* "a tragic novel, though of an unorthodox kind." Mizener himself contributes a fine comparison of Fitzgerald's late work to Eliot's *Four Quartets*.

A few of the essays, on the other hand, seem entirely useless. Eight of the first nine pages of John Aldridge's essay contain misquotations of Fitzgerald; why should we bother with the opinions of a critic who cannot even copy the text? Leslie Fiedler borrows (without credit) Troy's idea about failure, says (incorrectly) that "Every writer in Fitzgerald makes his first staggering entrance loaded," charges (falsely) that Fitzgerald never mastered "method and irony and detachment," and dismisses (wrongly) *The Last Tycoon* as an "over-rated fragment." D. S. Savage reduces Fitzgerald to "incestuous regression," explaining that the "Babylon" of "Babylon Revisited" is "Baby-land."

Most of the barriers to our appreciation of Fitzgerald are set up by the Fitzgeraldines. The first is a preoccupation with his life rather than with his works. Perhaps it was not always so, but right now Fitzgerald's life is a bore, and efforts to cast him in *The Drunkard's Redemption* are efforts to change the subject, on the part of people not interested in literature. The second barrier is a preoccupation with Fitzgerald as a voice, or even Eble's "social historian," of the 1920s. Mizener calls him "their most representative writer," and Fitzgerald himself wrote: "I really believe that no one else could have written the story of the youth of our generation." All this is true, but only true of Fitzgerald's poorer work; his best work is absolutely timeless, and is more relevant today than when he wrote it.

It is Fitzgerald's fate to appeal, for the most part, to inadequate critics, who celebrate him in prose that would have turned his stomach. They value him as a Jazz Age madcap pickling into "Our Poe" because they cannot tell how good a writer he is at his best, and because they do not much care.

Fitzgerald makes an instructive contrast with Hemingway, whose gifts and success he always envied. From the sad truthfulness of *The Sun Also Rises* to the slush of *The Old Man and the Sea*, the progress of Hemingway's novels is a progress in increasing dishonesty, fake glamor, and success. Fitzgerald began at the fake glamor and success end, with *This Side of Paradise;* and each novel after that marks a painful and unpopular step toward truth.

JOHN CHEEVER'S GOLDEN EGG

When a highly-esteemed short-story writer tries a novel and fails at it, in this amazing country, he is rewarded just as though he had succeeded. Thus Katherine Anne Porter's *Ship of Fools* became a rapturously-received bestseller, and J. F. Powers' *Morte D'Urban* and John Cheever's *The Wapshot Chronicle* won National Book Awards. In *The Wapshot Scandal*, Cheever has again tried, and again failed, to make short story material jell as a novel. As a two-time loser, he can probably expect the Pulitzer Prize.

The weakness is not any lack of plot. *The Wapshot Scandal* has enough plot for *War and Peace*. In the course of a year, from one Christmas Eve to another, the fortunes of the Wapshots change drastically. (The Wapshots, who are continued from the *Chronicle*, are a family of gentry centered in St. Botolphs, on the Massachusetts coast. They include two young brothers, Moses and Coverly, and their rich maiden aunt Honora.) Coverly's marriage has its ups and downs, as his wife Betsey turns moody or violent, but on the whole he comes off best during the year. Moses is cuckolded and deserted by his wife Melissa, and takes to drink. Honora is exposed as a comic criminal, and dies in contented disgrace. The "scandal" of the title is actually three: Melissa's adultery, Moses' alcholism, and Honora's banditry.

The changes wrought by one year are most effectively pointed up by the widow Wilston. On the Christmas Eve that begins the book, she and an itinerant carpenter named Alby Hooper, both naked and drunk, are trimming a Christmas tree. On the Christmas Eve that ends the book, she and Moses Wapshot are naked and drunk in a hotel room, although they seem to have forgotten the tree.

Such a narrative could clearly be a novel if it held together. It breaks into fragments, however, because of inconsistency of character and tone. People change character in the book to accommodate to each new incident. Dr. Lemuel Cameron, the world-famous atomic scientist who is Coverly's boss, is a good example. In one chapter, pursuing his mistress in Rome through a barrage of comic misfortunes and indignities, Cameron is a sympathetic and attractive figure. In another chapter, testifying before a Congressional committee, he is a mad monster. Both figures make perfect sense in their contexts, but they should not have the same name.

The inconsistencies of tone are equally disconcerting. A woman named Mrs. Lockhart is described to Melissa early in the book as a promiscuous slut, too poor to stay in the community now that the neighbors are applying economic pressure. Later Melissa hears that Mrs. Lockhart has hanged herself in her garage. When we are finally told Mrs. Lockhart's story, we discover that the Lockharts are rather well off, and that Mrs. Lockhart is an extremely sympathetic character, an unfortunate victim of circumstances. Fair enough: the woman who told Melissa about Mrs. Lockhart underestimated her husband's income and blackened her character.

However, the circumstances that drove Gertrude Lockhart to promiscuity and suicide are wildly funny: they result from her inability to get plumbers and repairmen when the household machinery breaks down. It is this shift in tone that is ruinous. Mrs. Lockhart can kill herself as the tragic victim of uncontrollable lust and consequent scandal, or as the pathetic victim of a neurotic sense of obsolescence and inadequacy, or as the comic victim of the oil burner repairman's bowling team and the washing machine repairman's Florida vacation. She cannot kill herself as all three, as Cheever would have it.

There is a similar failure of tone in the book's wonderful story of Emile, the grocery boy, and the plastic eggs. To promote the grocery store, Emile is to hide a thousand plastic eggs around the village during the night; all contain certificates good for prizes, and five gold ones are good for European vacations. In a series of hilarious misadventures, Emile succeeds in rousing the town. A pack of savage housewives in nightgowns pursue him, and he is forced to ditch the eggs in an empty lot, except for a single gold one, which he deposits on Melissa Wapshot's lawn. The incident is marvelously funny. Unfortunately, Emile is Melissa Wapshot's lover, and all the pity and terror of that affair evaporate in a scramble of plastic eggs.

The gold egg on Melissa's lawn, or Dr. Cameron's realization at the end of his Roman comedy that "there was some blessedness in the nature of things," is a proper end for a short story, not for a chapter in a novel. They do not develop *toward* a final resolution; they *are* a final resolution.

I have perhaps overemphasized one point, and in so doing have been unfair to Cheever. If *The Wapshot Scandal* is not a novel, it is a very impressive non-novel. Many things in it are quite fine. Melissa's affair with Emile is convincing and deeply moving (at least until the egg scene). Melissa's feeling for Emile's beauty, her torments of lust, her shame and self-contempt, her progress in degradation from dignified out-of-town weekends with Emile to quick straddles in a shack by the village dump, are all beautifully realized.

One character at least in *The Wapshot Scandal* is both consistent and memorable: the eccentric Honora. In *The Wapshot Chronicle* we learned that she throws her mail into the fire unread, and will only pay bus fares by annual check. In the *Scandal,* it turns out that she has other endearing idiosyncracies: she has never been photographed, and she has never paid an income tax. It is this last habit that is her downfall, since the Internal Revenue computers catch her. She is driven first to a suicide attempt, then to a flight abroad; brought back to St. Botolphs, she achieves a happy, drunken, and impoverished death. I suspect that Cheever is having a go at Edmund Wilson; in any case Honora Wapshot is one of the true comic creations.

Much of *The Wapshot Scandal* is extremely funny. There is a scene in which Coverly is told by his wife to take her new cleaning woman upstairs and show her how to work the vacuum cleaner. Betsey hears him start the machine, then hears his instructions: "Now we put it in here. That's right. That's the way. We have to get it into the corners, way into the corners. Slowly, slowly, slowly. Back and forth, back and forth." They are of course engaged in a more ancient pastime. This romp is out of character for Coverly, and the scene has been done before (Nelson Algren used a coffee grinder in *A Walk on the Wild Side,* which is closer to the origins of the joke in the double meanings of Negro blues). Out of character and unoriginal the scene may be; it is nevertheless uproarious.

Some of the humor in the book is pure slapstick. The income tax man confronts Honora while she is inspecting a basket of fireworks. Naturally, the fireworks go off, and in her efforts to extinguish them she catches him in the face with a vaseful of dirty water and a dozen hyacinths. Other funny scenes are almost surrealistic, as when Emile participates in a male beauty contest in Italy, after which the winners are auctioned off as homosexual concubines (fortunately for Emile, if not for the book's seriousness, he is bought by Melissa, who got to Rome with her golden egg).

Most often, the book's humor is edged, resulting in irony or satire. It is ironic that Norman Johnson, the tax man, throws the book at Honora because he stayed overnight at the Viaduct House, the soup at dinner had a burned match in it, the fight on television was terrible, his breakfast eggs were greasy, on his way to Honora's house he was attacked by a dog, and some children laughed at him when he ran. It is ironic that the alcoholic Episcopal clergyman displays the only attractive religion in St. Botolphs when, drunk at Mass and unable to remember the service, he improvises a prayer "for all those wounded by rotary lawn mowers, chain saws, electric hedge clippers and other power tools."

A good deal of the satire is directed against bureaucracy. At one point, Coverly is the victim of an airplane robbery, as a consequence of which he is given a police questionnaire to fill out, with forty questions ranging from "How often do you take a bath?" to "If you were forced to debase the American flag or the Holy Bible, what would be your choice?" The congressional investigation of Dr. Cameron manages to make nuclear scientists and congressmen seem about equally foolish.

At his best, Cheever is a marvelous writer. Here is the book's last look at Melissa, her hair dyed red, shopping for Emile in a Rome supermarket, and quietly weeping at her fate:

> No willow grows aslant this stream of men and women and yet it is Ophelia that she most resembles, gathering her fantastic

garland not of crowflowers, nettles and long purples, but of salt, pepper, Bab-o, Kleenex, frozen codfish balls, lamb patties, hamburger, bread, butter, dressing, an American comic book for her son and for herself a bunch of carnations. She chants, like Ophelia, snatches of old tunes. "Winstons taste good like a cigarette should. Mr. Clean, Mr. *Clean*," and when her coronet or fantastic garland seems completed she pays her bill and carries her trophies away, no less dignified a figure of grief than any other.

In "Some People, Places, and Things That Will Not Appear in My Next Novel," Cheever wrote that he was omitting various stereotypes because "they throw so little true light on the way we live." Melissa throws a great deal of true light on the way we live, but it is because of her uncovenanted heart, not because she buys Kleenex and frozen codfish balls. Cheever seems sometimes dazzled by the surface of American life, by its textures and glitters. But his best work shows that at the heart of that golden egg there is darkness and mystery.

THE AMERICAN ADAM

When John Barth's *The Sot-Weed Factor* was published in 1960, I appear to have been off hunting caribou near Baffin Bay, and reading nothing but the labels on cans of evaporated milk. Since then my students have been singing the book's praises. It has been reissued in paperback and, alert to the teacher's duty of following after the culture of his students at a decent interval, I dutifully sat down to read it. The result was four most pleasurable evenings.

The book's engaging title is an old term for "tobacco merchant," and is the name of the protagonist's satiric poem. *The Sot-Weed Factor* is a mock eighteenth-century picaresque novel, set mostly in colonial Maryland. I shall not attempt to synopsize the plot. Actually the book is a series of comic set-pieces, loosely strung on two threads of action: the efforts of Ebenezer Cooke, poet and virgin, to make his way in the world, and the efforts of his tutor, Henry Burlingame III, to learn his parentage. The plot contrivance is the most fantastic of any book I know, but Barth is not interested in making it convincing: it is at once preposterous and predictable, and that is part of the fun. Henry is a protean figure who assumes a variety of identities, but everyone in the book takes a turn or two at disguising himself: at one point three other characters are pretending to be Ebenezer, suggesting the scene in *Duck Soup* in which all the Marx brothers nightgown themselves as Groucho. There are dozens of recognition scenes, the climax of them Ebenezer's discovery that the attractive matron who has just attempted to seduce him used to be his wet-nurse.

The book is slow starting and too long, and it has its languors, but for the most part it is wonderfully funny. I was reduced to helpless laughter by at least half a dozen episodes, all improper. I shall list them, with the pages on which they begin, for the convenience of dippers. They include: the whore Joan Toast's story

(p. 66) of her defloration by a "great tom leech"; Henry's account
(p. 344) of his passion for a sow named Portia and his spirited defense of pansexuality; the mission of Father FitzMaurice to the
Ahatchwhoop Indians (p. 376), and his martyrdom at their
hands; Mary Mungummory's story (p. 431) of the spiritual exer-
cises that led to her conception; an eating contest (p. 597) to
determine the Ahatchwhoop kingship; and the wooing (p. 628) of
Ebenezer's twin sister, Anna, by an Ahatchwhoop called Billy
Rumbly.

    Barth loves lists, and even his lists are funny. When Ebenezer
goes to buy a notebook for poetry, he is undone by a choice of 16
varieties, from plain thin cardboard folio to fat ruled leather
quarto, with their various advantages and disadvantages, and he
goes after the proprietor with a short-sword. An English whore
and a French whore exchange insulting terms for their profession,
the exchange covering six pages. The long, annotated list of the
foods consumed in the eating contest is uproarious, as is the simple list of the foods not served: "No rabbitts."

    The language of the book sparkles with eloquence and wit.
In one of his disguises, Henry pretends to be Monsieur Casteene,
a French Canadian agent rousing the Indians against the English.
When a Roman Catholic priest mentions Casteen's Indian wife,
Henry says: "*Two* Indian women, Father Smith: 'tis a sin God
will forgive, in return for the massacre of Schenectady." When
Ebenezer, about to be tossed overboard by pirates, asks the pirate
captain to pledge to respect the ladies, he gets a proper pirate
answer. " 'I pledge to swive your pleasant ladies from sprit to
transom,' said Long Ben Avery. 'I pledge to give every jack o' my
crew his slavering fill o' them, and when they're done I pledge to
carve your little sister into ship's-beef and salt her down for the
larboard watch.' "

    As in all superior humor, there is a strain of melancholy just
under the surface. Barth produces a musical-comedy happy ending, in which Ebenezer and Anna recover their lost estate, and all
the separated lovers are united. Then, in an epilogue, he tears it
apart: Ebenezer has won his love, Joan, but she has become a
poxed and ugly opium-addict, and she soon dies, bearing a dead
child; Anna loses both men she loves; the other couples drift

apart; Ebenezer and Anna eventually sell the estate and move away. The book ends on Ebenezer's bitter epitaph for himself as a failure and a fool.

The Sot-Weed Factor conceals a number of preachments in its clowning, although in this deceptive book it is hard to tell just how seriously they are meant. One is that history tells glamorous lies. The book starts out as though it meant to affirm this generally, introducing us in an early chapter to two aged pederasts named Henry More and Sir Isaac Newton. It is soon clear that Barth's principal interest is in debunking American colonial history, specifically that of Maryland, his native state. The main instruments in this effort are two spurious manuscript journals in the book, Captain John Smith's *Secret Historie* and *The Privie Journall of Sir Henry Burlingame,* Smith's lieutenant and Henry's grandfather.

These scurrilous documents make it clear that Smith was a foul-minded lecher, that the compass with which he impressed Powhatan contained pornographic pictures, that Pocahontas saved his life out of lust, and that he introduced the Indians to the arts of sodomy, "learnt from the scurvie Arabs." We see him attempt to seduce one Indian queen with the delightful offer of "a lewd figure done in ivorie, a smalle coyne inscrib'd in filthie Arabick, and the pledge of twelve yardes of Scotch cloth, to be deliver'd on the next boat from London."

Where the comedy of these journals is not sexual, it relies heavily on our seeing Smith covered with urine or excrement. I am not as readily amused by scatological humor as some, perhaps because of the ferocities of Brooklyn child-rearing in the 1920s, but that does not dismiss the matter. It is not news that history glamorizes. There is something childish about this insistence on showing Captain Smith with his pants down, as though Barth were finally refuting his seventh grade history teacher. The debunking of colonial Maryland is wittier and funnier. Ebenezer's experiences show him a province containing "naught but scoundrels and perverts, hovels and brothels, corruption and poltroonery." At one point of desperation, he cries out, "Better the pistol than another day in Maryland!"

In the moral universe of *The Sot-Weed Factor,* it is public affairs that are wicked and sinful, while sex is harmless or benign. The jockeying for power in England and Maryland is shown as involving endless corruption, chicanery, intrigue, and betrayal. The sex, as represented by Joan's passion for the great tom leech, or Mary's joys with her Ahatchwhoop lover Charley Mattassin, or Roxanne Russecks asking her daughter's seducer only that he be gentle and discreet, seems morally innocuous.

Sex is preferably non-phallic, however. The three great lovers in the book, the two Ahatchwhoops and Henry, turn out to have in common not only that they are brothers (I warned you about the plot) but that they are all impotent; their mastery lies in other directions. Phallic sexuality is identified with sadism, and is typified by the book's pirates: they rape conventionally and kill afterwards. Indeed, the two acts are indistinguishable. When 100 pirates capture a ship bound for Mecca, carrying 1,600 young Moorish virgins, they spend a day and a night deflowering them, and "the deck looked like a butcher's block."

There is another kind of innocence, represented by Ebenezer, which consists of ignorance of the world; this is bad, destructive to the innocent and to those who come in contact with him. In one of its aspects, *The Sot-Weed Factor* is an allegory of American innocence and optimism, R. W. B. Lewis' "the American Adam," and Ebenezer might fairly be called what Henry James, Sr., called Emerson: "my fair unfallen friend."

In our fallen and paradoxical world, nothing is what it seems. When Anna marries the Ahatchwhoop Billy Rumbly, he becomes a handsomely dressed English gentleman, and she chooses to become a filthy squaw in deerskin and bear grease. When Ebenezer tries to write a *Marylandiad,* an epic to celebrate the province and justify his unauthorized title "Laureate of Maryland," he cannot. When, instead, he writes his satire, *The Sot-Weed Factor,* to revenge himself on the province, the poem gives Maryland a reputation for graciousness and refinement, and attracts good families to settle there. As a consequence, 34 years after he has given up poetry, Ebenezer really is commissioned Laureate.

Barth's novel has so many literary sources that it would be easier to list the books that it does *not* copy or burlesque. Basically, of course, it is a redoing of *Candide*, which is the archetypal American novel, as writers from Cooper to Salinger have demonstrated by rewriting it. At various times, *The Sot-Weed Factor* is a pastiche of Rabelais, *Don Quixote*, *Robinson Crusoe*, *Moll Flanders*, *Joseph Andrews*, *Tristram Shandy*, and *Fanny Hill*. At other times, it is reminiscent of Tarzan, the Rover Boys, and the Keystone Comedies. At still other times, it resembles nothing ever seen before.

The New American Novel, as I have remarked previously, tends to be a picaresque comedy of the anti-hero. It seems to be here to stay, and it has even produced a species of harmless snake that mimics its coloration: the first of them *Catch-22*, and the latest Elliot Baker's *A Fine Madness*. Of the species with venom, as *Stern* is the most profound, *The Moviegoer* the most honest, and *V.*, the most imaginative, so *The Sot-Weed Factor* seems to me the funniest yet. John Barth is young, and this is his third novel. His talent and learning are formidable, and although I cannot imagine what he could write after this book, I look forward to it eagerly.

ERNEST HEMINGWAY WITH A KNIFE

Seems like when they get started they don't leave a guy nothing. The first posthumous publication from the 50 pounds of manuscript that Ernest Hemingway left, A Moveable Feast consists of sketches about his life in Paris in the early 1920s, written (or rewritten) between 1957 and 1960. It is Hemingway's most insignificant book, worse than Green Hills of Africa. It is nevertheless interesting reading: at its best it has the interest of the minor work of an important writer; at its worst it has the interest of a bitchy remark overheard at a party.

The gossip interest centers in Hemingway's portraits of four writers, all dead: Gertrude Stein, Ford Madox Ford, Wyndham Lewis, and F. Scott Fitzgerald. These accounts are cutting and malicious, and if they are true, Hemingway was indiscreet and cruel to write them. His preface, however, raises the interesting possibility that they are not true. "If the reader prefers," he writes, "this book may be regarded as fiction. But there is always a chance that such a book of fiction may throw some light on what has been written as fact." If Hemingway spent the last years of his life inventing malicious lies about former friends and acquaintances no longer alive to defend themselves, one can only see him as contemptible.

Gertrude Stein is quoted in a childish defense of lesbianism. "The main thing," she says, "is that the act male homosexuals commit is ugly and repugnant and afterwards they are disgusted with themselves. . . . In women it is the opposite. They do nothing that they are disgusted by and nothing that is repulsive and afterwards they are happy and they can lead happy lives together." Hemingway later reports an overheard quarrel in which "I heard someone speaking to Miss Stein as I had never heard one person speak to another; never, anywhere, ever." Her response is a pathetic pleading and begging, and Hemingway has made his ironic point.

In addition, he shows, Miss Stein as desperately vain about her writing and pathologically jealous of other writers. Hemingway observes: "In the three or four years that we were good friends I cannot remember Gertrude Stein ever speaking well of any writer who had not written favorably about her work or done something to advance her career except for Ronald Firbank and, later, Scott Fitzgerald." "If you brought up Joyce twice," he adds flatly, "you would not be invited back."

Ford is presented, without explanation, as an image of vileness. "I had always avoided looking at Ford when I could," Hemingway writes, "and I always held my breath when I was near him in a closed room." "I took a drink to see if his coming had fouled it," he continues, "but it still tasted good." In an impressive bit of two-at-a-blow, Hemingway recalls Ezra Pound's assuring him that Ford "only lied when he was very tired," but he finds this reassurance difficult to keep in mind because of "the heavy, wheezing, ignoble presence of Ford himself."

There is no pretence that Wyndham Lewis is a friend; he is a vision of repulsiveness encountered once at Pound's studio. "I do not think I had ever seen a nastier-looking man," Hemingway writes. "Some people show evil as a great race horse shows breeding. They have the dignity of a hard *chancre*. Lewis did not show evil; he just looked nasty." Thinking about Lewis' appearance, Hemingway is reminded of "toe-jam," and he identifies Lewis' eyes as "those of an unsuccessful rapist."

These three are just a warm-up for Fitzgerald, who, as a good friend and as the successful writer who had recommended the unknown Hemingway to Scribners, deserves the full treatment. Fitzgerald had "a delicate long-lipped Irish mouth that, on a girl, would have been the mouth of a beauty. . . . The mouth worried you until you knew him and then it worried you more." On first acquaintance, Hemingway reports, Fitzgerald asked an intimate question about Hemingway's sex life (it was tactfully evaded). Later, Fitzgerald confessed to Hemingway that as a short-story writer he was a whore. There is a malicious (and, I am sorry to say, terribly funny) account of Fitzgerald off on a trip with Hemingway, drunk and convinced that he is dying. "With his waxy color and his perfect features," Hemingway writes, "he looked like a little dead crusader." Furthermore, Fitzgerald wrote illiterate letters, and Hemingway testifies: "I knew him for two years before he could spell my name."

If Scott Fitzgerald is presented as ludicrous, Zelda is simply vicious. She was jealous of Fitzgerald's writing, and tried to keep him too drunk to write; she spent her days "making him jealous with other women"; she told him, in order to destroy him, that he could never satisfy a woman (this leads to an extremely unconvincing scene in which Hemingway inspects Fitzgerald's equipment in a restaurant washroom and is able to reassure him).

It is with a certain shame that I reprint these reminiscences, since I believe them to be distorted and invented at least in part. Unfortunately, the reviewer cannot attack offensive material without giving it a little more currency, and there may even be some people who would not encounter these defacings of the illustrious dead except for my review. Beyond that, I do not doubt that there is some gossipy malice in me, too, to motivate the reviewing of this largely worthless book; it is not to Hemingway's credit to have stirred it up.

What sort of man was this overhear-and-tell, peek-and-tell, sniff-and-tell, invent-and-tell friend? The other interest the book holds is in the look it gives us at Hemingway in his last years (I do not think that we get much sense of the real Hemingway in his twenties). The first impression is of weepy self-idealization. Hemingway sees himself then as a "very poor and very happy" young husband, an intrepid writer who at work had "the air of a man alone in the jungle," a sensitive young heavyweight called "the Black Christ" by admiring peasants.

The constant and rather tasteless assurances of historic doings in the marital bed after a while come to seem protesting too much. Certainly a strongly defended-against homosexual impulse shows through the account of Hemingway in his teens carrying a knife to defend his virtue against "wolves." "When you were a boy and moved in the company of men," he writes melodramatically, "you had to be prepared to kill a man, know how to do it and really know that you would do it in order not to be interfered with." Underlying the mockery of Fitzgerald's good looks there is envy, and underneath the envy there is something curiously like desire. As for sublimation, it takes a classic form in Hemingway's statement: "After writing a story I was always empty and both sad and happy, as though I had made love." Elsewhere he talks of the danger of becoming "impotent" in his writing.

There is some very impotent writing in A Moveable Feast. Some of the prose exaggerates Hemingway's mannerisms until it resembles self-parody: "the hotel where Verlaine had died where I had a room on the top floor where I worked." Sketches sometimes end all portentous-pretentious: "But Paris was a very old city and we were young and nothing was simple there, not even poverty, nor sudden money, nor the moonlight, nor right and wrong nor the breathing of someone who lay beside you in the moonlight." The book includes the worst sentence Hemingway ever wrote (it is too long to quote here, but, for collectors, it occupies most of p. 65). The second-person style maddens.

Figures of speech are sometimes terribly arch: "a face fresh as a newly minted coin if they minted coins in smooth flesh with rain-freshened skin"; "soothing as the noise of a plank being violated in the sawmill." Or they are labored: "I showed the story to him as a curiosity, as you might show, stupidly, the binnacle of a ship you had lost in some incredible way"; "the considerably reconstructed face, rather like that of a well packed ski run." Or collapsible: "trying to read her [Katherine Mansfield] after Chekhov was like hearing the carefully artificial tales of a young old-maid compared to those of an articulate and knowing physician who was a good and simple writer." Or snide: Fitzgerald was excited by the adventure of drinking wine *from a bottle* "as a girl might be excited by going swimming for the first time without a bathing suit."

Some of the prose is simply inept. The unfortunate title is an example. It comes from a remark Hemingway made about Paris, that the experience "stays with you, for Paris is a moveable feast." A movable feast is a festival that does not come on the same day each year; Hemingway may have meant "portable" or even "immovable." Another example is his description of an attractive young artist's model "with a falsely fragile depravity." I cannot even figure out what he was trying to say. A fragile depravity would be one easily broken, perhaps that of a half-hearted sinner eager to be saved; a falsely fragile depravity must then mean an iron sinfulness that appears deceptively brittle—but what nonsense.

There is some good writing in the book, particularly a moving account of a sad professional fire-eater, met in a café, and a marvelously funny conversation with an aspiring writer, whom Hemingway tries to convert to literary criticism. There are effective descriptions and images. Yet on the whole this is Hemingway's worst piece of writing. As I wrote at the time of his death, at his best Hemingway left us, "in *The Sun Also Rises* and a handful of short stories, authentic masterpieces, small-scale but immortal." The publication of *A Moveable Feast* perceptibly diminishes Hemingway's reputation, and two more such will destroy it. I urge his widow and her advisers to temper their publication plans with mercy.

JEWISH, ALL TOO JEWISH

One of the reasons we read novels is to learn about the exotic world: how do Portuguese priests go about seducing their parishioners, why are the Japanese forever injecting themselves with vitamins? Wallace Markfield's first novel, *To an Early Grave,* is about a way of life just as exotic and glamorous as those, if one can stand away from it for a while: the life of New York Jewish intellectuals. Jewish? Indeed, to paraphrase Nietzsche, all too Jewish. The book is broad satire, wonderfully funny and mean; it is the most interesting first novel since Thomas Pynchon's *V.*

I do not think that *To an Early Grave* is a work of major importance, or that Markfield intended it to be. It is a small comic triumph, the sunniest novel about death that I know. The book deals with one Sunday in the life of Morroe Rieff, during which he and three other friends of Leslie Braverman, a gifted writer dead at 41, attend Leslie's funeral in Brooklyn. Markfield makes only the most perfunctory effort to unify the incidents: Morroe finds that he cannot cry over Leslie's death; everyone else cries at the funeral, but instead Morroe embarrassingly gets an erection at the sight of Sandra Luboff, Miss Social Welfare, and his memory of their dalliance; finally, at the end of the long day, rubbing his wife Etta with insect repellent, Morroe is able to cry. But this is less a serious development than Markfield's final irony: the tears come just as inappropriately as did Morroe's earlier reaction.

To an Early Grave is a *roman à clef,* and the originals of the dead genius and his wife Inez are people I knew slightly some years ago. I do not recognize the four principal mourners, which is perhaps just as well. Morroe is a City College graduate, who writes promotion for a Jewish fund-raising agency. He has all the sweet unworldliness of Krazy Kat. When Morroe tries to take down the number of a policeman for beating up a bum, he can find nothing in his pockets but dental floss and salt tablets. In the car on the way to the cemetery, Morroe has a beautiful meditation about his own mediocrity and the world's dangers, punctuated by "a splash of heartburn."

In the romp with Sandra, on the roof during a Braverman party, Morroe could hardly wait to get her panties off before reciting Cummings. In the cemetery during the funeral, he sees the grave of one Goldie Bromberg and he fantasies a life with her; he is then attacked by a squadron of geese; finally a mad old Jewish pretzel lady traps him into another fantastic romance. Morroe thinks, of his companions: "They may not respect me, but they like me." When we hear them mock him on the way back from the funeral, we realize that they do neither. Nevertheless Morroe, grinning "his shy and goofy grin," is eternal and enduring, and ultimately he overcomes them with innocence, as Krazy overcomes Ignatz Mouse.

The other three mourners are broad caricatures. Holly Levine, a most pretentious literary critic, owns the Volkswagen that takes the four to the funeral. Levine's Volkswagen is introduced with a marvelous soliloquy that begins: "To own a car in Manhattan is like towing a camel across the Sargasso." A seven-page scene in which Levine tries to write a review should be enough to drive anyone of decent impulse, susceptible to shame, out of the profession. Levine's form of mourning for Leslie is to say to a friend at the funeral: "We must first determine whether we want memoir or critique."

We first see Barnet Weiner, poet and critic of the arts, spending his Sunday morning in bed with a thin Bronx girl named Myra Mandelbaum, who had previously refused to stay the night, she explains, because her hair is oily and he has such hard water. Weiner "used to correspond with Gide in French and call him *Cher Maître*." In his criticism Weiner is fastidious and delicate, in reality he is a lecherous vulgarian, calling Morroe's attention to a girl walking by with the comment: "That little *tochiss*. I could bite into it like a piece of hot pastrami."

The fourth mourner, Felix Ottensteen, is an older man (the other three are about Leslie's age) who writes literary articles for a Yiddish daily and lectures to Hadassah groups. We first see Ottensteen refusing his son money; then we see him refusing to ride in the German automobile. Ottensteen is a refuser, but he is the most likable of Morroe's companions, he is the one most loyal to Leslie, and his rhetoric about Jewish woes is a relief from the culture-faking of the rest of them.

The most interesting character in *To an Early Grave* is of course the dead Leslie, who is endlessly resurrected for us. He was a small fat man, who walked like "a little *bubbe* loaded down with shopping bags." Leslie was dirty, tirelessly promiscuous, and a shameless sponge; he was a ruthless exploiter of his wife, who eventually evicted him; before his death he lived by writing pornography. But Leslie was also a brilliant critic and fiction writer, a conscientious stylist, and a man who saved his integrity for his work. (To Leslie, as to Weiner, art is the dream of a graciousness not attainable in life.) Above all Leslie was a character: a lover of egg creams, the master of a revolting dog named Kaplan, the man who lectured on *Lorna Doone* at a writer's workshop.

The women in *To an Early Grave* are all minor. Morroe's wife Etta comes through as a nagging voice and "absurdly large breasts." Leslie's widow, Inez, a Yiddish-speaking Gentile, is made "radiant, positively radiant" by her grief, and she is masterful at the funeral, inviting the mourners back to her apartment and instructing them to bring two large pizzas, "one all cheese, one cheese and anchovy." Sandra, Myra, and the other girls described or mentioned, are interesting only in their ready horizontality. The other women in the novel are ludicrous figures overheard in restaurants, or comic storeladies. This is accurate sociology: women are insignificant in the novel because they are insignificant, instrumental housekeeper-bedmates, in the Jewish intellectual subculture—to its shame.

To an Early Grave is enormously funnier than a review can convey, and perhaps the best review would be simply an anthology of quotations. This would have to include at least three wonderfully funny scenes. One is Morroe's childhood memory of the Jewish laundrymen outside the Norfolk naval base, forbidden to solicit the sailors, calling attention to themselves with costumes: Leo the Lumberman with an ax, Hershel the Hawaiian in a hula skirt, Moishe the Mexican in a Sam Browne belt and *huaraches*,

Morroe's father Cowboy Joe in a Stetson hat. Another is a splendid *pro forma* fight between Levine and a Jewish cab driver, who has dented Levine's car. A third is Leslie's funeral ceremony, which is climaxed when a Negro folksinger sings a Scottish tribute to Bonnie Prince Charlie.

One would have to include some anecdotes, particularly the two that broke me up. One is Weiner's tricking of an editor named Brucie Siskind by promising him the erotic delights of an Israeli amazon and giving him instead the phone number of Fat Gittel, Weiner's appetizing-store lady; Brucie's revenge is calling Weiner at four in the morning to stutter the names of various smoked fishes, accompanied by snatches of "Hatikvah." The other is the story, unfortunately not synopsizable, of what Leslie did when Inez came home early and found him and Minerva Turtletaub not reading page proofs together.

Markfield's comic descriptions are marvels of economy. He can compress all of Flatbush into a few words: "Kids gumming zwieback in wading pools." Here is an unfriendly Gentile: "She had on a narrow fur piece; its little beast jaws gaped open as though from great pain or rage." As for the cemetery, "even the young maples that lined the street seemed trimmed and pruned to the shape of menorahs." Here is a remark overheard in the washroom: "He was never a normal personality. A normal personality is not going to set fire to his mother's bathroom curtains when he's a big boy already."

Some of the funniest parts of *To an Early Grave* consist of tribal lore. The only art that truly interests Leslie's circle is popular culture. During the trip, Weiner challenges Levine to identify the nemesis of Bim Gump, the Green Hornet's driver, the words that Hop Harrigan radios to his announcer, and so on. Then Levine demands that Weiner name fourteen movies in which Bogart was featured but not starred, nine books by Albert Payson Terhune, the original Dead End Kids, and so on. Morroe is disturbed about not crying over Leslie's death, because he had cried when the planes shot King Kong off the Empire State Building; driving back from the funeral, Morroe dreams of encountering Leslie in a second-run movie theater, where he betrays him in a showing of *The Informer*.

The book bubbles over with comic rhetoric. In Leslie's apart-

ment "the very walls dripped troubles! You could peel them off
with the laths and tiles, they hung from the clothes dryer in the
kitchen, they stuffed up the drains, they killed the plants, they
brought in roaches!" The cab driver's sermon on his religion of
brotherhood, before his fight with Levine, is a comic masterpiece.
So is a rabbi's sermon, about the recalcitrance of the body, which
the four listen to until they discover that they are at the wrong
funeral.

At times there is too much rhetoric, and the topical and popular culture references overpower. But mostly the richness of language amuses and delights. Markfield has clearly taken *Ulysses* as
his model, but instead of trying to duplicate that encyclopedic
masterpiece, he has aimed more modestly at writing just Mr.
Bloom's Day in Brooklyn. As such, *To an Early Grave* is brilliantly
successful, and if you have not laughed since Fred Allen went off
the air, I prescribe this book.

THE SPIRE OF BABEL

I once described William Golding as the most maverick of novelists, a chooser of the least promising fictional subjects. My reference was to his first three novels; *Lord of the Flies,* about a group of English schoolboys reverting to savagery; *The Inheritors,* about the extinction of Neanderthal Man by Homo sapiens; and *Pincher Martin,* about the thoughts of a drowning sailor. Since then I have read *Free Fall,* a painter's melodramatic confessions, and *The Spire,* and I am prepared to modify my opinion somewhat. Golding is still the most maverick of novelists, but his subjects have become slightly more promising.

The Spire tells of the construction of a gigantic spire on an already completed cathedral during the Middle Ages. (The cathedral is that of Salisbury, where Golding lives.) This spire is the obsessive project of Jocelin, Dean of the cathedral, who tells the builder in a moment of prescience: "I see now it'll destroy us of course." The novel's action is the working out of that fate.

Jocelin himself is an elderly fanatic, mad in a brilliant and outwardly-controlled fashion. A guardian angel with six wings visits him occasionally, then settles into constant attendance. Despite this angel, Jocelin is tormented by evil forces. First an imaginary zany in motley strikes him in the groin with a pig's bladder; then a devil torments him at night; eventually all the demonic hordes in Wiltshire have a go at him. In the two years that it takes to build the spire, Jocelin goes without confession and the sacraments, and he ceases to function as a priest. When the spire is completed, Jocelin's spine, struck by his angel with a flail, collapses, and Jocelin is left disillusioned and dying.

Roger Mason, the master builder who designs and achieves the spire, is another of its victims. In the course of the work, Jocelin discovers that Roger has no Christian faith, and that he is terified of heights. Each time Roger gives up at some insuperable difficulty, Jocelin drives him on, and eventually Roger decides that Jocelin is the devil. As a result of the nervous tension of the construction, Roger takes to drink. At the end of the novel, he is a bedridden alcholic, and, after an unsuccessful attempt to hang himself in the outhouse, a blind and dumb one.

Perhaps the most important casualty is Goody Pangall, the red-haired wife of the cathedral caretaker, and Jocelin's beloved god-daughter. Early in the novel, a riot by the workmen results in the tearing of Goody's chaste dress and the exposure of her body. This vignette beautifully foreshadows her downfall as a result of the spire. When Goody's husband deserts in terror of the work-men, she has an affair with Roger. Jocelin overhears her adulter-ous dalliance with Roger in the incomplete spire one night, and is shocked less by the act than by her new wanton tone. Goody be-comes pregnant, and, assaulted by Roger's wife, she miscarries and dies in agony. Jocelin, who had come to give her money to enable her to go away, observes her agony and flees, leaving the money in a pool of blood on the cottage floor. Goody's body and blood replace Christ's as the sacrifice, in Jocelin's imagination, and he realizes that Goody has always been his true love, and that he has slain her.

If Jocelin destroys himself and those around him, this de-struction is the consequence of a mighty achievement. In the course of the building, Jocelin spends more and more of his time in the spire, first to bring the men luck, then to help them with the work, finally because their labor is his "service." The workmen are, in the Church's eyes, "murderers, cutthroats, rowdies, brawl-ers, rapers, notorious fornicators, sodomites, or worse"; Jocelin sees them as an Army of the Lord, "adding glory to the house." The projected spire was called Jocelin's Folly because the four stone pillars of the church that were to support it, themselves rested on no foundation. After the spire is built, these pillars are discovered to be hollow and filled with rubble. Yet by a miracle, perhaps because of a Holy Nail from the Cross, the spire goes up and stays up. (Critics of the Gospels, take note.)

Although Jocelin admits to the possibility that he is mad, *The Spire* is much more than a record of madness or obsession. Per-haps the best way to get at its complex significance, and one that is appropriate to its subject matter, is to look at it in terms of the medieval Four Levels of Meaning. On the first level, the literal or historical, the novel is a story of Christian sacrifice. Jocelin equates his call to build the spire with God's Kierkegaardian demands in the Bible: "But then out of some deep place comes the command to do what makes no sense at all—to build a ship on dry land; to sit among the dunghills; to marry a whore; to set their son on the altar of sacrifice." Jocelin has sacrificed himself, Goody, and the rest, to the Greater Glory of God. He may be a saint, or he may be a blasphemer. He is in any case guilty of the sin of pride: picturing his spire as "the apocalypse" to "complete a stone bible," even echoing Christ in "Now you shall have me always with you." But the spire stands.

On the next level, the allegorical or typical, Jocelin and his spire are Faustian man, man as he *aspires*. As Ibsen's Master Builder falls from *his* tower, so Jocelin pride-and-falls. On this level, the spire is not held up by God's grace but by man's will. Golding writes of Jocelin: "His will began to burn fiercely and he thrust it into the four pillars"; "In this dry air, his will, his blazing will, was shut down to a steady glow, which illuminated and supported the new building."

On the third level of meaning, the tropological or moral, *The Spire* is a story of Freudian repression and sublimation (as Golding is fully aware). Jocelin sees a workman cavorting, "the model of the spire projecting obscenely from between his legs." Jocelin has erotic dreams of Goody's red hair in association with his spire. His celibacy is a torment of the loins. Jocelin's final boast, as he lies paralyzed, is: "My spire pierced every stage, from the bottom to the top." In these terms the spire is Jocelin's enormous erection, vaster than Goody can contain and live, an impious spire of Babel to challenge the Yahvist's old phallic deity.

On the ultimate level of meaning, the anagogical or mystical, *The Spire* is a cautionary fable for the revolutionary or the artist (the partly autobiographical hero of *Free Fall* is both a painter and, briefly, a Communist). You can't make an omelette without breaking eggs—this novel concerns itself with the eggs. Take what you want, says God, and pay for it—this novel concerns itself with the payment. "Cost what you like," mad Jocelin cries out to his spire. He thinks bitterly, "The cost of building material," when he comes upon Goody and Roger in the spire. "I traded a stone hammer for four people," he recognizes at the end. Anagogically, *The Spire* is about the terrible human cost of vision, of creation—ultimately, of Golding's own vocation.

Two powerful mad scenes in the book show Golding at the height of his craft. In one, deserted in the spire because the men have inexplicably left work early, Jocelin sees fires spring up all around the countryside. He remembers that they are the balefires of Midsummer Night, "lighted by the devil-worshippers out on the hills," and he realizes where the men have gone. Jocelin weeps for the sins of the world, and decides that, as David could not build the temple because of Uriah's blood on his hands, so is his purpose similarly defiled by Goody's blood. Then Jocelin realizes that the twig he saw in the cathedral is pagan mistletoe; he tries to pray, but Goody appears in a sensual vision; when he runs down to the cathedral floor, the "paving stones were hot to his feet with all the fires of hell."

The other scene is even more powerful. As a storm begins to smash the spire, Jocelin braves the elements to go to the cathedral and protect it with the Holy Nail. "Satan in the likeness of a cosmic wildcat" appears, and dashes him to the ground, and all the devils out of hell attack him. Jocelin beats them off with the Nail, climbs to the top of the spire, and drives in the Nail. Then, with the spire safe, Jocelin is given over to the devils. In a sweet hot dance in devil "uncountry," Goody comes to him, "naked in her red hair." His love is finally consummated: "there was a wave of ineffable good sweetness, wave after wave, and an atonement. And then there was nothing."

Of living writers, only Golding and Isaac Bashevis Singer could bring off such a Witches' Sabbath, or would try to. It is these moments of glory that justify *The Spire*, not the pages of architectural description. The book is not accurate in its details of medieval life, nor is this sort of literal accuracy important to Golding (thus the fires lit with Piggy's concave eyeglasses in *Lord of the Flies*). For his own amusement, Golding will add an occasional artificial wormhole, such as spelling "tithe" "tythe," but if he wants Roger to mock a statement of Jocelin's with "Big talk," "Big talk" is what Roger will say.

After the spire is up, the book inevitably weakens, and Golding should have ended it sooner. There is an embarrassing scene between Jocelin and his confessor Anselm, in which they talk like two schoolgirls having a spat ("Why must you always have a very best friend?" "You were so—keen"). Jocelin attacked and stripped by a mob of townspeople, Jocelin arranging his tomb, Jocelin dying with the Host on his tongue—all are anticlimax after the book's tremendous events. Golding's touch is sometimes unsure. But he is the most interesting British writer today, and he baits his hook for Leviathan.

DANIEL CURLEY'S STORY

Daniel Curley is one of the most gifted American writers of my generation, although he has attracted surprisingly little attention. He published a volume of stories, *That Marriage Bed of Procrustes*, in 1957; then a novel, *How Many Angels?*, in 1958; finally a second novel, *A Stone Man, Yes*, in 1964. Curley is far more talented than a number of highly-touted novelists in our time, but he is apparently less talented than they in self-promotion.

One of the fascinating things about Curley's work is that he endlessly retells the same story, and in the course of his three books he has evolved from telling it tragically to telling it comically. As the example of John Updike should make clear, those writers who tell their own story over and over again do so, not because of any want of invention, but because their story is obsessive and compulsive, as was the Ancient Mariner's, and because they must tell it, to overcome it.

Curley's story has four principal strands, each with its key image: a failure with a prim nagging mother, curiously symbolized by a magnolia; a failure with an articulate bitchy wife, expressed in the image of an ambiguous grave; the loss of a fat whore to a more virile man, accompanied by the image of a beating; and the loss of a father figure, with an image of being initiated into mysteries.

These motifs first appear in the stories in *That Marriage Bed of Procrustes*. In "A House Called Magnolia," the narrator takes his mother to visit a decayed Southern mansion. Nothing he says or does impresses her, but she is overwhelmed by the gift of a magnolia blossom, incarnating all the beauty of the house, from the house's owner.

Three stories in the book deal with George Fuller, a professor of literature, and his awful wife, Alice. In "To Ask the Hard Question is Easy," she subjects him to a vicious tirade in bed; in "The

Fugitive," he deserts her to work in a can factory; in "That Marriage Bed of Procrustes," he fails her in bed, then tries to tell her about something important that happened when he was 12, while she mocks and insults him with terrible cruelty. The grave appears in the first of these stories when George digs a garbage pit, realizes that he could bash Alice with the shovel and bury her in the pit, and decides that that ambiguous pit-grave is his image of their marriage.

In "The Fugitive," George, in his new role as worker, tries to go off with a whore with enormous thighs, but he loses her to a hairy brute who wins her heart by slapping her, and wins her person by knocking George to the floor. The lost father figure is suggested in "A House Called Magnolia" by a courtly Judge Wilder, in whose house the narrator lives. The father figure who initiates into mysteries is an old barber, in the story that George tries to tell Alice in bed, and the mysteries are those of sex and excretion.

I do not mean to reduce the dozen stories in *That Marriage Bed of Procrustes* to these four motifs and images. A marvelous story, "Saccovanzetti," although obviously autobiographical, ignores these themes and explores the ironies of a group of boys playing payroll robbery and murder on the day that Sacco and Vanzetti are executed. "That Marriage Bed of Procrustes" is more than a story of failure with a bitchy wife, it is one of the finest short stories of our time, and its end, in which George brings delight to a little clown, is beautiful and heartbreaking.

How Many Angels? is a novel about Michael Pegnam, a trade paper journalist in New York, visiting his home town near Boston. He must make the difficult choice between settling there to teach school and marrying Nancy Hatcher, or leaving there and losing Nancy. Chapters of flashback in the first person alternate with present action in the third person, filling out Mike's earlier life and the complexity of the choice.

Mike's widowed mother, a school principal, is the prim nagging figure. With a fine symbolic rightness, he spends the weekend of the novel sick from her cooking; "there's no use trying to tell her" anything; at the end, Mike walks out on her and all that she represents. Curley works "A House Called Magnolia," rewrit-

ten, into *How Many Angels?* as one flashback, and once again the
narrator's mother visits Magnolia and gets a magnolia. Now, however, the ending openly admits failure: "And that was the last
time we spoke for the rest of our wonderful trip."

Nancy is a portrait of the awful wife in a larval stage. She has
memorized Mike's childhood, has moved into his mother's house,
and threatens to stay and take the teaching job if he does not.
Nancy wants to eat Mike's life and eat him, but Mike has better
sense than George: he realizes in time that she is a replica of his
mother, and he walks out on Nancy too. The grave image here is
George's old school, now a burned-out basement with a rubble of
his memories.

There are whores galore, all connected with beatings. When
Mike was in college in the South, the boys had a naked whore in
the room, but Mike was too badly injured from a beating received
earlier, and too drunk, even to look at her. In his night's wander-
ings in the present, Mike finds himself at a table in a roadhouse
with a whore, but he is too sick from his mother's cooking to do
anything about it. Shortly afterward Mike witnesses a savage cutting and kneeing, and identifies with the victim.

However, just as failure with a dominating mother and wife
is presented wishfully as rejecting *them* in *How Many Angels?*, so,
too, losing the whore is wishfully resolved. Mike ends his night's
wandering with a visit to Noreen, the girl he had dated and loved
in his teens, but had never dared to proposition. Noreen tells Mike
that he should have been more of a man, he tells her of the Southern beating (in which he turns out to have been quite a man),
and they pop into bed together, with impressive success. (Curley
tastefully does not describe their doings; instead he writes an
an elaborate description of Mike's inserting the key in the keyhole
before going upstairs to Noreen.) Noreen's bedroom "smells like a
whorehouse," but she is not fat; in fact, "she's too thin"; and she is
not a whore; in fact, Mike loves her and will marry her in place of
Nancy.

Instead of symbolic father figures, we have a flashback to the
real father, Mike's idol. That important Saturday at the age of 12,
which George started to tell Alice about, is fully recounted by
Mike to Noreen. It begins with the delicious mysteries in Frank
Lavalle's barbershop, continues with a sadistic priest explaining

religious mystery in confirmation class, initiates Mike into the
most beautiful mystery of all, when he and his father go fishing
and Mike catches an enormous pickerel with his father's rod, returns to religious mystery when Mike confesses to a kindly priest,
and ends in ultimate dreadful mystery when Mike's father is
killed in a car accident later that night.

How Many Angels? handles Curley's obsessive themes of
failure and loss by denying them wishfully. The happy ending
makes the book comic, although its tone is never more than wryly
funny. *A Stone Man, Yes* confronts these themes by embracing
them, exaggerating and caricaturing them, accepting life's mysteries in the vocabulary of broad comedy and farce. We are back
with George and Alice Fuller (now George and Alice Scott), with
an older George now chairman of the English department in a
miserable college.

The figure of the mother has merged into the wife who is her
replica, and the Freudian magnolia has wilted. Alice now takes on
monstrous proportions. She and George have separate bedrooms
on separate floors, since his marital embrace is odious to her. She
has become an alcoholic. She habitually addresses George as
"pig," and ceaselessly reproaches him with imaginary infidelities,
in tirades that crackle with mean wit. She has become fanatically
religious.

Actually, as the reader discovers long before George does, all
this is a facade, and it conceals an affair with Steven Pratt, one of
George's young instructors, an affair so physically demanding of
Pratt that he escapes it by drowning himself in the lake, or at
least by leaving his clothes on the shore and disappearing from
the novel. George eventually concludes that Alice's sanctity has
masked an endless chain of adulteries, heterosexual and homosexual. George's discovery of his cuckolding is the wildest farce: in
an official going-through of Pratt's papers after his disappearance,
George learns that Pratt had an unidentified married mistress of
insatiate passions, realizes that she would now be unemployed,
and tries to learn her identity in order to make her his own. When
he finally realizes that she already *is* his own, he resolves to shoot
her, instead.

The motif of losing that fat whore to the brute is easily introduced: Curley simply reprints "The Fugitive," rewritten, as an adventure of George's. The theme is later enlarged into mad farce in George's dream that he, a fellow undergraduate, and the old Judge in whose house they live, are in a hotel room with a whore so fat that a hand sinks to the wrist in the folds of her belly. George pretends to be asleep while the other two share her abundance, in an uproarious scene.

The beating by the brute finds a similar apotheosis in broad comedy, when George tries to seduce Pratt's girl, a big beautiful physical education teacher. He manages to get her clothes off, at which point she throws him over her hip (hurting his poor back) and straddles him on the floor, her lovely breasts in his face, telling him that she must remain virgin for Steven. Later, provoked beyond endurance, George punches Alice between the eyes.

The father figure is the old Judge, called Dean Percy in the dream and aged 100. He is a marvelous old Fat Knight. When George puts him to bed drunk after the hotel room scene, George thinks indignantly: "that old hypocrite, liar, sot, lecher, that fraud, that dirty, disgusting whited sepulcher. . . . father indeed—" He is indeed George's ideal farcical father, and he initiates George into the Oedipal mysteries of fat mama.

At the end, of course, George does not shoot Alice. Instead, he becomes reconciled with her in a perfect academic resolution: Alice will take over Pratt's classes for the rest of the year. George thinks: "nothing had changed but everything was different." In his final acceptance of Alice's past, George is enlarged, and one suddenly realizes that *A Stone Man, Yes* is a comic rewriting of Joyce's "The Dead," perhaps a conscious parody, with the same deep humanity. I never thought to find myself saying of an academic novel that it tells the truth, but *A Stone Man, Yes* is true, as the best caricatures are *true*, and terribly, terribly funny.

MAN CRITICIZING

"It would be presumptuous to claim that this mixture creates a new form of literary criticism," says the jacket of George P. Elliott's first book of essays, *A Piece of Lettuce*. Well, I am prepared to be presumptuous. Five of the book's 15 essays are examples of a fascinating new form of literary and cultural criticism that Elliott has invented: criticism by autobiography and parable. I cannot imagine other critics using the form, for reasons that I hope will become clear, but it is perfect for Elliott, and it is the first sign of blood in the veins of our criticism for many years.

Each of the five essays has its own uniqueness. "The Sky and a Goat" is an argument against formalism or aestheticism, a defense of "imperfect poems that contain a message." The example discussed is Winfield Townley Scott's "The U. S. Sailor with the Japanese Skull," and the poem is criticized technically but is ultimately justified as having "shown me a truth that matters." This literary argument is framed in what at first seems an irrelevant autobiographical excursion, Elliott's account of having grown up in a Southern California desert, on the edge of a carob plantation, and of a rude practical joke he once played on his parents.

A discussion of his youthful romantic tastes in poetry (desert nature was not *real* nature—no nightingales or wild thyme) leads into an account of his contrasting present views. Suddenly Elliott produces an emblem from the desert to explain his partiality toward imperfect poems. It is "Eva, our three-titted goat, whom I used to milk." Milking Eva's comically deformed udder taught Elliott that rich nourishment may spurt from the imperfect and the unbeautiful.

"Getting Away from the Chickens" is a defense of fantasy and escapist reading against the reality principle, and a critique of James' *The Princess Casamassima*. Elliott quotes a passage from this book and one from *Tarzan of the Apes*, and challenges the reader to tell which is which; his conclusion is that *The Princess* is "Burroughs for sophisticates." Interspersed with this jape is an account of Elliott's first job, the summer that he was 16, tending several thousand chickens. The details of the work are revolting, and the reader does not find it surprising when Elliott writes: "Most of my free time I spent getting away from the chickens." His refuge from the chickens was fantasy literature, and it is as fantasy that he defends James. The last two pages of the piece tell Elliott's bold parable: one night that summer a hen laid an egg in his mouth, and since then Elliott has been "*ab ovo*, a fantast."

The most ambitious of the essays, "A Brown Fountain Pen," is an attack on what Elliott calls "the muck-cult." More accurately, it is a defense of the tragic movement, going down into the pit in order to arise transformed, otherwise the Dantean movement, reaching Paradiso by way of Inferno and Purgatorio. Yeats' poetry is quoted and analyzed at length, and he is oddly compared to Elliott's father: both "believed and didn't believe" in mediums, both "believed history was not progressive but came in 2000-year cycles."

Then there is an attack on the muck-cultists, principally Henry Miller and Norman Mailer (the latter is given a blistering conjunction: "Who am I?" "Vote for me."). Finally Elliott tells the story of the brown fountain pen that his parents bought him for $5 out of their monthly income of $85 during the Depression. He lost it down the outhouse hole, and his father dug down, out of love, and recovered it for him—Elliott wrote with the pen for the next 20 years. It is a parable of love, and somehow a demonstration of why Yeats is "the greatest poet of the age."

"Coming of Age on the Carob Plantation" defends the rich complexity of life against oversimplification. It is cultural rather than literary criticism. Margaret Mead's anthropology is attacked as one sort of reductionism, imposing artificial patterns; Robert Penn Warren's *John Brown* is exposed as another, "saint-hating"; and personality-research in psychology is instanced as a third, quantifying the unquantifiable. There is a wonderfully funny account of the different ways each would wreck the story of Abraham going off to sacrifice Isaac. The answer to all this emerges as

Elliott's wrestling his father when Elliott was 15, and bigger than the old man. As they wrestled, the boy's "bones melted" and his "knees buckled," and the senior Elliott threw him. Was that the son's coming of age, as the simplifiers would have it? Certainly not. "I guess I came of age in the usual, unshapely American way —that is to say, by turning twenty-one."

The title essay, "A Piece of Lettuce," argues chance against design, and the work of literature it concentrates on is *War and Peace*. The theme of mediocrity is mysteriously introduced. It is the danger inherent in the mode of realism employed in *War and Peace;* Elliott at 13 suspected that his father might be mediocre; at 19 he decided that he must be mediocre himself. Next chance is pursued: Elliott discovers the gaps in determinism by seeing a cigarette butt blown onto a clump of dandelion; his baby brother looked as though his eye had gone blind, but it was only a piece of lettuce stuck to the eyeball; the son of friends died as the result of a fantastic series of coincidences. Then it turns out that chance is one of the great themes of *War and Peace,* but that it is all controlled and determined by Tolstoy's art; as for mediocrity, Tolstoy "is not dedicated to hatred of mediocrity as was Flaubert." If God is not protecting the Elliotts, Tolstoy is, in a sense, and the story of the piece of lettuce is a parable of the powers of the omnipotent artist.

This highly personal critical form is right for Elliott because it perfectly fits his message: the affirmation of Life and Love. This is a very unfashionable message at present, and Elliott is stating it as a corrective to what he sees as our Alexandrianism. That is, he is writing counter-statements, in the tradition of George Orwell, whom he places "as a sort of corrective to the esoterics who have been overrunning literary criticism." Elliott's life, with its history of family love, bears witness to his views, and its events are emblematic because nothing is meaningless, because everything that lives is holy.

In briefly synopsizing these essays, I have not done justice to the complexity of Elliott's juggling, the intricacy of his weaving. "Getting Away from the Chickens" has not only its final emblematic egg but a whole clutch of eggs: there is a Freudian egg, a

Gravesian egg, a Jamesian egg, a dyed Easter egg, even a candy
egg with a scene inside that becomes an ironic subplot. In putting
his life and beliefs in the foreground, Elliott becomes something
like an Emersonian figure of a Man Criticizing. "A Brown Fountain Pen" not only tells its parable of love and redemption, it is
also a comprehensive intellectual history of its author.

Let me say, if it needs saying, that my high opinion of Elliott's essays is not based on their speaking for me. I am formalist,
materialist, and rationalist, where he is content-oriented, fantast,
and Christian. I am as deeply skeptical of Life and Love as I
would be of Hearts and Flowers. The Scott poem Elliott praises in
"The Sky and a Goat" is a bad poem, and not because it is "true,"
but because it is badly written, as Elliott partially demonstrates,
and because its raw shock has not been digested into art.

Beyond that, these essays do not fully express Elliott's views
either. If Henry James is only a tonier Edgar Rice Burroughs in
"Getting Away from the Chickens," another essay in the book
makes it clear that Elliott believes him to be preeminent among
"a few writers of excellence" in his age. If "Getting Away from
the Chickens" argues for escapist reading, another essay in the
book dismisses the habit as using "literature as a drug for killing
time and dulling anxiety." Elliott's positions are stances, necessary
correctives.

The danger is of falling into Philistinism, as when Elliott declares in "The Sky and a Goat" that he "would rather have a
bucket full of goat's milk" than a Greek vase. Ultimately he is
limited by a preference for the representational over the abstract
and for spirit over nature. "I cannot imagine a statue of a reptile
or of no-thing," he writes, "which could please as *David* does." I
can, having seen quite a few of them in ancient and primitive
art.

The remaining ten essays in the book are of a more routine
sort. Even here Elliott cannot entirely keep himself out. There is
a brief account of the carob plantation in "Raymond Chandler,"
and "Who is *We?*" (a silly essay) interrupts its discussion of Leslie
Fiedler's theories to tell the story of a chaste night Elliott once
spent in bed with a truck driver named Smitty. The essays are
studded with insights, but these insights tend to be into life rather

than art. Elliott writes, for example, of Southern California: "The sex is mostly in the nerves, very little in the heart. In the heart, if nothing else, there are cars."

The best of the traditional essays is "Ezra Pound," which keeps a perfect balance of admiring Pound's technical mastery and despising the late *Cantos* as "muttery humming, with snarls," of admiring Pound's "generosity of soul" and detesting his fascism. For some reason, Elliot dismisses the explanation "He suffered from paranoia" as "vapid." (Would he similarly dismiss "He suffered from gallstones"?) The essay "Getting to Dante" is almost as good: it is hurt by a curious analogy of Dante with Freud as a reporter of the unconscious.

Ultimately Elliott's strength lies not in straight criticism, but in following the bent of his genius (to borrow a pun from Thoreau) in the autobiographical pieces. "I see a paradigm of man," he writes in "A Brown Fountain Pen," "in one hand a puddle of mucus with a blood kernel, in the other a spiral of stars." It is far too long since we have heard such a voice in American criticism.

NEW VOICES OF ISAAC BABEL

Whoever may be the foremost major writer of our century, Isaac Babel is surely its foremost minor writer. In his lifetime he published 60-odd stories and sketches, the best of them of matchless mastery. Babel was part of that astounding wave of Jewish creativity in Europe that included Freud and Einstein, Proust and Kafka. Babel has been called "the greatest Russian stylist since Pushkin": I am in no position to judge that, but Babel is certainly (if one classifies Nabokov, his only peer, as an American) the greatest Russian fiction writer since Chekhov.

Babel's daughter, Nathalie Babel, has edited *The Lonely Years 1925-1939*, consisting of eight new stories, several hundred of Babel's letters to his mother and sister, and an appendix of relevant documents. The stories are of considerable interest. The best of them, "Froim Grach," is a melancholy conclusion to Babel's earlier stories of Benya Krik and the colorful Odessa Jewish gangsters. In it, Froim, the legendary one-eyed leader of the Moldevanka gang, goes to the Cheka to complain that they are ruthlessly executing his men (so unlike the comic-opera Czarist police in the earlier story, "The King"). While Borovoi, an Odessa interrogator for the Cheka, is rounding up other officials to show them the remarkable Froim, Simen, the 22-year-old Moscow-bred head of the Odessa Cheka, has Froim summarily taken out and shot. The tiny perfect story ends with Simen justifying himself to Borovoi ("What good was this man for the society of the future?"), and Borovoi, after a moment of doubt, spiritedly telling the Moscow Chekists stories of Froim and the bandits, "all those extraordinary stories that are now a thing of the past."

Two sketches in the book, "Kolyvushka" and "Gapa Guzhva," were to be parts of a "novel" (that is, a series of related stories and sketches after the fashion of *Red Cavalry*) called *Velikaya Krinitsa*, about a village being reorganized as a collective farm.

Both deal with types unsuitable for collectivization: Ivan Koly-vushka is a peasant evicted by the collective, and Gapa is a lusty widow. Ivan's reaction is to kill his horse with an axe and to wreck his machinery, meanwhile shouting to the bystanders: "I'm a man, a peasant— Haven't you ever seen one before?" Gapa's reaction is to confront the official in charge of collectivization with a desperate question: "Will they be left in peace, the whores, or not?"

Two other stories demonstrate Babel's mastery of economy, in the second case by a negative example. The first, "Answer to an Inquiry," is a brilliant four-page account of the narrator's going to bed with a Tiflis whore, improvising a story of having been a male concubine for Armenians, and getting his ten rubles refunded out of professional courtesy— "This was my first author's fee." "My First Fee" is a later and much less successful rewriting of the story at twice the length. For example, there is a perfect sentence in the first version: "In a small glass bowl filled with a milky liquid flies were dying—each in its own way." In the second this becomes four sentences, with descriptions of the death throes. (The most charitable guess is that "My First Fee" is one of the pieces about which Babel wrote to his mother and sister in 1931: "The scribblings are rather trivial—they've been padded in order to cover the advances.")

The three remaining stories are early slice-of-life realism. "Mama, Rimma and Alla" and "Ilya Isaakovich and Margarita Prokofievna" were Babel's first publications in 1916, when he was 22. "The Tale of a Woman" was published somewhat later. There are touches that announce Babel's genius in all three, but he had not yet found his wry personal form.

The letters are immensely important, the first real look that the English-speaking world has had at Babel himself. These letters are not themselves works of art, as are those of Keats (perhaps only a very young writer can write such letters). Instead they are a look behind the works of art into the desperate conditions of their manufacture, as are the letters of Fitzgerald. Their most frequent tone is hysteria. As personal documents, Babel's letters are primarily a record of what he calls in one of them his "one true, unchanging and indestructible love"—for his mother ("I'd beat myself into a pancake for her sake," he writes). After

1929, when Babel's daughter was born, he had two true loves.

The great interest the letters have is as a record of the same ambivalence we find in the fiction. There is quite an autobiography in the comic pseudonyms with which Babel signs letters: "Worker for Enlightenment no. 3929," "Hermit Crab," "Isaac Spinoza," "Ivan Karpovich Babel" (Ivan Karpovich was a stableman), "I. Diogenov." One of the great ambivalences in Babel, the subject of that beautiful story "The Awakening," is between culture and nature, his culture-centered Jewish heritage and the world of Russian nature that it rejected. (Babel refers in a letter to "one of Papa's rules—to stay clear of nature.")

Culture is represented in the letters by a ceaseless preoccupation with reading and writing. But the attraction of nature is equally powerful. As a result of his cavalry experience, Babel was mad for horses: he lived in the village of Molodenovo because of a stud farm nearby; he hung around racetracks and jockeys; in Moscow he could only regain "peace of mind" by visiting a stable. The Russian countryside had a comparable appeal for him: he writes endlessly to his mother and sister in Brussels of "the beauty of the Russian winter," of a landscape "lovely, cool, reassuring, so Russian," of "the amazing beauty spread out around me" at Molodenovo.

This complex and ironic man had the most unsophisticated pastoral feeling about countrymen. He writes: "I'll meet the New Year at the stud farm as is fitting, in the company of simple and therefore good people." Babel did his best to become one. "Under the direction of a stableman," Babel boasts, "I am learning a new profession—the handling of horses. It's a delight that isn't comparable with any other." At another time: "At Molodenovo they still use sickles for reaping. I have learnt the knack and handled one with infinite delight."

Babel's greatest ambivalence, however, is a dichotomy within culture: the rival appeals of communism and Judaism. (This is seen despondently in the story "The Rabbi's Son" in Red Cavalry, more optimistically in the later story "Karl-Yankel.") At times in the letters Babel seems quite firm in the Soviet faith. He writes in 1934, for example, of "this boundless, forward-streaking, never-before-seen land called the USSR," and announces: "Real miracles are taking place in our country. There is an incredibly rapid rise in the general welfare and the world has really never seen such an outburst of energy and cheerfulness." At the same time Babel is full of nostalgia for the Jewish religion and for "that old crook the Jewish God." He keeps the Passover, the years that he remembers to, by buying matzos and attending the seders of relatives; in 1937 he sends his mother and sister Rosh Hashanah greetings, and he promises to go to the synagogue on Yom Kippur.

In part, both these stands are deceptions. The praise for the Soviet Union is certainly written for the censorship: in 1925, when censors were not a problem, Babel writes of Moscow as "an environment devoid of art or creative freedom"; writing from abroad in 1933, he wastes no words on forward-streaking. The letters speak of the glories of "total collectivization," of "unforgettable Velikaya Staritsa" and the "limitless vistas" opening up—but we know Babel's true feelings about collectivization from the stories of Ivan and Gapa in his fictitious Velikaya Krinitsa. Similarly, the seders and synagogues, if they are not jokes, are put in to please his mother. Babel was an atheist.

There is no doubt, however, that he really was pulled in both directions. Babel steadfastly refused to emigrate when he could, or to stay abroad the few times that he was allowed out to visit his wife and daughter in Paris and his mother and sister in Brussels. As for those anachronisms the Jews, Jewish memories are the subject of every single one of Babel's best stories.

After the hysterical tone of the letters, it is a relief to get back to the iron control of the stories. A new collection of Babel's stories was published in paperback in 1963, translated by Andrew R. MacAndrew, who translated most of *The Lonely Years*. It is called *Lyubka the Cossack and Other Stories*. It includes three stories not in Walter Morison's *The Collected Stories*, two of them rather trivial, and a third, "The Road There," the brilliant shocker that appeared in Blake and Hayward's *Dissonant Voices*. MacAndrew leaves out five of the 35 pieces in *Red Cavalry* (while assuring the reader that "all of them are included"), along with four others in the Morison book. His translation appears to be more accurate than Morison's: at least it is earthier (where Morison's *barin*, for example, says "I've tickled all your maternal parents," MacAndrew's says "I've tumbled your ma and the mothers of the likes of you"). For style, I still prefer Avrahm Yarmolinsky's translation in *Benya Krik* to either. Inexplicably, MacAndrew has put the stories "in an order that reflects the chronological sequence of Babel's life."

As a writer during the first two decades of the Russian Revolution, Babel is primarily the chronicler of its misfits, of those eggs that are broken but then not used in the omelette. Nathalie Babel has made available some new misfits: implacable Froim, crazed Ivan, drunk and dissolute Gapa. Babel is in the position of his character Borovoi, knowing that they are useless elements for the socialist future, but also knowing how much the socialist future is thereby diminished.

"My life is easy, happy and privileged," Babel writes to his mother in 1935, and indeed it was, in some respects. In 1939 he writes that he is finally settled in the fancy *dacha* built for him as an honored writer, at work on a film about his dead friend and protector Gorky, resolved to make this his final filmscript and get back "to my true work." It is Babel's last letter. He was denounced, arrested, and never seen again. Stalin's Russia had decided that four-eyed Babel was as useless an element in the socialist future as one-eyed Froim.

REASON IN MADNESS

Scented Gardens for the Blind, by the New Zealand writer Janet Frame, is the most remarkable novel that I have read in many years. If it is not a work of genius (I feel that all such heady possibilities should be kept in pickle for a few years), it is surely a brilliant and overwhelming tour de force. I was held captive by it from the first page to the last, as they lightly say of thrillers. Although it is certainly not a novel for everybody, it is assuredly for anybody who values in the novel the qualities more often associated, in our diminished time, with poetry: intellectual complexity, ornate and figurative language, and intense moral seriousness.

This amazing novel consists of three strands, in successive chapters. The first is an interior monologue by Vera Glace, a middle-aged woman who lives alone in a house in a New Zealand town with her adolescent daughter, Erlene. Vera suffers from the fact that Erlene has lost the power of speech, and Vera herself is greatly tempted by the attractions of psychic blindness: in what she calls "a marriage with darkness" she sees not only greater safety, but the possibilities of a purer light, "a light that does not suffer the stain of human vision; a pure light resting, like a bandage, close to the deepest wound of the dark."

Vera's obsession is a terrible undefined guilt, related to Erlene's dumb state. "If I knew that her first words were to be judgment upon me," Vera thinks, "I would kill her, I would go now to the little room where she sits alone in the dark, and kill her, and she would not be able to cry for help." "Erlene must be prevented from telling the truth about me," Vera resolves. Yet we never learn what that truth is. Sometimes it seems a universal human guilt, an Original Sin. "It is a condition of human life that blame rests, like a butterfly on a leaf," Vera thinks. At other times it seems some specific guilt connected with Erlene's condition, or with the long-drawn-out death of Vera's father, or with Vera's

once having drowned a sack of kittens. Somehow, Vera is doomed
if Erlene speaks, but equally: "If she does not speak I am
doomed." The last words we hear from Vera in the book are brave
rather than reassuring: "But I am innocent. How can I convince
the world that I am innocent?"

Vera's characteristic voice, immediately distinguishable from
the others, is preoccupied with inhumanity. Its central vision is of
homeless beggars attacked by "strange menacing dogs," while the
respectable householders keep their doors safely barred. Vera
often hears the beggars pleading outside, and she asks herself desperately: "How soon shall we learn enough to be able to open the
door to them without putting ourselves in more grave danger?"

The second strand, in chapters following Vera's, consists of
Erlene's thoughts and actions. Although she is speechless, she has
long conversations with a blackbeetle on the window sill—her
Uncle Blackbeetle, in fact. She also has sessions with a therapist
named Dr. Clapper, although the question of whether or not she
speaks a few words to him is in dispute. Erlene is as much in love
with death as her mother is with blindness, and death is rarely out
of her mind. She wishes herself dead; she sees a fly mashed on
Dr. Clapper's window and imagines the doctor threatening to kill
her similarly—soon there are two more dead flies on the window,
then four, then the window is opaque with blood.

Erlene's typical voice is the voice of Uncle Blackbeetle telling
her a story, never about anything but death. He summons up a
vision: "It's the soldiers passing in twos and threes, with iron
bands round their foreheads and little sachets of diseases and lav-
ender flowers tied to their waists, and their teeth cleaned with
white ash." "Wood ash?" she asks. "People ash," he answers. Erlene dreams of these soldiers, who become her image of the
human condition, as chilling and impersonal as her mother's beggars and dogs are chilling and personal.

The third strand, in chapters following Erlene's, consists of
the thoughts and actions of Edward Glace, who deserted his wife
and daughter eleven years before to go back to England. His
chosen life work is compiling the history of a family named
Strang, and by the time of the novel he has progressed to the
living Strangs. Edward's hobby is playing war with plastic sol-

diers. Where Vera and Erlene are roaring mad, Edward is only
meekly mad, to the extent that he comes in the course of the novel
to hear imaginary voices, which sometimes mutter obscenities
about the Strangs.

Edward is a conventional humanitarian, worried about The
Bomb, and his aimless recording of the Strangs is somehow a shor-
ing of human fragments against global ruin. Vera recalls "a husband who keeps people, like hens or pigs, in an enclosure of Time,
hoping to protect them from extinction; he feeds and fattens their
histories; all has been well; only now they have strayed into the
present—how will he cope with them?" Erlene thinks: "He is preserving the human race in syrup, heavy syrup, but the weight on
the container is false, and nobody realizes." Edward's distinctive
voice is petulant, and his vision of mankind centers in illness: "old
bronchial fluey men and women." A crowded bus becomes his
metaphor: "So this was humanity—tension, disagreement, dis-
comfort, the common cold."

For fifteen marvelous chapters, five devoted to each character, this symphony of mad voices goes on, reminding us of the
blending of three different pitches of derangement on the heath
in *King Lear*. Then it is all abruptly resolved in the sixteenth and
last chapter, given to Dr. Clapper. All the voices, he reveals, are
those of Vera Glace, a spinster of sixty who has been a patient in
his asylum since she was mysteriously struck dumb thirty years
before. Another patient named Clara Strang looks after her. For a
moment we feel a pang of disappointment, a sense of being
cheated, as we do at the end of William Golding's *Pincher Martin*
when we discover that Martin died instantaneously and that all
his stubborn survival has been imaginary.

I am still not sure that the formal break is right. But the revelation is. We had known that Vera was a paranoid schizophrenic
("I believed, in my powerless state, that I had once been in control of the world," she thinks); surely it is fitting for her to be a
dissociated personality in addition, with her stubborn silence and
death wish projected onto an imaginary daughter, and her faint
and scattered life impulses identified with an imaginary former
husband. Throughout the book we have felt a unity under the
rhetorical variety that is more than the unity of authorship. Ed-

ward has been seen as "a lighthouse keeper whose beacon shines upon three wrecks and he must choose which to rescue first, not realizing that he has been deceived and there is only one wreck." "Erlene knew," we were told, "that there were no Strangs, that her father was a myth and a dream, that he would never return, and that neither she herself nor her mother was real."

Vera is in fact a monstrous parody of the Trinity, an Unholy Family at once three persons and one. Midway in the book Erlene fancies herself pregnant from Dr. Clapper's stare, and she imagines herself giving birth to Jesus in the garden shed. Later she fancies herself pregnant by Uncle Blackbeetle, but Uncle Blackbeetle has always looked like a black aspect of Dr. Clapper, and eventually the two merge. In our last view of Erlene, her father returns to New Zealand and appears in her room to persuade her to talk—of course he too is now Uncle Blackbeetle.

Nor is Miss Frame yet through with us. In the last chapter, after her thirty years of silence, Vera Glace is restored to speech. Britain has been destroyed by The Bomb, and Vera is then seen sitting up cheerfully, speaking the "new language of mankind": "Ug-g-Ug. Ohhh Ohh g. Ugg." Ultimately Vera is a shocking yet deeply compassionate symbol for Thermonuclear Man, or Woman: struck dumb by the threat, struck babbling by the reality.

There are great risks in an ascent of this sort: the climb is laced with crevasses, and Miss Frame falls into some of them. The grotesque may melt into whimsy, as when Uncle Blackbeetle tells of his literary cousin who lived in the dictionary, or his cousin Albert Dungbeetle who believed that dung fell from God. Images are sometimes heaped until they topple, or they lie labored and flat. Those mad voices telling us profundities occasionally slip in a pseudo-profundity.

But the rewards are comparably great. So much of *Scented Gardens for the Blind* is truly, marvelously, *imagined*. One great theme is a vision of terror embracing the meekest creatures. The danger is from "moth grubs which chew your face in the dark and spit out the wishbones behind your eyes"; pigeons cry "Fail-curdle" as rooks cry "Flaw"; the fate of Icarus today is not melting in the sun but being "forced down into a paddock full of strange cattle who have devoured him, flesh, bone, skin, and left only one torn paper-and-paste wing."

Answering this nonsense of terror is a counter-nonsense full of the deepest human compassion. Uncle Blackbeetle's work on Erlene's window sill is making little coffins for the beans who die daily, principally from thirst. They shrivel and die, they go blind in their one black eye. The tiniest beans, who die without opening their eyes, will fit three in a coffin, but Uncle Blackbeetle would never put three together, since that would be mass burial.

It is hard to guess at the influences behind this amazing book. Lewis Carroll, primarily. Certainly Golding, probably Djuna Barnes (if Dr. O'Connor wrote a novel, this would be it), possibly Virginia Woolf, perhaps William Faulkner, maybe even John Hawkes. It remains a unique and unclassifiable work. I have not read Miss Frame's earlier books, and I am almost afraid to start.

THE BIBLE AS HISTORY

I am, and have been for a long time, an amateur student of the Bible and of archaeology. When Dr. Werner Keller's *The Bible as History* appeared in 1956, I somehow missed it. I resolved not to miss its sequel, *The Bible as History in Pictures,* translated by Dr. William Neil. My reward was the experience of reading, with mounting shock, one of the most ignorant and fraudulent books I have ever encountered.

Keller's principal trick is illustration by false syllogism. He demonstrates the historicity of Abraham by showing the ruins of Haran and a statue of its governor at the time. He confirms God's punishment of Sodom and Gomorrah with a photograph of a pillar of salt near the Dead Sea, captioned, "Among the many remarkable salt formations, some of them surprisingly human in appearance, is one which still to this day recalls the punishment of Lot's wife." (But *is* it Lot's wife, and if so, who are the others?) Was Joseph really in Egypt? Here are photographs of the Sphinx and some pyramids, "which Joseph and many of his kinsmen must have seen." And the bondage? Just take a look at this photograph of a brick with wisps of straw in it.

How can anyone refuse to believe that David killed Goliath as described, after one has seen a photograph of an ancient sling stone from the area? Solomon *must* have built the Temple, because at a place now called "Solomon's quarries," "traces of quarrying are plainly visible." How about Jesus calming the wind and waves on the sea of Galilee? Here is a photograph of the sea itself, and its sudden squalls "can be quite dangerous." We can no longer doubt that Jesus healed a paralyzed man at the pool Bethesda, by saying, "Rise, take up thy bed, and walk," since Keller shows us a picture of the very pool. (Why not the very bed?)

Nor is this the only sort of slyness and deceit. Reconstructions drawn from Bible descriptions are cleverly interspersed among the photographs, as though those things too had been dug up. Only a careful reader will discover that the page of the Epistle to the Romans pictured is not St. Paul's autograph letter.

When Keller deigns to argue, he is foolish. He takes the historicity of the patriarchs as established by the fact that Peleg, Serug, Nahor, and Terah turn up as place names in the Mari Cuneiforms. (This should suggest the opposite conclusion, that the Bible's geneologies are constructed out of anything that came to hand.) Keller propounds Breasted's theory that there is "not even the barest mention" of Joseph in "the otherwise meticulously accurate Egyptian records" because the events occurred when Egypt was under the Hyksos occupation. (This solves the problem by raising a much more severe one: why then does Genesis describe, not Egypt turned topsy-turvy by the Hyksos, but a traditional Egypt ruled by the Pharaohs?) But Keller rarely argues. His custom is to assert, usually with maddening vagueness: "Many scholars today reckon." "This is thought to have been," "Experts believe," and so on.

Keller is a German journalist, and I do not know of what branch of learning he is a doctor. He is unbelievably ignorant of Bible scholarship and criticism. He thinks that Assyrian kings fought lions hand to hand, because they are shown doing so on reliefs, and he is impressed by their bravery. (This is on the order of believing that Egyptian kings habitually stood on the heads of their enemies.) Keller has no idea what history is, or what might be considered historical evidence. Nor does he know a syllable of Hebrew, to judge by his statement that the name Seraiah "suggests that this dignitary was an Egyptian." (It is a typical Hebrew name, meaning "God strives.") Keller is so credulous that he believes in Herod's Massacre of the Innocents.

Keller's real interest, as the book makes clear, is custom and costume, and he keeps insisting on "the astonishing accuracy of the biblical record of the life and customs." There is no mention in his index of Covenant or Passion, but there are 29 entries under "Hairstyle," in ten categories.

Where earlier writers of books of this sort have had the humility to give them such titles as *Daily Life in Bible Times*, Keller has the effrontery to claim that he is *confirming* the Bible. Archae-

ologists given to *schliemannizing* (claiming to have discovered
Agamemnon's Tomb or Priam's Treasury when they have dug up
an anonymous burial), in order to make a splash in the newspa-
pers, must share some of the blame for Keller. A stable with stalls
for 450 horses excavated at Megiddo is King Solomon's Stable
(Solomon has stalls for 40,000 horses in I Kings 4:26; where are
the other 88 stables?); a copper mine found at Ezion-geber is
King Solomon's Mine. These claims are the excavators', not Keller's.

To the believer, I should imagine, all this is irrelevant or distasteful. Keller is convinced that Leonard Woolley found the
Flood in Mesopotamia, and he shows a photograph of a thick de-
posit of clay that it left at Ur. But the Flood in Genesis is not a
Mesopotamian inundation, but a story of God's destruction of all
flesh for its wickedness, of the salvation of the righteous Noah and
his family, in an ark containing breeding pairs (or sevens) of all
the animals in the world, and of the covenant afterwards established with Noah. It is a story, in short, of divine justice and
mercy, not of water and mud.

The small part of the book devoted to the New Testament, 30
pages out of more than 300, largely ignores the Gospels to concen-
trate on The Acts of the Apostles: the events of Holy Week are
passed by in silence, with the barest mention of the Crucifixion
and none of the Resurrection, while St. Paul's travels are illustrated in detail. But the New Testament is not a travelogue to
Christians; it is an account of Christ crucified, risen, and to come
again.

Keller does one positive disservice to believers: in his eagerness to show the Prophets as prophetic, he makes them seem
pseudepigraphic (later false attributions). One by one they are
credited with foreseeing the rise and fall of Assyria and Babylon,
the captivity and return; Zephania even "foresaw with horror" so
unpredictable an event as the Scythian invasion of Palestine. The
Book of Daniel is conventionally dated about 164 B.C. because
that is the date of its last accurate "prophecy"; the accurate
prophecies of the Prophets would seem to suggest that their
books too were written *after* the events they "predicted," that
they are all post-Exilic. (This has always been the contention of

the radical critics, who date the Priestly compiler late and the Prophetic books later, seeing them as nationalistic and Pharisaic reactions to Hellenism, written from 350 to 150 B.C.)

If *The Bible as History in Pictures* is irrevelant or a disservice to the religious, it is an insult to the intelligence of the rationalist. Actually, archaeology confirms little in the Bible, and nothing of any significance. Before the ninth century B.C., there are only two items. The Canaanite Amarna letters, about 1400 B.C., mention the "Hapiru," who may or may not be the Hebrews; the stele of Pharaoh Merenptah, about 1230 B.C., mentions a people of Israel, perhaps, living in Palestine. In the ninth century some real history begins to appear in the Bible, in Kings and II Chronicles, and it has been confirmed by archaeology. The Moabite Stone (which is probably a fake, but no matter) boasts a victory by Moab over King Omri of Israel, about 840 B.C. The Black Obelisk of Shalmaneser III of Assyria, a few years later, shows King Jehu of Israel paying tribute. The annals of Tiglath Pileser III of Assyria, about 730 B.C., describe his conquest of Israel and name kings named in the Bible, as do the annals of his successor Sargon II. Babylonian cuneiform records of 592 B.C., describe the captivity of King Jehoiachin in Babylon. That is all, except for a few Hebrew finds. A seal names King Jeroboam II; King Azariah's tombstone has been discovered, as has his son Jotham's seal; and the Lachish ostraca (inscribed potsherds) tell of the Babylonian conquest of Lachish in the sixth century.

Utterly unsubstantiated, and obviously "sacred history"—that is, myth believed to be history—are not only Adam and Noah and Samson, but Abraham and Isaac and Jacob, Joseph and Moses and Joshua, David and Solomon and the First Temple. The archaeological find that made this clear (*The Bible as History in Pictures* does not mention it) was the discovery, around the turn of the century, of some Aramaic papyri from the island of Elephantine in Egypt. (A. Cowley published them in 1923 in *Aramaic Papyri of the Fifth Century* B.C.) They are the letters and documents of a Jewish colony there contemporary with Ezra. The colonists were orthodox Jews, as their correspondence with the high priest at Jerusalem makes clear, yet their papyri show that they had never heard of Moses or the Torah, the Exodus, the Sabbath, the Patriarchs, the Twelve Tribes, or of any festival except Unleavened Bread. They had their own temple in which they performed blood sacrifices, and they worshipped Yahveh, his female consort Anath, and three other gods.

Archaeology may eventually expose Christian sacred history similarly. Meanwhile, John the Baptist and Jesus, Paul and Peter, remain equally unsubstantiated by archaeology or history. The Christian first century disappears at a touch.

After *The Bible as History in Pictures, The Bible as History* proves an anticlimax. It documents, or at least explains, some of its sequel's unsupported assertions. I now know why Keller believes in Herod's Massacre of the Innocents: "it fits in perfectly" with Herod's "revolting" character.

Keller has become somewhat more sophisticated, or been much corrected, in the eight years between the two books. The drawing of Solomon's Temple in the first book is pure de Mille; the drawing in the second suggests a discreet reformed temple in Scarsdale. Keller has given up his explanation of manna as tamarisk exudations produced by a plant louse; in the new book, which does not mention manna, he limits himself to explaining the quail. He has learned that ostraca are not "baked clay tablets." He no longer identifies two Assyrian soldiers on a relief as "Tiglath-Pileser II (with bow and sword) besieging a fortress." (Did he think that one was Tiglath and the other Pileser?) The first book claims to be addressed to "churchmen and agnostics alike." This one, with 329 illustrations, is more openly addressed to Keller's true public, the nitwits.

RALPH ELLISON IN OUR TIME

Ralph Ellison has always insisted that he is primarily a writer of fiction. Thus he offers a harvest of essays and reviews, *Shadow and Act*, as secondary gleanings from the novelist's life. If these essays do nothing else, he writes modestly in the introduction, they have saved him from cluttering up his fiction "with half-formed or outrageously wrong-headed ideas." Bosh. As a cultural critic, taking his examples mainly from literature and jazz, Ellison is first-rate. His mind is unfailingly interesting, in addition to its special interest to readers of his fiction. While we await the novel with which Ellison has been occupied for many years, we can nourish ourselves very well on these gleanings.

"I lay no claim to being a thinker," Ellison writes with the same habitual modesty. It is true that he is not characteristically an original thinker (how many of us are?) but an applier and extender, and a peculiarly sane and wise one. Ellison's vision is informed by three great truths: a proposition and its two corollaries. These are all so unfashionable at present, in this country at least, that Ellison's is a unique voice, so that the least page of his essays could have been written by no one else.

The proposition is that freedom is the recognition of necessity. In this phrasing, by Engels out of Spinoza, it sounds alien and ideological; but in other language it was early discovered by Ellison in the experience of American Negro life, and was confirmed by his later reading of writers as diverse as Emerson and Malraux. In the introduction to *Shadow and Act*, Ellison writes of the jazz musicians he grew up with in Oklahoma City as "artists who had stumbled upon the freedom lying within the restrictions of their musical tradition as within the limitations of their social background." "Wright was able to free himself in Mississippi," Ellison points out, in a debate with Irving Howe, "because he had the imagination and the will to do so."

In art, the necessity that must be recognized in order to bring freedom is craft, technique. Ellison identifies art as "an instrument of freedom," and defines "the writer's greatest freedom" as "his possession of technique." He writes of the paradoxical necessity that the jazz musician learn "the fundamentals of his instrument and the traditional techniques of jazz," in order "to express his own unique ideas and his own unique voice." Technique, Ellison informs LeRoi Jones, is "the key to creative freedom."

A recognition of necessity similarly brings freedom in life. "Negro American life," Ellison writes in his introduction, is "bearable and human and, when measured by our own terms, desirable." Sometimes he defines this consciousness as a tragic vision. Ellison told Richard G. Stern in an interview in 1961 that American Negroes share "certain tragic attitudes toward experience and toward our situation as Americans." At other times the recognition seems closer to stoicism. "But there is also an American Negro tradition," Ellison reminds Howe, "which teaches one to deflect racial provocation and to master and contain pain. It is a tradition which abhors as obscene any trading on one's own anguish for gain or sympathy; which springs not from a desire to deny the harshness of existence but from a will to deal with it as men at their best have always done."

Most characteristically, Ellison describes this consciousness as neither tragic nor stoic, but as "a tragicomic confrontation of life." He sees this as best exemplified by the blues. "Being initiates," Ellison writes, "Negroes express the joke of it in the blues." The blues, he adds elsewhere, "are, perhaps, as close as Americans can come to expressing the spirit of tragedy." In another essay Ellison talks of "the secular existentialism of the blues." "They are the only consistent art in the United States," he writes, "which constantly remind us of our limitations while encouraging us to see how far we can actually go."

Ellison makes clear that the freedom he talks of is not an escape into the imagination, a flight *from* life, but a freedom *in* life. "The work of art," he writes, "is a social action in itself." It leads to further social action in the real world by broadening the scope of possibility for its readers. The aim of *Invisible Man* was "to explore the full range of American Negro humanity"; if it succeeds even partially in that great aim, no reader, Negro or white, remains unaltered by the book. If American life contains "the very essence of the terrible," a Negro writer can assist the process of transforming it by "defining Negro humanity." This is, of course, Kenneth Burke's dramatistic concept of symbolic action in which art is a naming that transforms attitudes, and attitudes in turn eventuate in actions.

The first corollary that follows from the proposition that freedom is the recognition of necessity is that consequently the writer's responsibility is to write. "The real question," Ellison observes in answering Howe, is: "How does the Negro writer participate *as a writer* in the struggle for human freedom?" In response to Howe's statement that "there may of course be times when one's obligation as a human being supersedes one's obligation as a writer," Ellison replies: "I think that the writer's obligation . . . is best carried out through his role as writer."

I first discovered this truth for myself in the career of Henry Thoreau, and I argued the same unpopular view in "Henry Thoreau in Our Time" in 1946 (the essay is reprinted in *The Promised End*). Now I am delighted to see that Ellison not only echoes Thoreau but often sounds like him. "It is not necessary for even the most unimaginative of us to be consumed by flame in order to envision hellfire," Ellison writes in connection with Stephen Crane; "the hot head of a match against the fingernail suffices." "I could escape the reduction imposed by unjust laws and customs," Ellison tells Howe, sternly, "but not that imposed by ideas which defined me as no more than the *sum* of those laws and customs." (The only change Thoreau would have made in the sentence would have been to italicize the "me.")

It is unfortunate that all this had to be stated in controversy with so limited an opponent as Howe (who is not really interested in literature, and has not the dimmest understanding of symbolic action), since this resulted in defining the issues far too narrowly. By the nature of Howe's charges Ellison was forced to emphasize his aesthetic differences with Wright, rather than his aesthetic indebtedness to Wright; he was forced to talk about activism in the Freedom Movement, rather than the fact that art and the imagination *inspired* the Freedom Movement.

The second corollary that follows from Ellison's proposition is that fraternity in the world of the imagination is the necessary preparation for fraternity in society. "I learned very early," Ellison told Stern in the interview reprinted in *Shadow and Act*, "that in the realm of the imagination all people and their ambitions and interests could meet." As *Moby-Dick* and *Huckleberry Finn* are "great dramas of interracial fraternity," so are they social forces as real as sit-ins. "The way home we seek," Ellison said when he received the National Book Award in 1953, "is that condition of man's being at home in the world, which is called love, and which we term democracy." Jazz similarly creates "images of black and white fraternity," not only simply, in the mixed band and the unsegregated club, but more complexly in jazz's essential nature as a marriage of cultural traditions, and thus "the most authoritative rendering of America in music."

Ellison and I have been friends for almost a quarter of a century. In *Shadow and Act* he praises me once or twice, then in one essay identifies me as "an old friend and intellectual sparring partner" and does his best to beat my brains out. I would be faithless to that friendship and tradition, and would earn my readers' distrust in addition, if I failed to point out that the great virtues of the book are accompanied by many faults. These essays and reviews are a mixed lot, not rewritten, and they vary considerably in quality. The two occasions when Ellison is reduced to counting the Negro characters in the works of American writers are not on the level of sophistication of the rest of the book; a previously unpublished piece turns out to be a 1944 attack on Gunnar Myrdal for ignoring the class struggle and for taking essentially the line that Ellison himself now takes; the old chicken joke at the end of the piece about Charlie Parker is ruinous.

A more important criticism is that these essays, by their occasional nature, their glancing references to books and authors, do not offer the full confrontation of Melville or Dostoevsky or Malraux in Ellison's terms that he owes us and that only he can do. Faulkner's *Intruder in the Dust*, by an accident of journalism, is tackled only in the film version. Beyond that, Ellison has limits: he is too respectful of received opinion; he is not at his best in polemic; he is reluctant to recognize the African elements in American Negro culture. If Ellison's prose sometimes has great beauty and eloquence, it sometimes has great clumsiness; if his similes are at times effective, they are more often strained and farfetched.

But these are the prices to be paid for the novelist's life, for what Ellison calls (in reference to Jimmy Rushing's blues style) the "romantic lyricism" of the Southwest, for the autodidact's fresh eye. Ultimately, Ellison's faults are insignificant weighed against his virtues. *Shadow and Act* is a monument of integrity, a banner proclaiming "the need to keep literary standards high." In his insight into the complexity of American experience, Ralph Ellison is the profoundest cultural critic that we have, and his hard doctrine of freedom, responsibility, and fraternity is a wisdom rare in our time.

THE CORRECTION OF OPINION

It appears to be generally believed that James Purdy is an important American writer. The publication of his third novel, *Cabot Wright Begins,* offers an occasion for dissent. Purdy is a terrible writer, and worse than that, he is a boring writer. The only reason for reviewing bad books is to attempt the correction of opinion, one of the traditional functions of criticism, which has fallen into abeyance in our sleazy literary age. This review will attempt to show the vast discrepancy between the praise of Purdy by so many prominent literary figures and the reality of his work, and will then try to get at the causes of that praise.

Purdy's first book of stories, *Color of Darkness,* appeared in 1956. (There was an earlier private printing of some of the stories, and an English volume.) The book was greeted by a rapturous chorus. "I think that his is a first-rate talent," said James T. Farrell. "A rich and passionate talent," added Winfield Townley Scott. Katherine Anne Porter praised Purdy's style: "Style as fluid and natural as a man thinking to himself in the dark, yet controlled, coherent, with an innate sense of form, and great powers of concentration." "He has the priceless gift of compassion," she added.

Horace Gregory wrote that Purdy's stories "are the only *new* and deeply moving stories written in this country in the 1950's." Dudley Fitts, who had apparently been reading more stories than Gregory, said: "Purdy's stories are the real thing, the veritable real thing, the kind of excitement of art that only J. F. Powers has shown us in recent years, and Flannery O'Connor." Dorothy Parker called Purdy "a striking new American talent, sure and sharp and powerful."

Angus Wilson described the book's novella, "63: Dream Palace," as "a small masterpiece." Dame Edith Sitwell, in an introduction to a paperback edition of *Color of Darkness,* added that the novella is a masterpiece from the first sentence to the last, and she found two other masterpieces in the volume. She put Purdy himself "in the very highest rank of contemporary American writers." John Cowper Powys called him "the best kind of original genius of our day." Kenneth Rexroth said of the book: "I sincerely believe it is one of the best first books of short stories I have ever read." "He will surely enchant the reader who values a new expression of new feeling and experience in our very new times," said Tennessee Williams.

Purdy's first novel, *Malcolm,* appeared in 1959. "The most prodigiously funny book to streak across these heavy-hanging times," wrote Dorothy Parker, going on to commend Purdy's realism, originality, insight, and power. R. W. B. Lewis classed Purdy with Saul Bellow and Ralph Ellison, and compared Malcolm to Billy Budd. David Daiches announced: "It is a very funny book, and whatever else the careful reader will find in it, he will find the delight of true original comedy."

The Nephew, Purdy's second novel, was published the next year. William Carlos Williams wrote to Purdy: "You have squeezed us into a ball, tenderly, heart and soul, and laid us bare with complete understanding." "A complex, reverberating work," said Angus Wilson. "A genuine surprise; an instance of the difference between the creative and the merely literary," wrote Terry Southern.

A volume of stories and plays, *Children Is All* (1962), seems to have disappointed many of these enthusiasts, but Dame Edith Sitwell was loyal to the last. She found "at least three" additional masterpieces in the new book, including one of the plays, and announced: "I think it undoubted that James Purdy will come to be recognized as one of the greatest living writers of fiction in our language."

Cabot Wright Begins (1964) was welcomed by Susan Sontag as "a literary event of importance" by "one of the half dozen or so living American writers worth taking seriously," and Theodore Solotaroff (once himself a corrector of opinion) characterized its ending as "a great moment in contemporary writing." Both compared Purdy to Nathanael West. "*Cabot Wright Begins* is a delight all the way through," said Paul Bowles.

The contrast between all these incandescent words and the

lumpish reality of Purdy's books is shocking. The early stories are ineptly written, but several of them have a raw power that comes from Purdy's imaging domestic hostility and potential violence as *overt* violence. Thus a son kicks his father in the groin, a husband beats his wife bloody at a party, a boy breaks the neck of his younger brother, and (in "Why Can't They Tell You Why?," the best story in *Color of Darkness*) a mother drives her son literally mad.

The later stories, in *Children Is All,* have lost even this power. In its place there is only verbal violence, as in a story that ends with a virtuous wife's rejecting the advances of her wealthy father-in-law with "You whoring old goat!" Or there is the chic shock that begins another story: "Pearl Miranda walked stark naked from her classroom in the George Washington School where she taught the eighth grade, down Locust Street."

The novels are not novels but contrived sequences of visits to grotesque households in quest of someone's identity, and before long Purdy becomes bored with the contrivance and ignores it. "Texture is all, substance nothing," says Madame Girard in *Malcolm,* and her creator appears to agree with her. In *Malcolm* the hero visits, in quest of his own identity, a series of exotic addresses given him by a peripatetic astrologer, then marries and dies. The book is an inconsequential *Candide,* or, more accurately, a pretentious *Candy.* In many respects it is an expansion of "63: Dream Palace," in the genre of sad farce rather than pathos-bathos. Its predominant style is the sort of cuteness that Truman Capote has made peculiarly his own.

The Nephew (which reads as though it had been written before *Malcolm,* and published as a result of *Malcolm's* success) is Midwest small town soap opera. A retired schoolteacher named Alma, living with her brother Boyd, goes on a series of visits in the town to learn more about their dead nephew Cliff (that is, A, B, and a quest for C). Alma learns principally that life is pretty hard on everyone, and she is broadened by the discovery. If Malcolm is a pretentious *Candy, The Nephew* is a pretentious *Peyton Place,* or, to use a borrowed trope, a Burne-Jones allegorical painting entitled "Rigidity Yielding to Compassion."

Cabot Wright Begins is a bad sick joke, a portrait of the Yale man and Wall Street broker as mass rapist. The visits are made by two Chicagoans who come to Brooklyn to interview Wright and *write* his story *right*. The book is a garish scrapbook of Purdy's opinions on the wickedness of our civilization, written in mock-Alger style (an interloper leaves "cursing his assailant roundly") whenever Purdy remembers. An elaborate and complex structure of narratives within narratives serves no purpose beyond introducing the jeremiads. If *The Nephew* is an allegorical painting, *Cabot Wright Begins* is Pop Art.

Purdy's writing is so careless that by p. 172 of *The Nephew* he has forgotten what occurred on p. 159. His prose is ungrammatical, clumsy, graceless, and often unintentionally funny. Here is a sentence from *The Nephew;* "They all sat drinking now with the exception of Alma, who having tasted from her glass gingerly, only made pretense from then on to imbibe any more." Here is one from *Cabot Wright Begins:* "Stooping to pick it up, her eyes were riveted to the irregularly margined triple-spaced words, giving the effect of having been branded on the paper by an iron."

Purdy specializes in the inept simile. In *Malcolm,* Madame Girard's eyelids flutter "like a medium who sees the ghost she had never thought to catch." A woman's life in *Cabot Wright Begins* "had been as unpleasant as though she had been tied under the posterior regions of a huge mammoth, such as a rhinoceros." In general, Purdy writes like a careless undergraduate. Malcolm is warned not to expose his tattoo "to the unprotected sun." Alma keeps "a replenished store of nuts for the squirrels." (Here Purdy is clearly trying to write two sentences at once, one saying that Alma keeps a store of nuts, the other saying that she replenishes the store whenever it runs low.)

Ultimately, Purdy is neither a novelist nor a fiction writer. He is a social satirist, and at times a funny and effective one. The last third of *Cabot Wright Begins* suggests that he missed the true vocation for which his combination of passion and bad taste qualify him, that of sick comic.

The question is, then, why do all these celebrated writers assure us that this ugly duckling is a swan, an ornament of our letters comparable to Nathanael West or Flannery O'Connor (not to speak of Herman Melville)? The answer, I am afraid, allows them the choice of being fools or knaves. Some of them (Farrell, Dr. Williams) are themselves writers so tin-eared that they cannot see anything wrong with Purdy. Others (Gregory, Daiches) are indiscriminate critics sore-legged from climbing on bandwagons. Some (Rexroth, Southern) are loosely of Purdy's school, and thus promote their own work in promoting his. Quite a few are fraternity brothers.

The most hardened offender, Dame Edith Sitwell, spent many decades exposing her literary incapacities to the world. (As a plummy example, I offer her introduction's explanation of the end of "63: Dream Palace," involving one of Lenny Bruce's favorite polysyllables.) As for Katherine Anne Porter: her remarks about Purdy's style are shamelessly irresponsible; on the subject of his compassion, the author of "Flowering Judas" might have enlightened us, not the author of *Ship of Fools*. But what is Dorothy Parker doing in this crowd, or my old friend Dick Lewis? I wish I knew.

SNOPESLORE

"He had never thought of it [the sea] before and he could not have said why he wanted to go to it—what of repudiation of the land, the earth, where his body or intellect had faulted somehow to the cold undeviation of his will to do—seeking what of that iodinic proffer of space and oblivion of which he had no intention of availing himself, would never avail himself, as if, by deliberately refusing to cut the wires of remembering, to punish that body and intellect which had failed him."

No literate reader, I suppose, could fail to recognize that sentence as the unique and curious language of William Faulkner. It is easy enough to deride the wretched grammar and syntax, the tortured tropes, the affected and often incorrect use of words. I did so in *The New Leader* in a review of *The Reivers*. To my great regret, that review appeared on the stands the day that Faulkner died. Alas, everything I said about that poor book is true, but since then I have felt that I owe the record some compensating appraisal of Faulkner's more significant work.

The reissue of the three novels of the Snopes trilogy as a boxed set entitled *Snopes* furnished an opportunity. Faulkner may have written monstrous prose, but at his best it is transcended by an imagination almost Melvillean in its power and audacity. Faulkner's best work attains to greatness by the intensity of its tragicomic vision of man, and in that canon the Snopes trilogy has a place as Faulkner's fullest exploration of natural evil, what Coleridge called (in characterizing Iago) "motiveless malignity."

Snopes is about the inundation of Snopeses that befell Yoknapatawpha County, Faulkner's writing preserve in rural north Mississippi. The first volume, *The Hamlet* (1940), takes the story from the appearance of the first Snopes, Ab, in the hamlet of Frenchman's Bend late in the last century, to the departure of Flem, whose social rise is the central action of the trilogy, to the wider opportunities of the nearby town of Jefferson.

Two sections of *The Hamlet* are among the boldest and most brilliant things Faulkner ever wrote. One is the killing of Jack Houston by Mink Snopes, Flem's small vicious brother or cousin (all Snopes interrelationships are obscure). Mink ambushes Houston with an old shotgun and shoots him in the belly, then drags the corpse a great distance and hides it high in a hollow tree. Mink drives his wife and daughters away, and during the days that he is disposing of the body Mink lives on cold stale coffee and raw meal out of the barrel, and finally on sweetened water and the grains of meal in his stubble of beard.

When buzzards reveal the location of the corpse, Mink goes with an axe in the night to chop it out and hide it elsewhere. In a fantastic scene, the starved and maddened man fights off Houston's wounded, starved, and maddened dog, and gets the body, but it has decomposed and one arm remains in the tree. When Mink returns to the tree, he is captured. His only comment on his act is a marvel of macabre and terrifying humor. "I was all right," Mink says, "until it started coming to pieces. I could have handled that dog. But the son of a bitch started coming to pieces on me."

The romance between the idiot Ike Snopes and Houston's cow is quite as remarkable. Ike falls in love with the cow, and bravely saves her from a grass fire in a grotesque scene that ends with the terrified cow defecating on Ike. He then steals the cow and runs off with her. We see Ike and the cow eat feed from the basket together, then Ike gathers flowers, clumsily stripping off the petals of some, and makes her a crude garland that disintegrates into fodder as he puts it on her head. It is funny and touching, and an absolutely convincing account of the love an idiot might feel for a cow. Nor is that the limit of Faulkner's audacity. As Ike watches the dawn rise, Faulkner writes him an idiot *aubade*, the lover's dawn song.

The Hamlet's sequel, *The Town* (1957), is much inferior imaginatively. One can see the difference most clearly by comparing the stampede of I. O. Snopes' mules in the second book with the stampede of Flem's Snopeslike spotted horses in the first, which it imitates. *The Town* covers Flem's rise to respectability as president of a Jefferson bank, and, I am sorry to say, respectability is intrinsically less interesting than depravity. Gavin Stevens' love for Flem's wife Eula and then for her daughter Linda is poor stuff, and the book contains a variety of hokum, including one or two spoofs of the Faulknerians. *The Town* is saved by a fresh infusion of pure Snopesism in the last few pages; the arrival in Jefferson of four savage and frightening little Snopes children, born to a Jicarilla Apache squaw, and their fantastic depradations, including the eating of a $500 Pekinese (Flem pays for it), and a good try at burning at the stake a young Snopes who had been training them as a hunting pack.

The final volume, *The Mansion* (1959), shows Faulkner even further from his sources of strength, in a world where Linda Snopes frequents Twenty One and the Stork Club, and Flem displays his penchant for blackmail by stealing her membership card in the Communist party. Much of it is absurd, and some of it is disastrous. But just as *The Town* is redeemed by the Snopes Indians, so *The Mansion* is saved by Mink Snopes, and its first and last sections come alive with Mink's demonic vitality. In the first we see the outrage to his humanity that made Mink kill Houston; we watch Houston's arrogance drive Mink step by step into the corner of murder. Flem deserts Mink at the trial, and for 38 years Mink bides his time in jail, waiting to be released, so that he can kill Flem. The last section of the book, Mink's overcoming one by one of all the insuperable obstacles between him and a shot through Flem's head, is one of the wonders of our literature.

The heart and power of the trilogy, the whale in this *Moby-Dick*, is the Snopes family. They are a matchless gallery of portraits. The progenitor is Ab, the sullen and spiteful old barn-burner, who establishes the family in Frenchman's Bend. From the first look we get at him, deliberately tracking horse manure on Major de Spain's fancy rug, to the last, an old man raising water-melons for the pleasure of punishing the boys who steal them, Ab is a model of nastiness and the spiritual ancestor of every church-burner in Mississippi.

Then there is Flem. Flem is so mean that when he cheats a poor farm wife out of $5 he forces her to thank him by giving her a nickel bag of candy for the children. He is so greedy that when he is made superintendent of the power plant he steals the brass safety valves off the boilers. Jefferson believes that when Flem bought a black felt hat on being made vice president of the bank, he did not throw away the cloth cap he had worn for 17 years, but sold it to a Negro boy for a dime. Flem has been sexually impotent all his life, having perfectly sublimated all other passions into his one pure lust.

Most important, there is Mink, who is compared by everyone in the book to every sort of deadly small animal, but is a man for all that, and a perverse tribute to the indomitable human spirit. Mink's heroic ability, characteristic of Odysseus, is to endure patiently until his moment comes. He has learned that "a man can bear anything by simply and calmly refusing to accept it, be reconciled to it." After the fashion of a Homeric hero, Mink will kill but he will not steal. He is illiterate, but the will is so fierce in his small frail body that when he must read a name to get to Flem, he reads it.

Around these mighty antagonists are lesser Snopeses. I. O. is a bigamist who talks a half-educated jargon. When schoolteaching palls, he goes into the trade of getting his mules killed on the railroad tracks. His fat son Saint Elmo is an insatiable maw, and his twins Bilbo and Vardaman seem aptly named. His son Clarence becomes a Silver Shirt state senator. Another son, Doris, is the joker who tried to train the Snopes Indians. The last son, Montgomery Ward, progresses from running a YMCA canteen in France, during the first World War, as a front for a brothel, to running a photography studio in Jefferson as a front for a pornographic peepshow, to success in Hollywood.

Launcelot, called Lump, is a chivalrous storekeeper who violates Negro women customers behind the counter as part of a nickel purchase, and sells peeks at Ike and the cow. Lump is horribly shocked at Mink's murder of Houston, not because Mink killed him, but because Mink neglected to rob him afterwards; Lump nevertheless plans to help Mink by framing a Negro for the crime and assembling a mob to torture the Negro into confessing.

Wesley Snopes has the distinction of having been tarred and feathered for the statutory rape of a 14-year-old girl at a revival service. His son Byron absconds with money from the Jefferson bank and flees to Mexico, where he fathers the Snopes Indians.

His other son Virgil does sexual exhibitions for small wagers. The last Snopes named in the trilogy, Orestes, sets booby traps. At the end, ominous new Snopeses are glimpsed at Flem's funeral.

In Faulkner's view, Snopeses are Mississippi poor whites—tenant farmers and sharecroppers, crackers and rednecks—who have the vitality no longer possessed by the gentry of Sartorises and de Spains that he so much admires. Faulkner detests Snopeses, and in some moods he dreads them, and sees them proliferating like cancer cells. But in saving moods he is able to laugh at them, and to make us laugh at them. As the example of Mink makes clear, Faulkner never forgets that they are men too. The Snopes who shot Medgar Evers in the back was a man, not an animal, although we need not be proud of the fact. William Faulkner's *Snopes*, and Mink in particular, is a contribution toward understanding these new murdering Snopeses, and thus eventually getting them back between the pages of books, where we can laugh at them again.

THE AUSTERITIES OF THE NEW NOVEL

I am perhaps not the best audience for the French "new novel." I do not believe that the traditional novel is dead, or that the psychological novel is outmoded, or that literature needs—or in fact could endure—a modern revolution of the sort we have had in art and music. I found the film *Last Year at Marienbad* so slow and boring that I walked out. Nevertheless, one ought to give the new and experimental a fair hearing. On that dangerously open-minded principle I tackled the latest novel to be published in this country by the film's author, Alain Robbe-Grillet. It is *The Erasers*. This is Robbe-Grillet's first novel, originally published in 1953; his other novels, with their dates of publication in France, are *The Voyeur* (1955), *Jealousy* (1957), and *In the Labyrinth* (1959). All have been translated by Richard Howard. I have now read all of them but *The Voyeur*.

The Erasers is not easy to synopsize. A band of terrorists in a French town on the Channel coast have taken to killing a public figure every evening at 7:30. The ninth of these, an economist named Daniel Dupont, escapes with an arm wound; so that he may work against the gang, the government announces that he is dead. A detective named Wallas, whose odd habit is buying erasers, is sent from Paris to investigate Dupont's murder. As the result of a wild series of coincidences, among them Wallas' physical resemblance to one of the killers, Dupont and Wallas manage to confront each other with pistols in Dupont's house at 7:30 the next night, and Wallas shoots Dupont dead.

An amusing idea, one thinks: the detective murdering the corpse. Perhaps even a commentary on the paradoxes of identification, on the order of Chesterton's *The Man Who Was Thursday*. But Robbe-Grillet aspires to much more. The novel hints strongly that, unknown to either, Wallas is Dupont's illegitimate son. It is full of references to Sophocles' *Oedipus the King*: its epigraph is the Chorus' moral to Oedipus, "Time that sees all has found you out against your will"; a drunk in a café plays variations on the Sphinx's riddle; and so on. All this suggests that *The Erasers* is Robbe-Grillet's perfectly serious version of the Oedipus story, and that all the *roman policier* contrivance is his version of the power of fate.

Jealousy is very different. The narrator is a banana planter on a Caribbean island, and the novel consists of his observations of his wife A . . . and a neighboring planter named Franck with whom the narrator believes her to be having an affair. A few simple events recur endlessly: Franck visits for drinks or meals; he and A . . . discuss a novel set in Africa; Franck kills a centipede on the wall, leaving a stain; Franck and A . . . drive to town for a day's shopping and have to stay overnight when the car breaks down; while they are away the narrator erases most of the centipede stain; one day Franck is expected for lunch but does not appear.

This sequence is nowhere given in the book; it was constructed for me by an ingenious puzzle-loving lady of my household, dating events by whether the centipede stain is absent, present, or faintly present on the wall. From such a chronology it is possible to suspect that Franck has been killed by the jealous narrator, but Robbe-Grillet nowhere says so, and Franck may equally have been killed by his jealous wife, or may have been kept from coming to lunch by a nasty sniffle. The novel is a curious *tour de force*, powerful and disturbing but limited and monotonous. It is more like a fugue or a villanelle, or a pioneer surrealist movie, than it is like a work of fiction.

In the Labyrinth tells of a demobilized soldier come to a provincial city in winter to deliver, to a man who is to meet him on a street corner, a box containing a dead soldier's belongings. He misses the meeting and for several days—during which time the enemy occupies the city—he wanders the streets looking for someone to whom to deliver the box. He is half-frozen, exhausted and feverish; he gets wounded by an enemy patrol, and he soon dies, his package undelivered. After his death the narrator identifies himself as a retired doctor who treated the soldier. He has inherited the box, and he may have (or he may not have) inherited the soldier's mission. In its restriction for most of its length to the soldier's painful and delirious perceptions, or the doctor's reconstruction of them, *In the Labyrinth* is indescribably tedious. It is the *least* novel that I have ever read.

Robbe-Grillet's revolution does not lie in his subject matter, which from Fated Parricide to Quest is the traditional material of literature, nor in his uses of form, which include conventional symbolism (the erasers, the centipede, the box), and a great deal of repetition with variation. The revolution lies in four curious austerities which he imposes on the novelist. I can best express them in the form of slogans.

The first is: things not thoughts. Thus when Wallas looks into a store window we are told not the contents of his mind, but the contents of the window; when Wallas walks in a cold wind we are not given his emotions but the shrinkage of the skin on his face. We never learn the feelings of the lovers in *Jealousy*, if indeed they are lovers, but we are invariably told the location of their chairs, and the angle at which the chairs are set. We learn, of the soldier in *In the Labyrinth*: "It suddenly seems very important to make an exact inventory of the room." It is so important that it replaces psychology.

A second principle is: measurements not metaphors. There are a few figures of speech in these novels, but they seem to be oversights, since Robbe-Grillet aims to replace all figuration with exact mensuration. Thus Wallas walks the town, not lonely as a cloud, but "a half second for each step, a step and a half for each year, eighty yards a minute"; the doctor does not find his room a cage for the spirit, instead, "It is five steps from the table to the corner of the bed; four steps from the bed to the chest."

The other two austerities seem to have been inaugurated after *The Erasers*. One is: spatial limitation not omnipresence. Thus A . . . brushing her hair is described only to the extent that the narrator can see her, and when she steps away from the window the description stops (Robbe-Grillet even uses the theatrical term "sight-lines" for this). A woman who befriends the soldier is described only when she comes into the light; when a door is opened a few inches her son appears as a "vertical strip" of a boy.

A consequence of this camera-eye restriction, and the last of

these odd principles, is: uncertainty not omniscience. Thus A
. . . is "probably" holding a letter because the narrator cannot see
clearly, Franck is "probably" thanking her for a drink because the
narrator cannot hear him. The husband can try to reconstruct a
remark from the situation, and he will give alternative possibilities
if he has not heard a remark clearly, but he has (and we have) no
access to what goes on out of his sight and hearing. In *In the
Labyrinth*, the soldier tells us that a boy in a café is "not the same
as the one" he met earlier; later the narrator tells us that it probably was the same boy, "despite slight contradictions"; we have no
way to tell.

   Why does Robbe-Grillet impose these limitations on his fiction? In his view, he is not narrowing the novel but enlarging it,
with the resources of musical form (a long description of a native
song in *Jealousy* is clearly an aesthetic for the novel), the abstrac-
tion of modern painting, and the immediacy of film. Robbe-
Grillet has published two manifestoes for his practices in *La Nouvelle Nouvelle Revue Française:* "Une voie pour le roman futur"
(July 1956), and "Nature, humanisme et tragédie" (October
1958). These make clear that he is against the use of psychology
because visual experiences give a truer account of inner reality;
that he objects to metaphor as sentimentalizing the material universe, which should only be quantified; that the omnipresent and
omniscient author, with his traditional characters and plot, has
been replaced by observers and objects. Thus Robbe-Grillet's revolution is in part technical, to produce a modern form for the
novel, and in part philosophical, to come closer to the truth of our
experience.

   I do think that there are certain gains. Technically, these
methods can produce a smoldering intensity, as in *Jealousy*. Philo-
sophically, a world of limited and distorted sense perceptions is
undoubtedly truer to our present sense of experience than a solid
world surely known. But the losses are massive. The whole fascinating world of the mind is made off-limits to the novelist, along
with metaphor's recognition of similarity in dissimilarity, which
Aristotle saw as a mark of genius. Trivialization seems inevitable
in the method: with the devotion of a nineteenth-century Russian

novelist describing the ice breaking up on the Neva in April, Robbe-Grillet describes an ice cube melting in Franck's drink. No subtlety of characterization is possible, since only familiar shapes are recognizable in these murky waters: Detective confronts Victim in *The Erasers;* the trio in *Jealousy* are the stock triangle of harlequinade and French bedroom farce; the soldier of *In the Labyrinth* has no shred of individuality.

Worst of all, the results quickly become monotonous and boring. Robbe-Grillet's freedom from the conventions of the novel is the freedom of deprivation. It binds the novelist with the tightest new constraints, until he cannot even perform his primary function, which is to be interesting. A prefatory note to *In the Labyrinth* insists that the story 'is subject to no allegorical interpretation." We must take Robbe-Grillet's word that these events are not meant to have any larger meaning, that they stand for nothing beyond themselves. But in themselves they are trivial and tedious, so that finally they have *no* interest for us. I regard these novels as serious experiments and Robbe-Grillet as a very clever man; in my opinion they are failed experiments of limited value, and Robbe-Grillet has been sadly misled by his cleverness.

T. S. ELIOT'S IMMORTALITY

The death of Thomas Stearns Eliot diminishes us considerably. In 1950, Eliot appeared on the cover of *Time,* having achieved that dubious eminence as the result of his first Broadway hit, *The Cocktail Party.* In the accompanying story, an anonymous entrail-reader took the long view. "Is Eliot a great poet?" he asked, and promptly replied, "His own age would not call him so, and doubts that posterity will." Fifteen years later it is possible to say that *Time* was as wrong in 1950 as it had been in its first issue in 1923, when it reported rumors that *The Waste Land* was a hoax.

The reason for beginning with these whimpers is that they may call up an appropriate bang. Eliot was a great poet, a poet of increasing mastery right through *Four Quartets,* and ultimately a great devotional poet. This is not as I would wish it, necessarily, but it is no less true for that. In a moving tribute to Eliot in *The New Leader* (December 9, 1963) Howard Nemerov wrote:

> He set us an example of the art of poetry, which by its seriousness and ambition successfully pressed the claim of poetry itself to be taken seriously in the world. For better or worse, there must be ever so many of us who would not have attempted poetic composition except for that example, that voice, and the somewhat dour and wry ascetic charm which it conferred upon the art.

The public voice was dour and ascetic, certainly. Where one's heart went out to Joyce, and one's hat at least went off to Yeats, what could one offer the remote figure of T. S. Eliot, O.M., but a genteel nod? Yet the poetry strongly suggests that this frosty image was artificial, masking a passionate nature and great emotional turbulence. The figure of Sweeney, apeneck and gross, is as much an aspect of his creator as is timid and fastidious Prufrock, and the two coexisted in Eliot very much as Bloom and Stephen coexisted in Joyce. As early as 1927, with great perception, Francis Fergusson wrote of Eliot in *The American Caravan* as "romantic" and "passionate."

An imagery in the poetry that is always associated with gratification and release is the New England coast, where Eliot spent boyhood summers. Prufrock has seen the mermaids "riding seaward on the waves": alas, away from him. The old man in "Gerontion" recalls "Gull against the wind, in the windy straits/of Belle Isle." The fructifying rain never comes in *The Waste Land*, but there is a beautiful freeing of the waters in the imagery of sailing near the end:

> Damyata: *The boat responded*
> *Gaily, to the hand expert with sail and oar*
> *The sea was calm, your heart would have responded*
> *Gaily, when invited, beating obedient*
> *To controlling hands*

The same imagery of New England sailing as mastery and freedom, strongly nostalgic and erotic, reappears in *Ash-Wednesday* and "The Dry Salvages" in *Four Quartets*. "Marina," which Elizabeth Drew calls "the only purely joyous poem Eliot has ever written," is also his most sea-drenched poem, transferring the recognition scene of *Pericles* to the Maine coast.

The other pervasive sense that the poetry gives of the concealed personality is its terrible suffering and guilt. Eliot's wife, a ballet dancer named Vivienne Haigh Haigh-Wood, whom he married in 1915, was in a nursing home from 1930 until her death in 1947. Eliot was separated from her in 1933, and lived as a bachelor until he married his secretary, Valerie Fletcher, in 1957. Before his first marriage the imagery of loneliness is overwhelming in such poems as "The Love Song of J. Alfred Prufrock." After 1930 the imagery of guilt predominates. At all times there is a curious lovely image of remembered happiness, most fully expressed in lines from *The Waste Land:* "when we came back, late, from the Hyacinth garden, / Your arms full, and your hair wet."

"Let me also wear / Such deliberate disguises / Rat's coat, crowskin, crossed staves," Eliot wrote in "The Hollow Men" in 1925, his time of greatest desperation and misery. Eliot's disguises

have included the celebrated "four-piece suit" of which Virginia
Woolf made fun; the bowler and rolled umbrella of the City bank
clerk, gentleman publisher, and connoisseur of Stilton; the striped
trousers proper to a Kensington churchwarden, a vestryman at
fashionable St. Stephen's.

The two rival ways of Christianity, mystic and humanitarian,
can best be characterized by the statement of St. John of the
Cross, "Hence the soul cannot be possessed of the divine union,
until it has divested itself of the love of created beings," and by its
direct opposite in I John 4:20, "If a man say, I love God, and
hateth his brother, he is a liar." Eliot seems to have had a strong
impulse toward Christian brotherhood, but to have been driven
by his backward devils to place a higher value on the Christianity
that denies the world; it is St. John of the Cross' terrifying sentence that precedes the fragments of *Sweeney Agonistes*.

The central doctrine of Christianity for Eliot, we learn from
Four Quartets (where it is the only dogma named), is Incarnation;
but where Christian humility flows naturally from Incarnation
(man must humble himself as God did), what followed from it in
Eliot's theology was transcendence rather than immanence. This
otherworldly Christianity combined very well with a variety of
most unattractive social and political views that Eliot held; I have
attacked them in *The Armed Vision* and I shall not recapitulate
that attack here. Oscar Cargill is probably right in taking the end
of the second movement of "Little Gidding" to constitute (however adequately) repentance of, and apology for, Eliot's racism.
The third movement is certainly a reconciliation with "one who
died blind and quiet," who is at once Milton, Joyce, and all such
regicides, dissenters, levellers, puritans, socialists, atheists, and
free-thinking Jews.

Ultimately it is the poetry that matters. I do not think that
the criticism, with the possible exception of one essay, "Tradition
and the Individual Talent," has the same permanence. The criticism was invaluable in its time, as I argue in *Poetry and Criticism*,
in changing the taste of our age and creating an audience for the
"low seriousness" of Eliot's early poetry. The critical doctrines,
with their emphasis on escape from emotion and from "personal

and private agonies," are too narrowly, as *The Armed Vision* says, "the aesthetic of a suffering man." One cannot have a high opinion of the plays, except for the wonderful eloquence of the Chorus in *Murder in the Cathedral*. The light verse about cats, and such infrequent late verse as "The Cultivation of Christmas Trees," were never more than curiosities.

At every period of his life, until his interest switched to drama, Eliot wrote lyric poems of rare magnificence: "La Figlia che Piange" in *Prufrock and Other Observations* (1917); "Sweeney Among the Nightingales" in *Poems* (1920); "Journey of the Magi" (1927) among the *Ariel Poems*; "Triumphal March" (1931) from the unfinished *Coriolan*—those are merely the first that come to mind. Beyond those, Eliot produced three ambitious "major" works, in some cases by combining lyrics previously published independently. (It was this that Yeats, to his detriment, could rarely bring himself to do.) Eliot's major poems are *The Waste Land* (1922), *Ash-Wednesday* (1930), and *Four Quartets* (1936-1942). They are among the glories of our age.

In my view, *Four Quartets* is the finest of the three, and it increases in power and beauty as it progresses. "Burnt Norton," the first, developed out of fragments discarded from *Murder in the Cathedral* during rehearsals. It lacks a close personal involvement, as its title place, a Gloucestershire manor house that an eighteenth-century owner set on fire, lacks personal associations for Eliot. "East Coker," named for the Somersetshire village where the Eliots lived before they emigrated to America, is enormously better. The ancestral involvement (key images come from *The Boke named The Gouvernour*, by Eliot's East Coker kinsman, Sir Thomas Elyot) releases a remarkable eloquence, as in the short fourth movement, from which I quote part of the first stanza:

> *The wounded surgeon* plies *the steel*
> *That* questions *the* distempered *part;*
> *Beneath the* bleeding hands *we feel*
> *The* sharp compassion *of the healer's art*

The wounded surgeon is Christ (in a metaphor adapted from a sermon by Bishop Andrewes). All that the rigors of space permit me to do with the complex miracles of language in the passage is to call attention to them with roman type.

"The Dry Salvages," named after a group of rocks off Cape Ann, Massachusetts, develops with mounting authority after its magnificent beginning: "I do not know much about gods, but I think that the river / Is a strong brown god." "Little Gidding" is named after a seventeenth-century Anglican community in Huntingdonshire, now the site of a restored chapel, where Eliot went to pray in 1937. To my taste, it is Eliot's masterwork. I do not think that there has been any verse in English in our century better than its second movement, in which a lyric of profound tragic acceptance is followed by an *Inferno* encounter after a London air raid, or its fourth movement, a Pentecostal fire sermon.

Nemerov reminded us, in his tribute, that Eliot enlarged our concept of poetry beyond the limits of an English country churchyard, but nevertheless returned us to one in the *Quartets*. Now Eliot's ashes, in accord with his wish, have been deposited in the church in East Coker. In 1958, on the occasion of his 70th birthday, Eliot modestly told V. S. Pritchett, in an interview for the *New York Times Book Review*: "But my poetry is American. Purely American. I hope my poetry will last. I don't think my criticism will." His poetry *is* American, and it *will* last. It is the only immortality in which I can share his belief, and it is surely the only one worth having.

NORMAN MAILER'S YUMMY RUMP

"There are nights when one comes home after a cancerously dull party, full of liquor but not drunk, leaden with boredom, somewhere out in Fitzgerald's long dark night. Writing at such a time is like making love at such a time. It is hopeless, it desecrates one's future, but one does it anyway because at least it is an act. Such writing is almost always unsprung. It is reminiscent of the wallflower who says, 'To hell with inhibitions, I'm going to dance.' The premise is that what comes out is valid because it is the record of a mood. So one records the mood. What a mood. Full of vomit, self-pity, panic, paranoia, megalomania, *merde,* whimpers, excuses, turns of the neck, flips of the wrist, transports. It is the bends of Hell. If you purge it, if you get sleep and tear it up in the morning, it can do no more harm than any other bad debauch."

This is Norman Mailer in *Esquire* not long ago, ostensibly talking about the work of a contemporary, but obviously telling us the genesis of his new novel. Instead of tearing it up in the morning, Mailer published it as *An American Dream. An American Dream* is a dreadful novel, perhaps the worst I have read in many years, since it is infinitely more pretentious than the competition. Mailer's novel is bad in that absolute fashion that makes it unlikely that he could ever have written anything good. Since its awfulness is really indescribable, instead of trying to describe it I will try to communicate its quality by allowing three of its constituents to represent the whole. These are: its plot, its mystique of human smells, and its tropes.

The novel covers several days in the life of the narrator, Stephen Richards Rojack, a New Yorker in his early forties. He was briefly a Congressman, and now makes his living as a professor of existentialist psychology at a city university, where he offers a seminar in Voodoo, and as master of ceremonies on a far-out television interview program; he is the author of one popular book,

The Psychology of the Hangman. Rojack was a hero in the Second
World War, and is in fact "the one intellectual in America's history" with a Distinguished Service Cross. He is separated from his
wife, a beautiful rich Roman Catholic of Hapsburg ancestry,
Deborah Caughlin Mangaravidi Kelly.

Rojack begins the novel's action by a wrestling match with
his wife, occasioned by her boasting of perversities with her lovers, in the course of which he strangles her. He leaves the corpse
on the carpet, goes downstairs and buggers the maid, who in her
enthusiasm admits to being a Nazi, and tells him that he is absolutely a sexual genius. Then he goes back upstairs, cleans his
wife's corpse up a bit, and pitches it out the window.

This piles up traffic on the East River Drive, and one of the
cars involved contains Eddie Ganucci, a statesman in the Mafia,
and a beautiful blonde nightclub singer named Cherry Melanie,
who looks "like a child who has been anointed by the wing of a
magical bird," and with whom Rojack promptly falls in love. As
soon as the detectives release him, Rojack goes to the club where
Cherry sings, outfaces a burly prizefighter, and takes Cherry
home to bed.

The next day there is another interview with the detectives,
in the course of which Rojack defends himself so skillfully that he
is told: "You missed a promising legal career." Then he learns
that his wife's murder has been declared a suicide as a result of
his father-in-law's influence. He returns to Cherry, who confesses
to being a fan of his television program, and expresses her feeling
for his talents by biting pieces of skin out of his ear. She tells him
that she was raised by an incestuous half-brother and half-sister,
after which he succeeds in bringing her to the first orgasm she
has ever experienced in genital intercourse.

While they are engaged in mutual congratulations, Cherry's
former lover, a gifted Negro singer and "stud" named Shago Martin, walks in on them. He pulls a switchblade on Rojack, but Rojack, unarmed, overcomes him, beats him up, and throws him
down the stairs. Rojack then goes to visit his father-in-law, the
mysterious tycoon Barney Oswald Kelly, another former lover of
Cherry's. While Rojack is at Kelly's, President Kennedy (called
"Jack") telephones to express his condolences. The Nazi maid is

now working for Kelly and simultaneously blackmailing him, and she tells Rojack that at the time of her death Deborah was involved with lovers high in American, Soviet, and British espionage circles. "Last night there must have been electricity burning in government offices all over the world," she adds.

Kelly compels Rojack to listen to his life story, spiced with father-daughter incest, and Rojack then demonstrates his courage (he intends "to blow up poor old Freud" by showing that cowardice is the root of neurosis) by walking a dangerous parapet near Kelly's terrace. Kelly tries to push him off the parapet with an umbrella, but Rojack smashes Kelly in the face with the umbrella and departs. He goes back downtown and learns that Shago has been beaten to death by an unidentified assailant in Morningside Park, and Cherry has been beaten to death in her apartment by a confused friend of Shago's. Rojack arrives just in time to hear her last words. He then drives to Las Vegas, where he is highly successful at the dice tables. The book ends with his telephoning Cherry in Heaven; we know it is Heaven because "Marilyn says to say hello."

These are merely a few of the simpler strands in the plot. Synopsis cannot convey the unbelievability of the characters (Kelly, for example, seems based largely on Fu Manchu: he says "me" for "I," but asks "do you know that phrase of Kierkegaard's of course you do—I was in a fear and trembling"). It cannot convey the genteel double standard of the sex (sodomy is for servants), or the windy occultism that accompanies the sex acts (going to bed with Rojack must be like going to bed with Madame Blavatsky). It particularly cannot convey the dreamy unreality of the conversation ("You black ass ego," says Cherry sternly to Shago).

The book is full of mystiques, Rojack has powers of telekinesis and precognition; the deaths of Shago and Cherry seem to be caused by a posthumous curse of Deborah's, which Rojack escaped by walking the parapet; there is a great deal of pajama-party demonology, including an encounter with "the most evil woman ever to live on the Riviera," who justifies the title by keeping a scorpion in a cage.

The most curious of these mystiques is the spirit odors that the characters emanate. Before he cleanses himself by strangling Deborah, Rojack smells "like the rotten, carious shudder of a decayed tooth." Deborah's smell is compounded of "sweet rot," "burning rubber," and "a bank." The Nazi maid has "a thin high constipated smell," as well she might. A pair of detectives give off, respectively, "a kind of clammy odor of rut," and "the funk a bully emits when he heads for a face-to-face meeting." Ganucci exudes "an essence of disease, some moldering from the tree of death." Cherry smells "of something sweet and strong," among its elements "the back seats of cars." The principal detective smells "sour with use, and also too sweet." Shago's odor is "a poisonous snake of mood which entered my lungs like marijuana," later "a smell of full nearness as if we'd been in bed for an hour." Kelly emits "some whiff of the icy rot and iodine in a piece of marine nerve left to bleach on the sand," varied by "the stench which comes from devotion to the goat."

These phrases should give some idea of Mailer's prose, which is additionally distinguished by poetic inversions ("Neat and clean was his blue shirt"), unidiomatic tenses ("Whatever Deborah would deserve"), and sentences without a fig leaf of syntax ("Enormous, and stared at one with a clear luminous look, an animal's fright, some creature with huge eyes.") The similes, however, deserve special attention. Some of them are Homeric, for example, a passage that begins, "Once, in a rainstorm I witnessed the creation of a rivulet," and concludes six lines later: "That was how the tears went down Cherry's face."

Many of the similes are tritely romantic: "narrow and mean as the eye of a personnel director," "the look of a rock-hard little jockey recollecting an ugly race," "faint as the ghost of a jewel box." Others are excessively labored: "as if drunkenness were a train which rocketed through the dark and I was sitting in a seat which gave out backward on the view and so receded further and further from some fire on the horizon: thus came each instant nearer to the murmur one hears in the tunnel which leads to death."

Some of the similes seem deranged. "Hot as the gates of an icy slalom" is one such; others are: "I cried within like a just-cracked vase might shriek for cement," which is ungrammatical in addition; and "with the insight of an ice pick the precise thought came to me." Two woeful herpetological tropes suggest that Mailer has never seen a snake: Shago's switchblade "opened from his palm like a snake's tongue"; "The umbrella lay like a sleeping snake across my thighs."

Mailer's slovenly misuse of language creates non-existent characters and stories. "Like sitting to dinner in an empty castle with no more for host than a butler and his curse" is the single mysterious reference in the book to The Butler's Curse. "I was close to a strong old man dying now of his overwork" does not mean that an old man is dying near Rojack, in fact there is no old man; it is Mailer trying to say that Rojack feels poorly. Other tropes are notable for their spit-on-the-Harvard-crimson vulgarity: "a delicious pain clean as a mistress' sharp teeth going 'Yummy' in your rump" is perhaps my favorite, although an orgasm "fierce as the demon in the eyes of a bright golden child" has a lot to recommend it.

I do not think that all of this is due to simple ineptness. Some of it surely represents Mailer's immortal longing, to be a *big* fancy writer like Thomas Wolfe. I submit one further simile in evidence: "as if the terrors of men were about as admirable as the droppings of hippopotami." This has everything: turns of the neck, flips of the wrist, transports, *merde,* even an elegant Latinate plural.

Enough. Why didn't Mailer pitch the whole preposterous mess out the window after he read it over? Ask *Esquire* and Dial Press and Dell Books and Warner Brothers, which have guaranteed him half a million dollars for it.

AFTERWORD

For slightly more than four years, from May 1961 to June 1965, I wrote regular lead reviews for *The New Leader*, a bi-weekly journal of opinion. I took the task seriously, and worked very hard at it. At the end of that time I gave it up, exhausted in both senses: tired and emptied. The column occasioned a surprising amount of interest and praise—less a tribute to my merits, I suspect, than to the rarity of sustained serious reviewing in our day.

This collection of a representative sampling of the reviews, slightly more than half the total, is made in response to that interest. It is submitted as the record of an experiment in regularly confronting the literature of our time with a hard eye, so to speak, insisting on standards of excellence at a time of general cultural debasement, trying to tell the truth at a time when truth has become unfashionable in literary journalism.

The reviews have been rewritten for style, and errors have been corrected, but no opinions have been changed. In some cases, another paragraph or two, omitted from *The New Leader* because of the exigencies of space, has been restored. The order is chronological.

I have known for a long time that my talents, such as they are, are mainly of a destructive order, with a highly developed instinct for the jugular, but I have sternly restrained them. The reviewing of worthless books must in each case be justified (the world says otherwise, or the book just won an important prize, or the author is a major figure); otherwise why waste the space? If the work of destructive criticism is to be done at all, it should be done by the fierce and hungry young, not by such benign old grandfathers as myself. But few young seem either fierce or hungry, and at times the old bloodlust sweeps over me.

Apart from this observation, some other generalizations can be made. A few persistent ideas, about art, life, or the relationship of the two, recur again and again: that form, as the ordering of disorder, is a moral act; that all true humor is deeply tinged with melancholy, with, in consequence, my respect for such ambivalent forms as the blues and the impure forms of the New American Novel; a very bleak view of my *moment* and *milieu,* and in consequence an insistence that only accounts of inadequacy and alienation can be true or honest. This last surprised me. I knew that I was not enthusiastic about The American Century, but I was quite surprised to discover how often I demanded "truth" when I would have thought I asked only "art."

The rigid confines of two pages (burst through only on rare occasions), about 1,500 words, were no doubt beneficial in forcing me to select and compress what I had to say, but the reviews complain regularly that the "rigors" or "tyranny" of space prevent this or necessitate that. I found it frustrating to review collections of stories or essays, because of the amount of space that has to be expended in synopsizing or characterizing individual units, and after a while I either avoided it or got around the problem by limiting myself to a sampling. For the same reason, I came to find round-ups unrewarding, and in the last year I did none. I have reprinted few reviews of collections, and no round-ups.

An important difference between reviewing and criticism is that the reviewer must depend on a single reading. This is wonderfully challenging and sharpening (one must begin to figure out the book from the first sentence), but it is also nerve-racking and wearying, and the result is usually not equal in merit or permanence to the product of repeated readings and study. (I can see the difference in the few reviews that I did of old books that I know thoroughly.)

The greatest joy in doing such a column is the discoveries made reading for it: writers I had somehow missed (Singer, Barth); foreign writers little known in this country (Sologub, Tanizaki, Eça de Queiroz); writers I had read but did not fully appreciate (Svevo, Nabokov); writers no one seemed fully to appreciate (Curley, Miss Frame); gifted first novelists (Percy, Friedman, Pynchon, Markfield). In some cases, this pleasure was augmented by finding my remarks reprinted to introduce the book to other readers, or receiving a warm, sometimes moving, letter from the author.

The other side of this coin is the disillusionments. Few of my disillusionments got reviewed, but for one reason or another I dealt with some highly-praised writers whose experiments turned out unprofitably (Robbe-Grillet, Hawkes), or whose appeal proved mainly nonliterary (Grass, Donleavy), or whose reputations remained inexplicable (Storey, Purdy). Considering the general absence of standards and the corruption (ranging from friendly log-rolling to the purest venality) of our reviewing, I am most proud of those reviews, such as that of Hemingway's posthumous *A Moveable Feast,* in which I stood up for the truth amid a chorus of lies.

From the perspective of time, some corrections and second guesses are in order. The only evaluations I would revise, to my surprise, are a few downward. I now think that I overpraised Anthony Powell's Music of Time series, which on further reading seems something less than the "work of art" I called it; I surely was too hopeful about Warren's coming out of his wilderness; I either did not perceive or could not make clear the emptiness of Katherine Anne Porter's *Ship of Fools.* That is all. I have not reprinted these pieces. On reconsideration I stand by every other opinion expressed, including some that have been almost unanimously attacked.

A few mistakes required correction. The worst, by far, was my failure to recognize the Russian roots of the language in Anthony Burgess' *A Clockwork Orange;* this has since been corrected in a revision of the review printed as an Afterword to a paperback edition of the book. In the review of Henry Miller, I misfigured the franc (shocking in a coin collector), and accused Miller of stealing five or six hundred dollars from a friend, when in fact he stole considerably less. Surely, as an English teacher, I should have known better than to misspell Poe's middle name, or to credit Bloom's "knockmedown" cigar in *Ulysses* to his antagonist.

In other cases, where there is no visible error, I would have been helped by knowing or remembering more. I reviewed a Joyce Cary novel and said everything about it except the important thing, its debt to *Lord Jim;* I praised Updike's story "Flight" but never mentioned Lawrence's *Sons and Lovers.* To

my sorrow, I credited Stephen Dedalus with a joke he had borrowed from Nietzsche; I named Whitney Balliett and Nat Hent-
off as our two best jazz critics and forgot Martin Williams; I did
not learn until after my review of Barth's *Sot-Weed Factor* that
the poem and its author were historical realities. I predicted that
a novel by Jean Cau, which I have never heard mentioned since,
would be endlessly discussed; I predicted that Donleavy's second
novel would be as popular as his first; I will not be numbered
among the prophets.

Some omissions are regrettable, a few of them my own fault.
What could have persuaded me to pass up a chance to review
Nabokov's *Pale Fire*, which I later found to be a work of genius?
I am embarrassed to discover that I reviewed two Japanese and
a Senegalese but never reviewed a Latin American book. Other
omissions could not be helped: four years are not a large enough
net to catch every worthwhile writer. An absurd convention kept
me from dealing with the work of one novelist, Shirley Jackson,
whom I think important and about whom I have quite a bit to
say. Beyond that, I may have missed significant books because
of my lack of interest in realistic family chronicles, or because
good books tend to be published in scattered bursts, or simply
because I had too little time to explore. Finally, I regret that I
never produced tributes to two writers whose deaths were great
losses to the culture as well as to me personally, Lord Raglan
and R. P. Blackmur.

Still, I did what I could, and the results, if flawed, do not
seem to me without merit.